JOURNAL WITH PURPOSE

DRAW QUICK & EASY
Modern Florals

Over **100** botanical motifs to doodle,
draw and decorate your journals,
sketchbooks, and crafts

Helen Colebrook

DAVID & CHARLES
—PUBLISHING—

www.davidandcharles.com

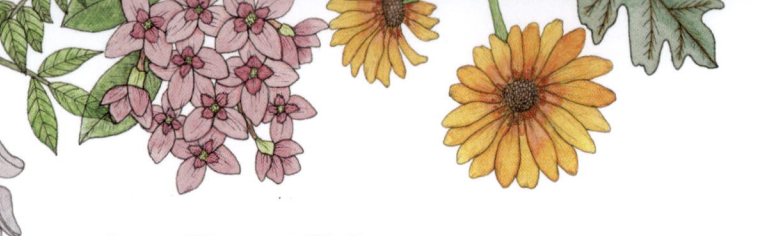

CONTENTS

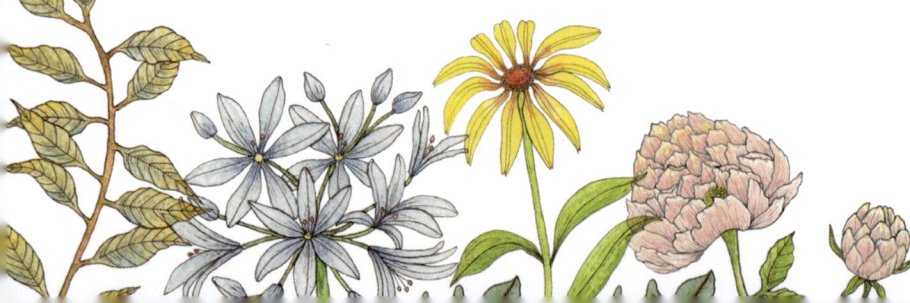

INTRODUCTION

I'm so excited to share this book with you, which is full of step-by-step tutorials for drawing a lovely variety of plants. I hope you find lots here that you want to try out in your own sketchbook. I also hope that going through these exercises gives you the confidence and skills to draw the flowers and leaves that you see around you.

I've spent many years keeping journals and one of my favourite things to document is the changing seasons and what I'm observing in nature on my daily walks. It helps me to feel connected to the wider world and I just love seeing those drawings brighten up my journal pages.

Throughout this book you will see the drawing outline broken down into lots of steps, so that you can get a feel for how the design comes together. I always use a waterproof drawing pen so that I am free to use any medium on top, with my most commonly used being watercolour paint.

It wasn't that long ago that I didn't consider myself to be creative at all. However, I've learned that if you take things slowly, have patience with yourself, and practise regularly, it really is possible to improve your skills and come up with drawings that you're proud of.

As well as showing you how to draw a wide variety of individual flowers, I've also included some projects in this book that will help you take your floral drawings in new directions — there are so many wonderful possibilities for your creativity once you get stuck in.

I hope you enjoy going through this book as much as I enjoyed creating it.

Helen

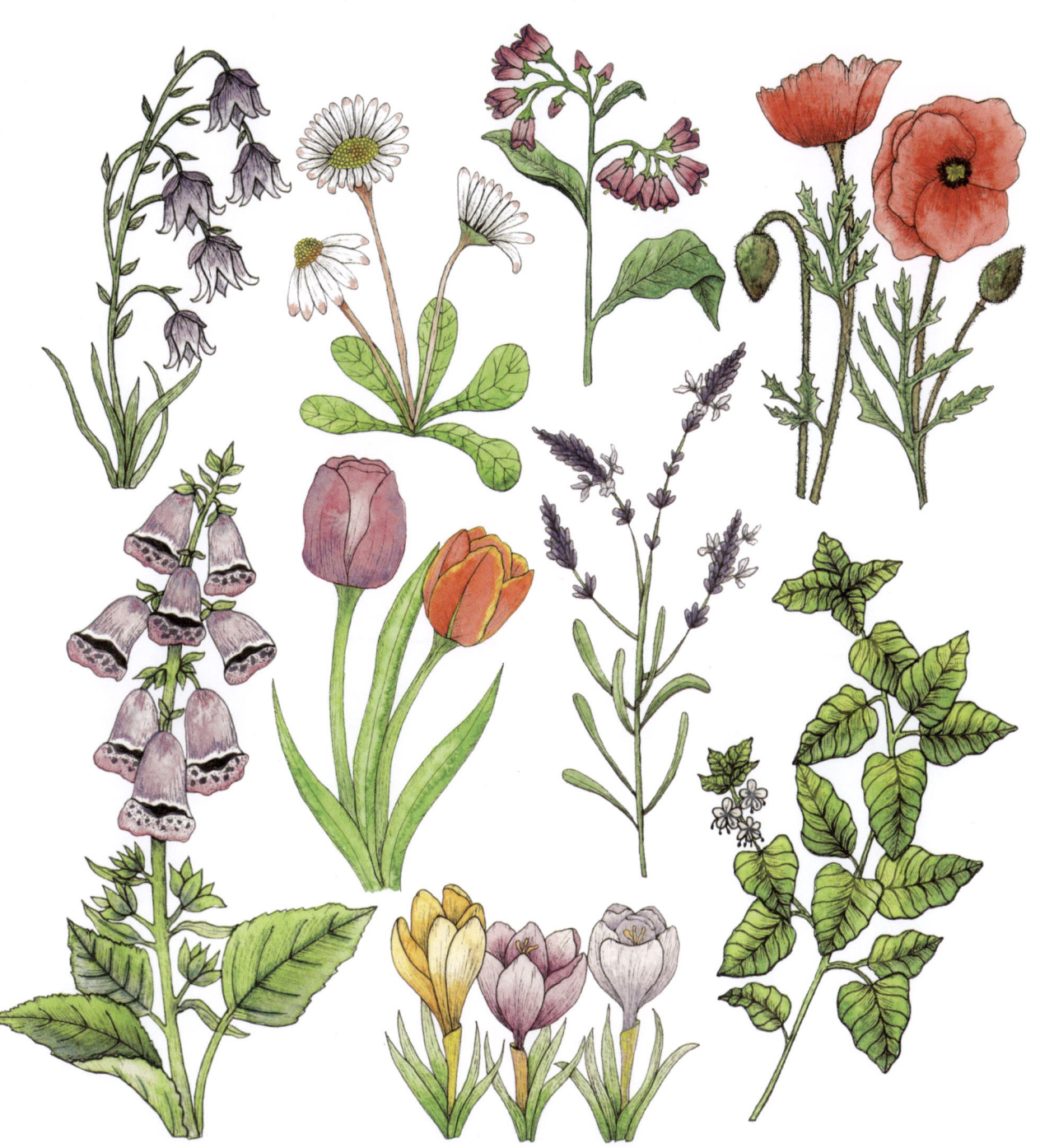

TOOLS & MATERIALS

When it comes to choosing art supplies, there are so many wonderful options available. However, I also think it's important not to overthink things or end up buying lots of new stationery that you don't end up using.

I always like to use a mechanical pencil and eraser for the initial sketching of my drawings. For inking I like to use a waterproof black fineliner and I usually have a variety of nib sizes on hand. I tend to use a medium nib for outlining and a finer nib for adding all the little details.

My favourite medium for adding colour is watercolour paint, with occasional coloured pencil shading on top. However this is definitely the area where you can choose whichever supplies you most enjoy working with. I would always encourage you to just begin with whatever tools you already have.

I create a lot of my drawings in a watercolour sketchbook, but I also love the challenge of working on different backgrounds - like book pages, vellum, fabric, and cardstock - so I would definitely encourage you to have a play.

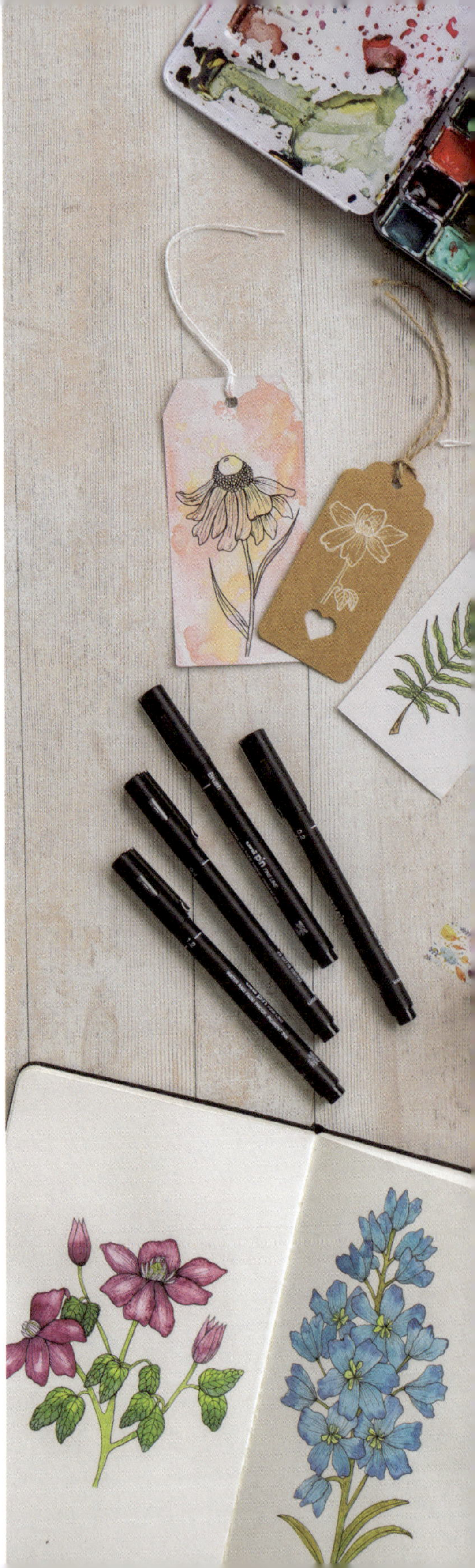

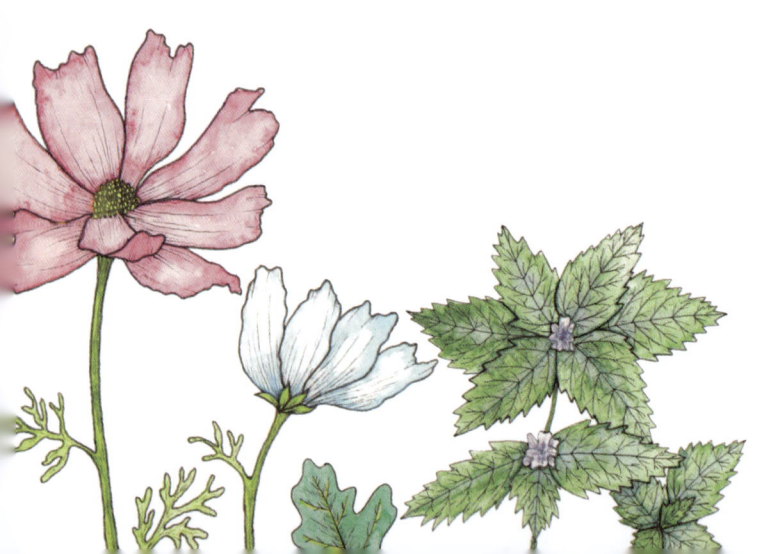

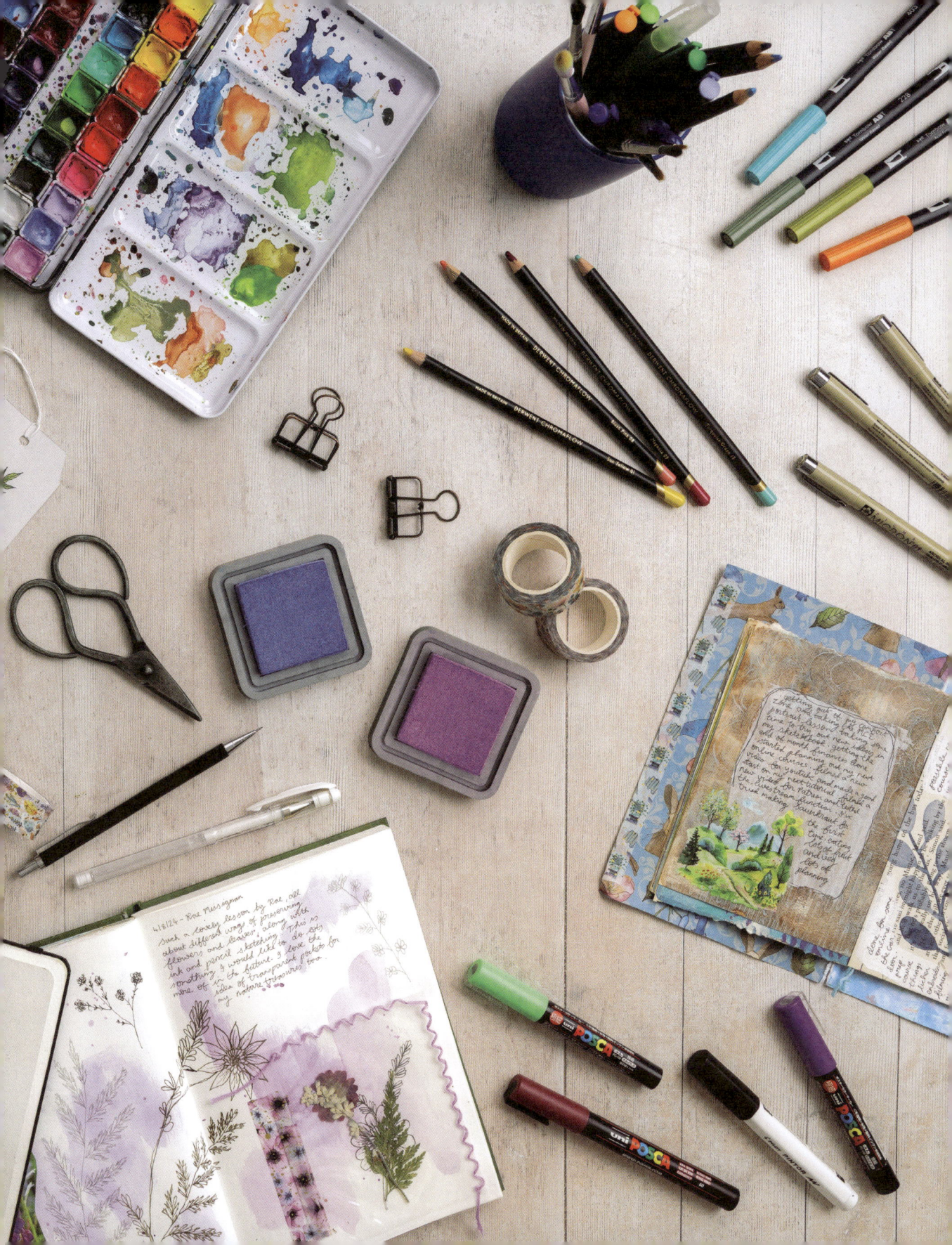

Florals

I've included lots of my favourite plants in this section and I hope you find some of yours here too. Once you've gained confidence by drawing the flowers in this book I hope you will try sketching the plants you see around you, as this will bring a really personal feel to your sketchbooks and journals.

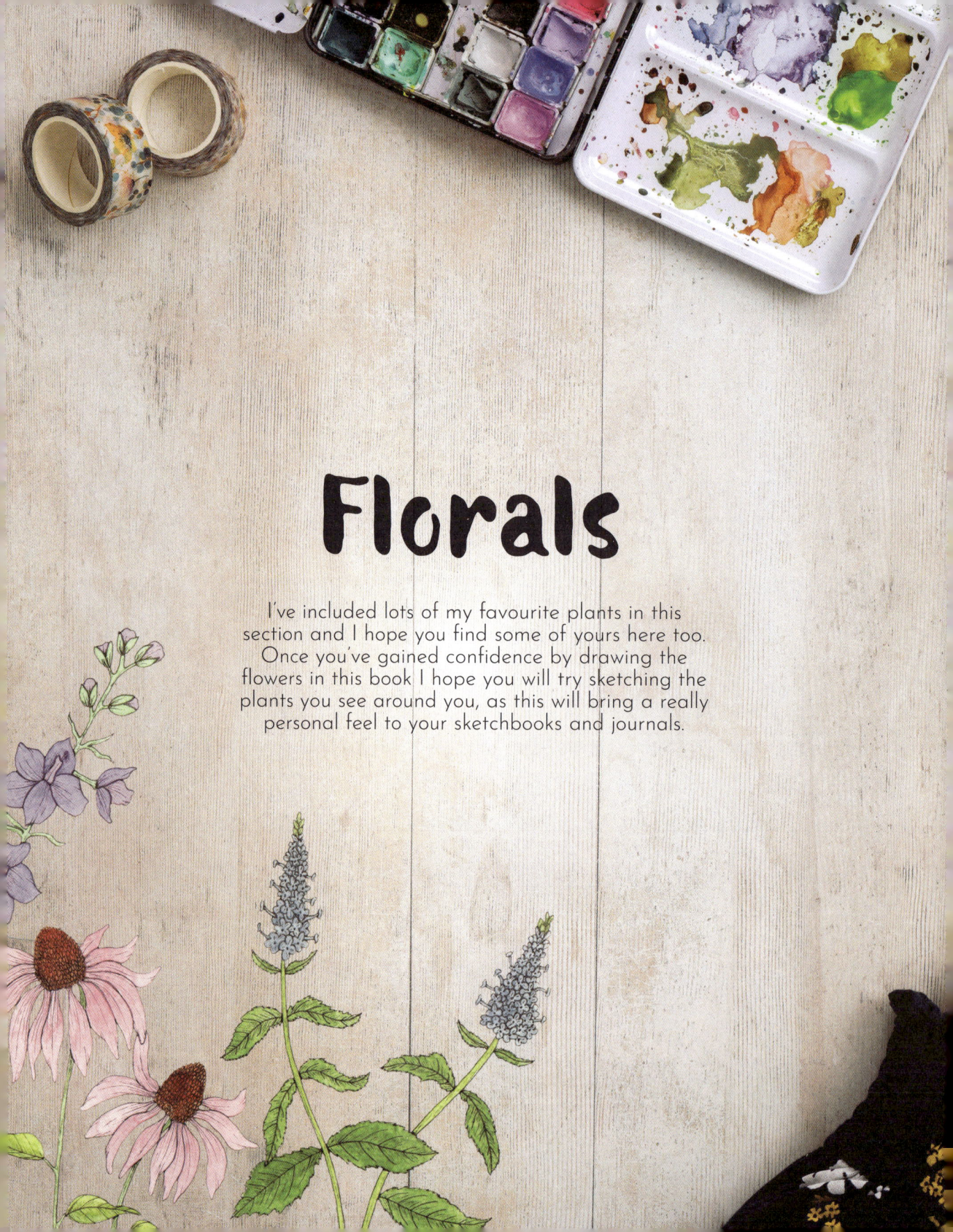

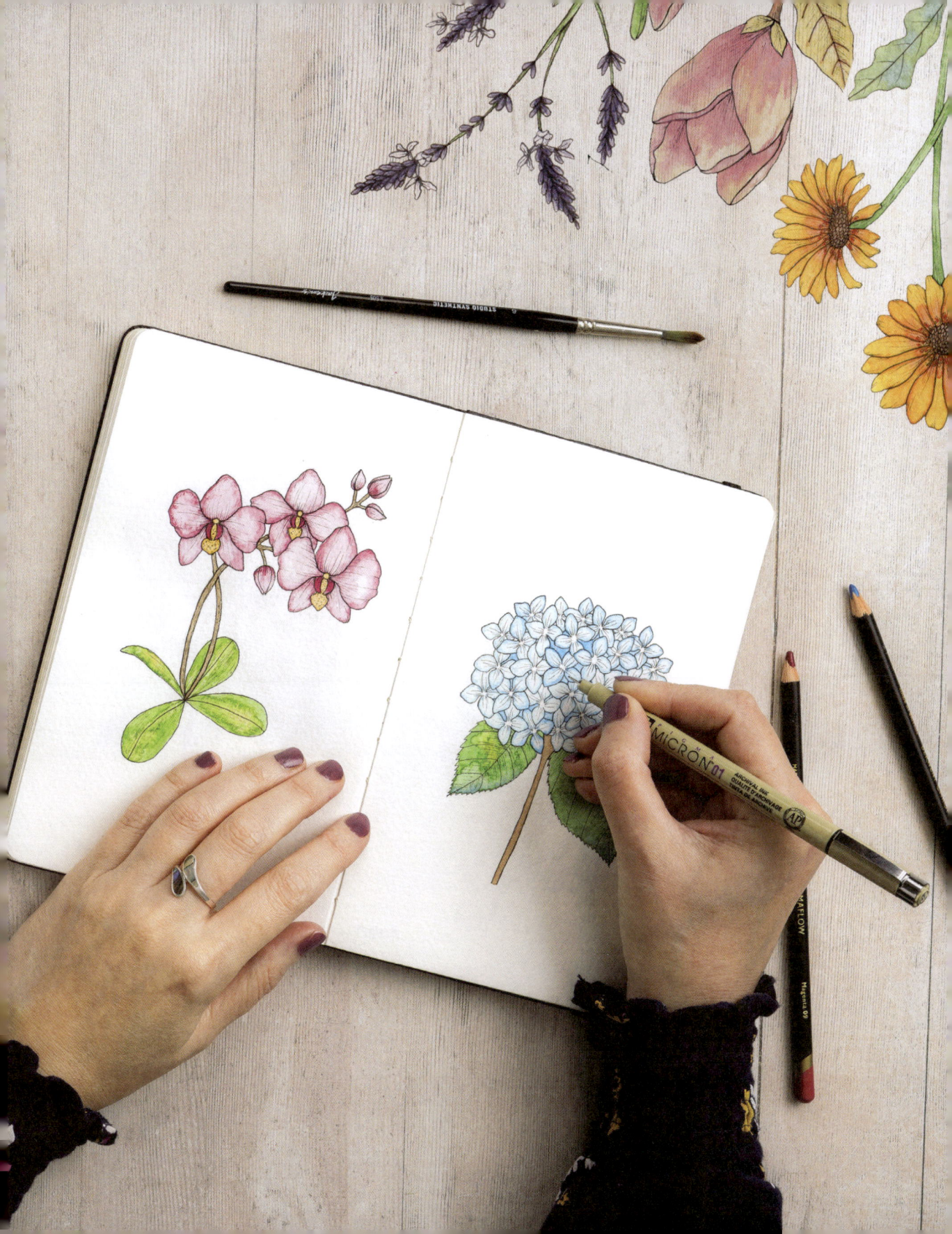

Daffodil

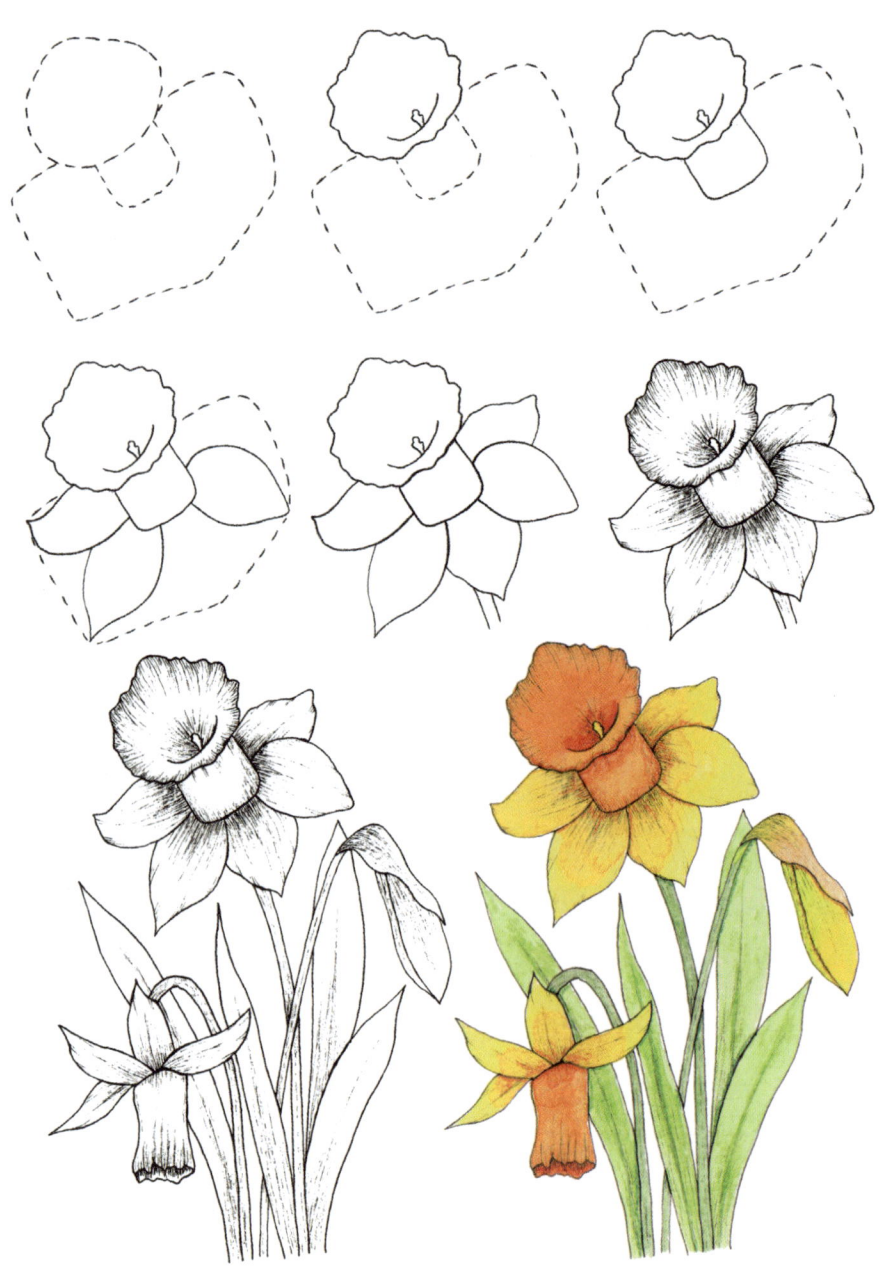

Iris

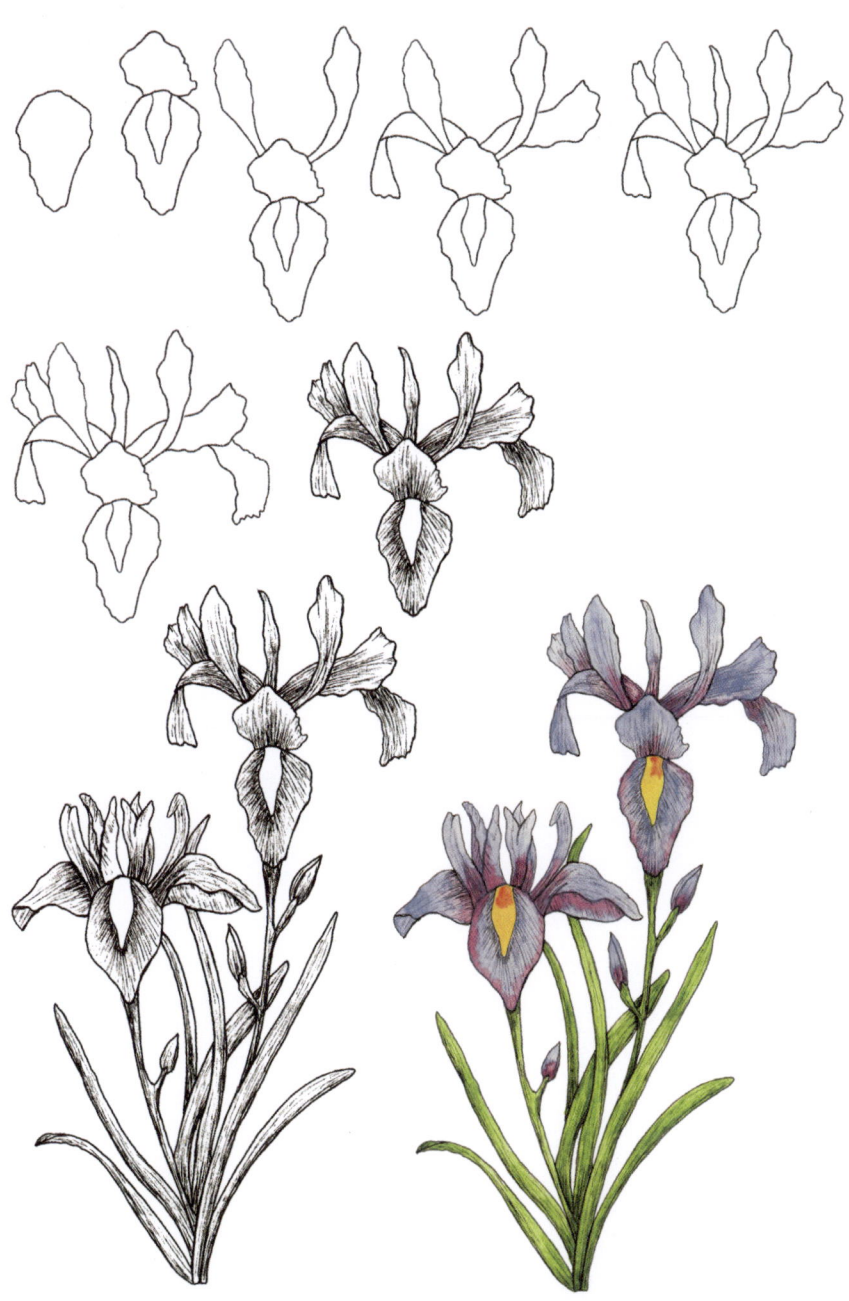

Snowdrop

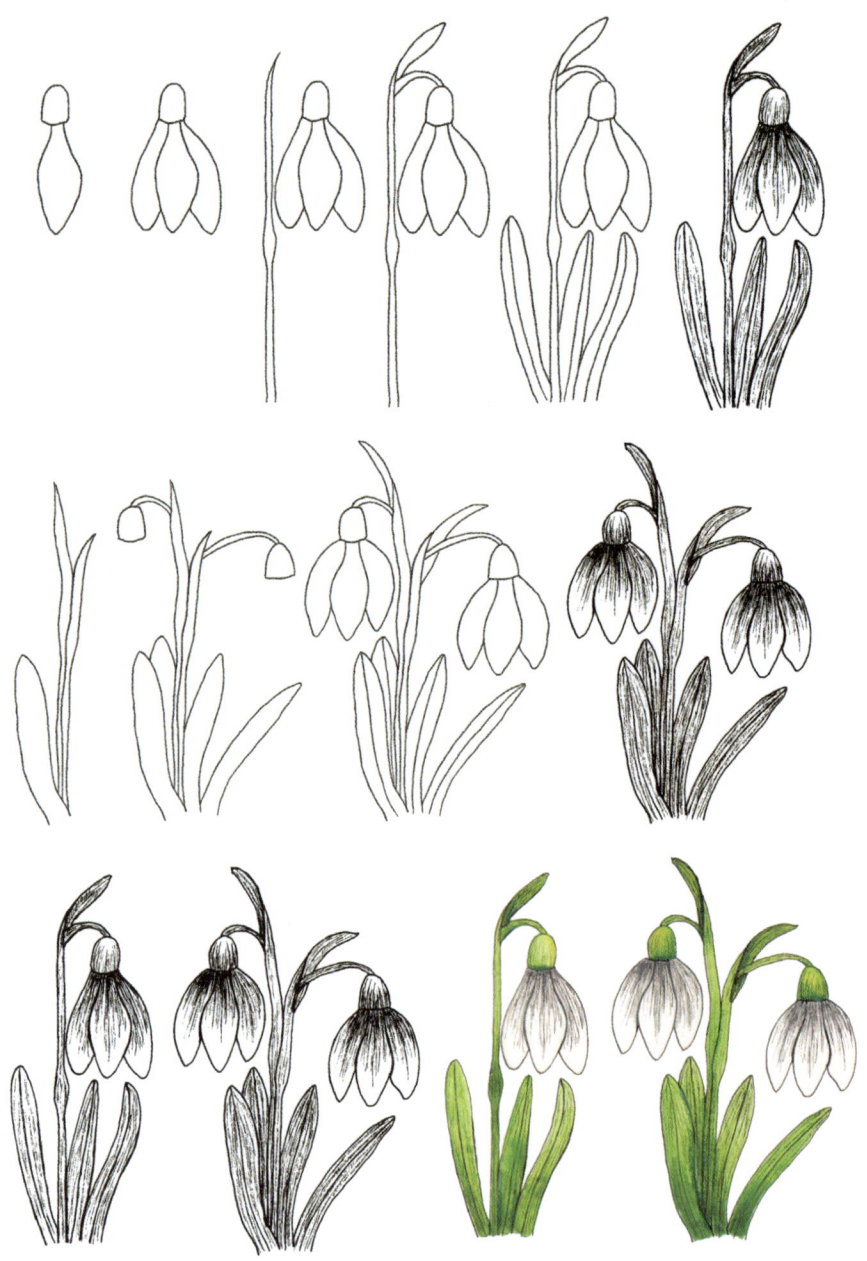

Tulip

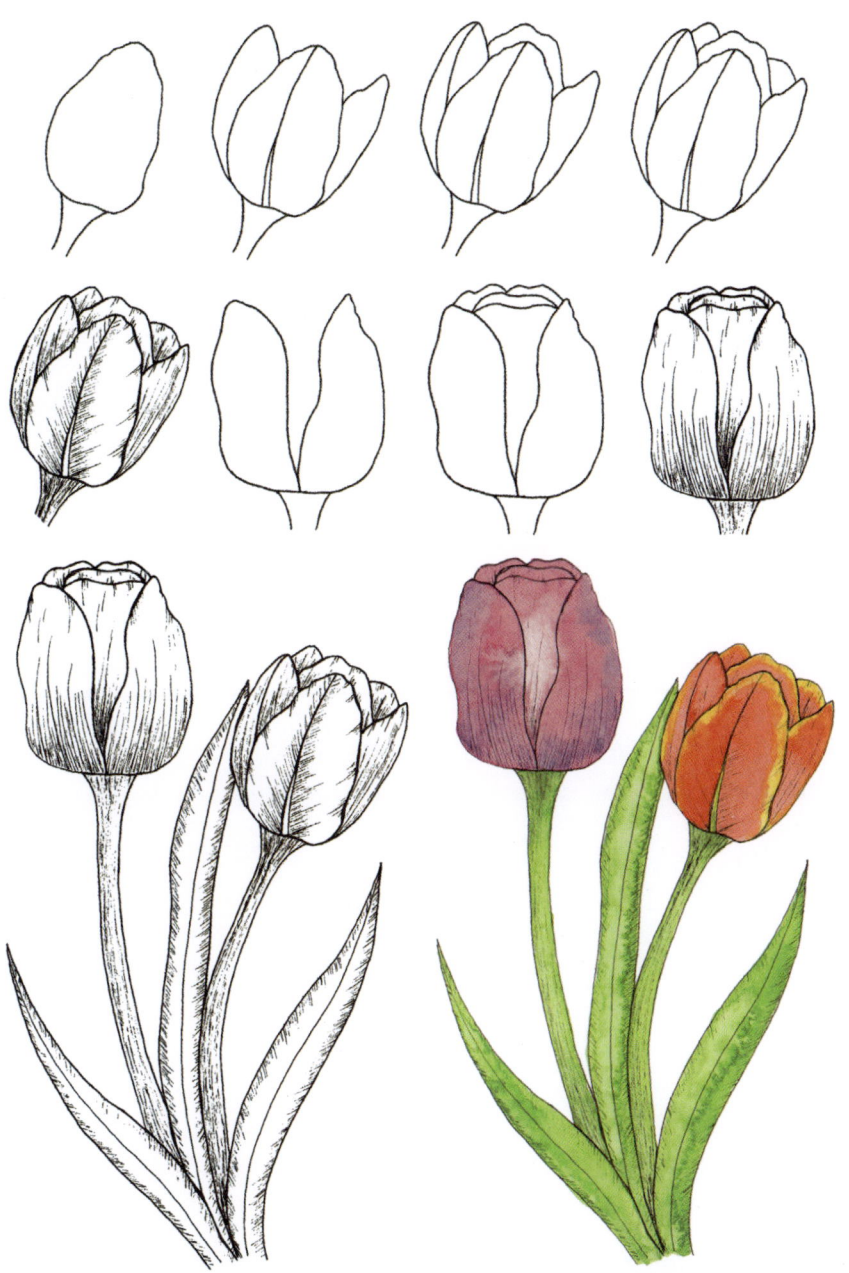

Pansy

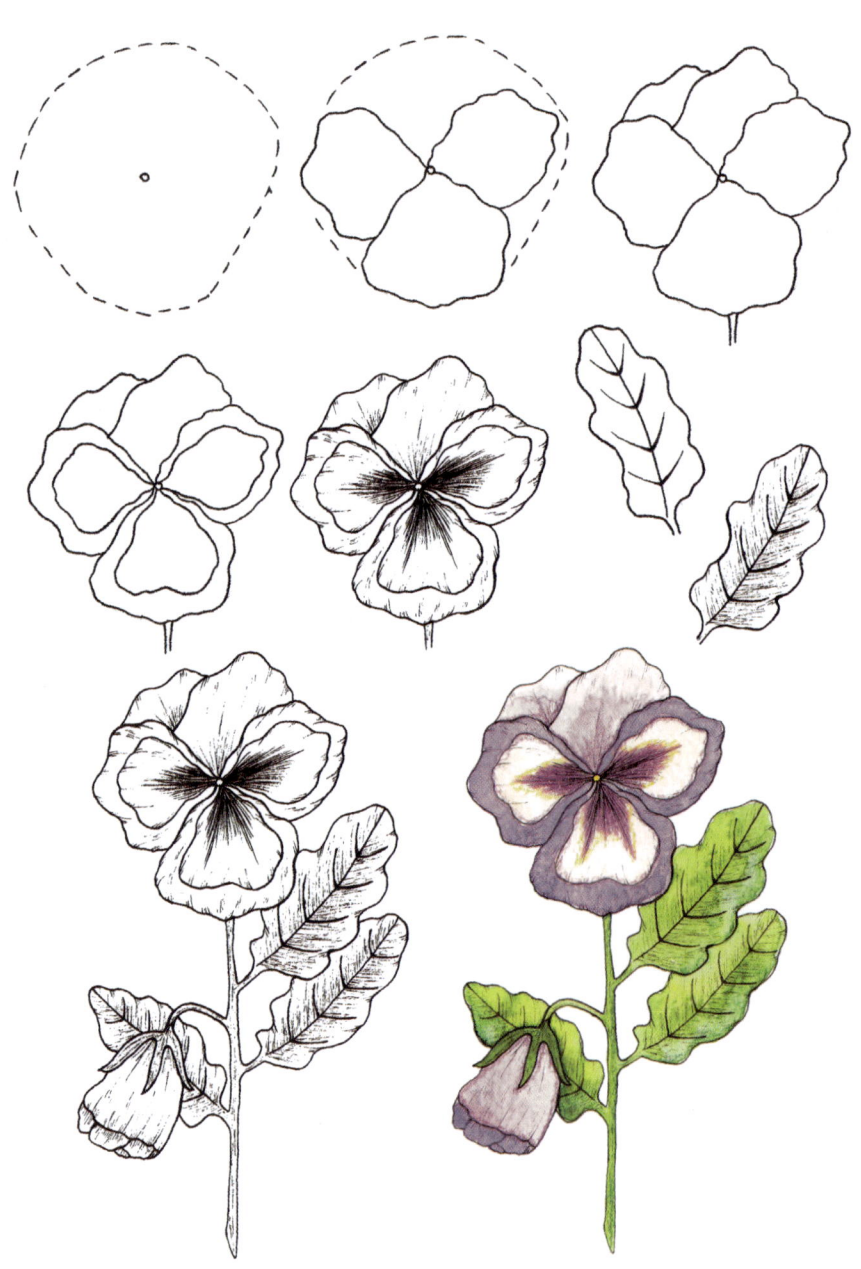

Common Daisy

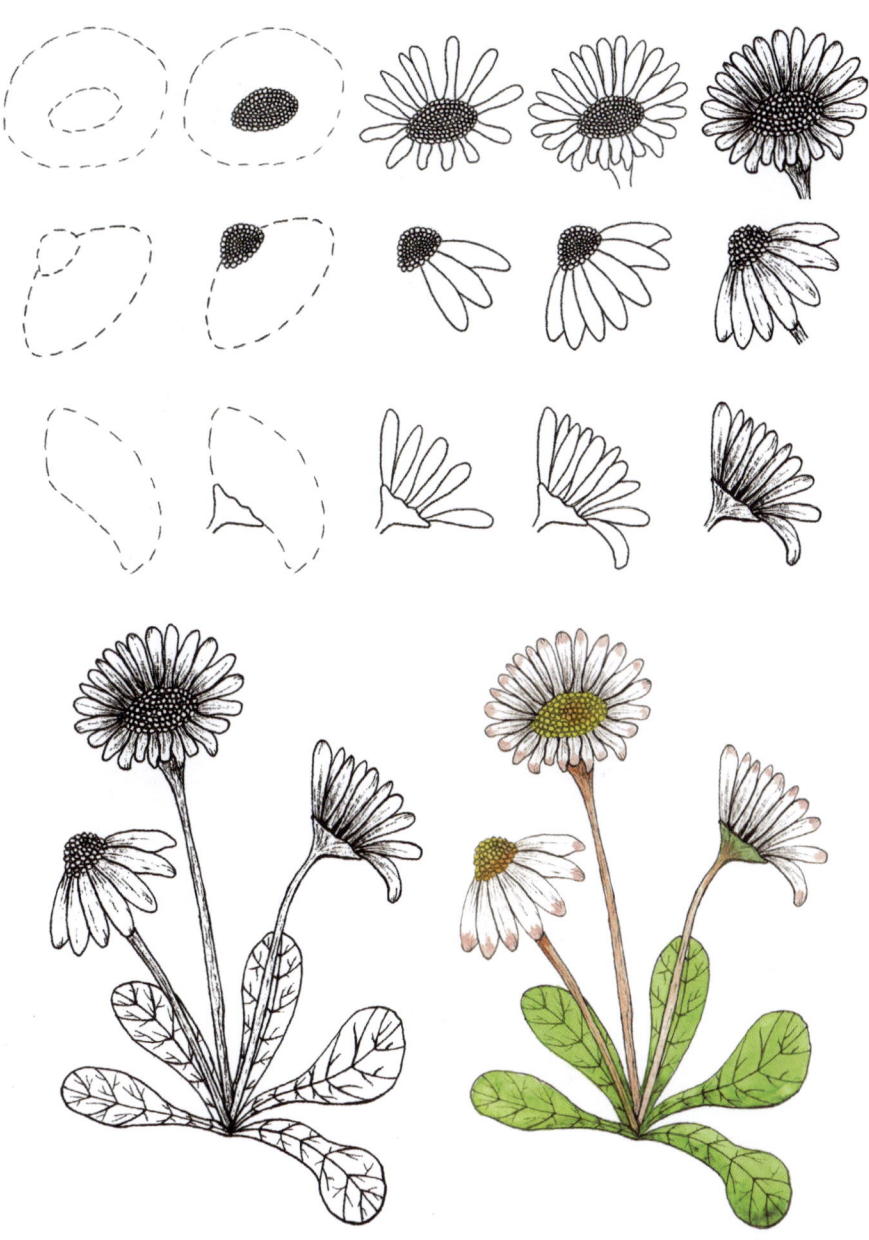

Sunflower

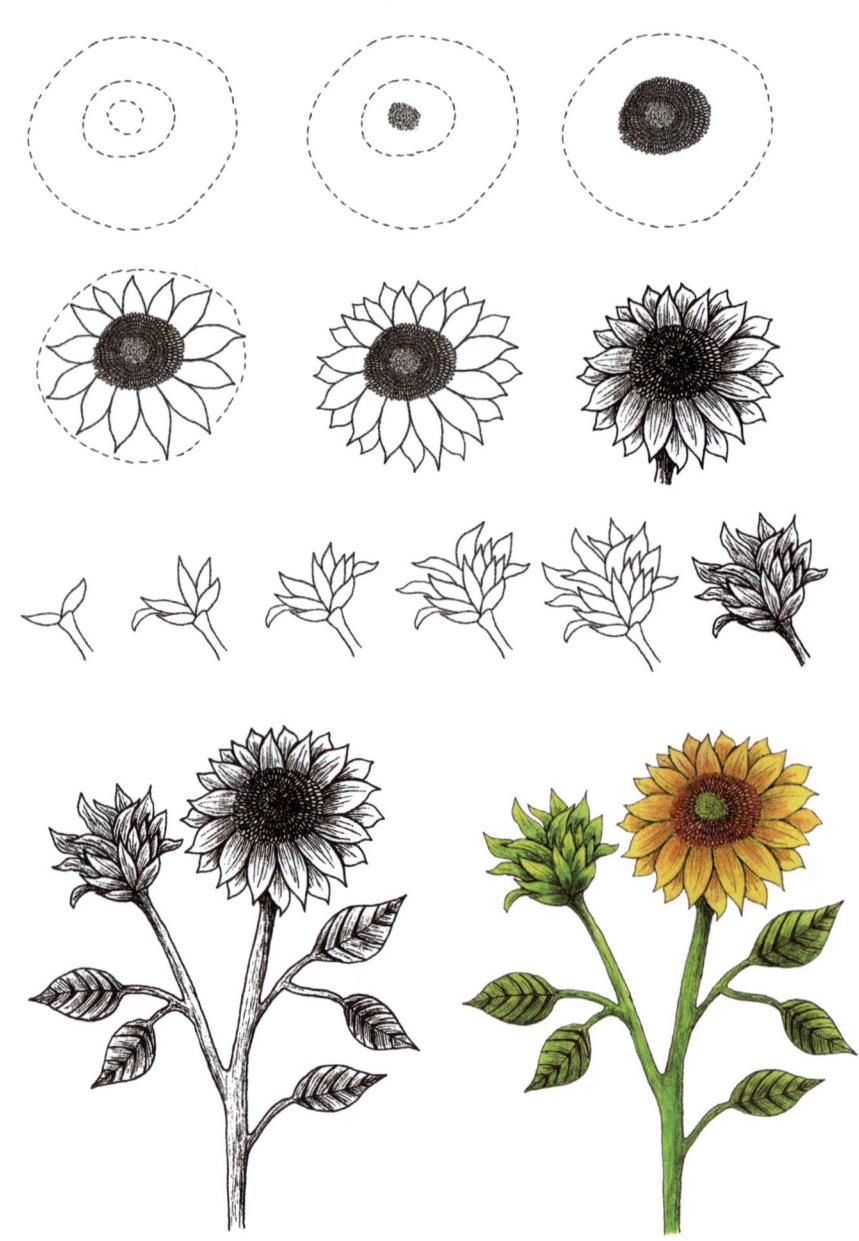

Dandelion

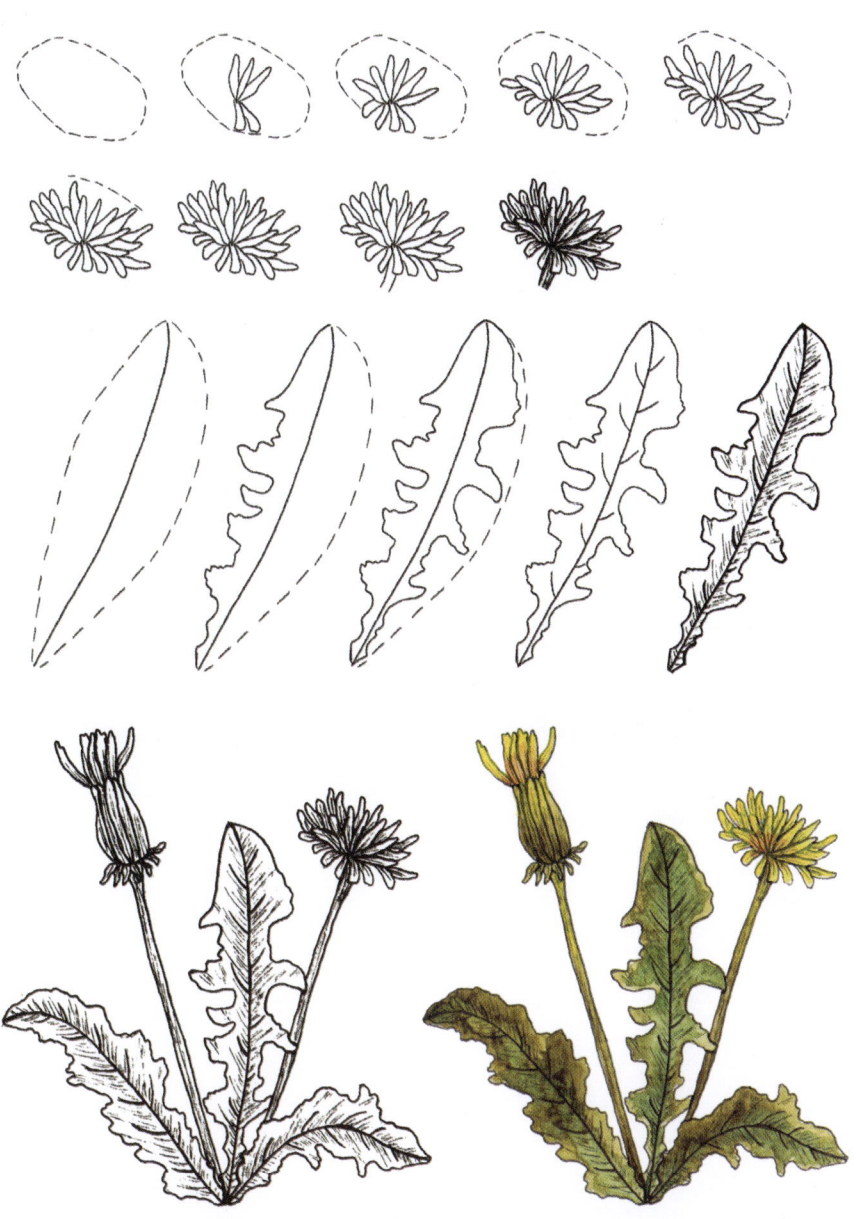

Dahlia

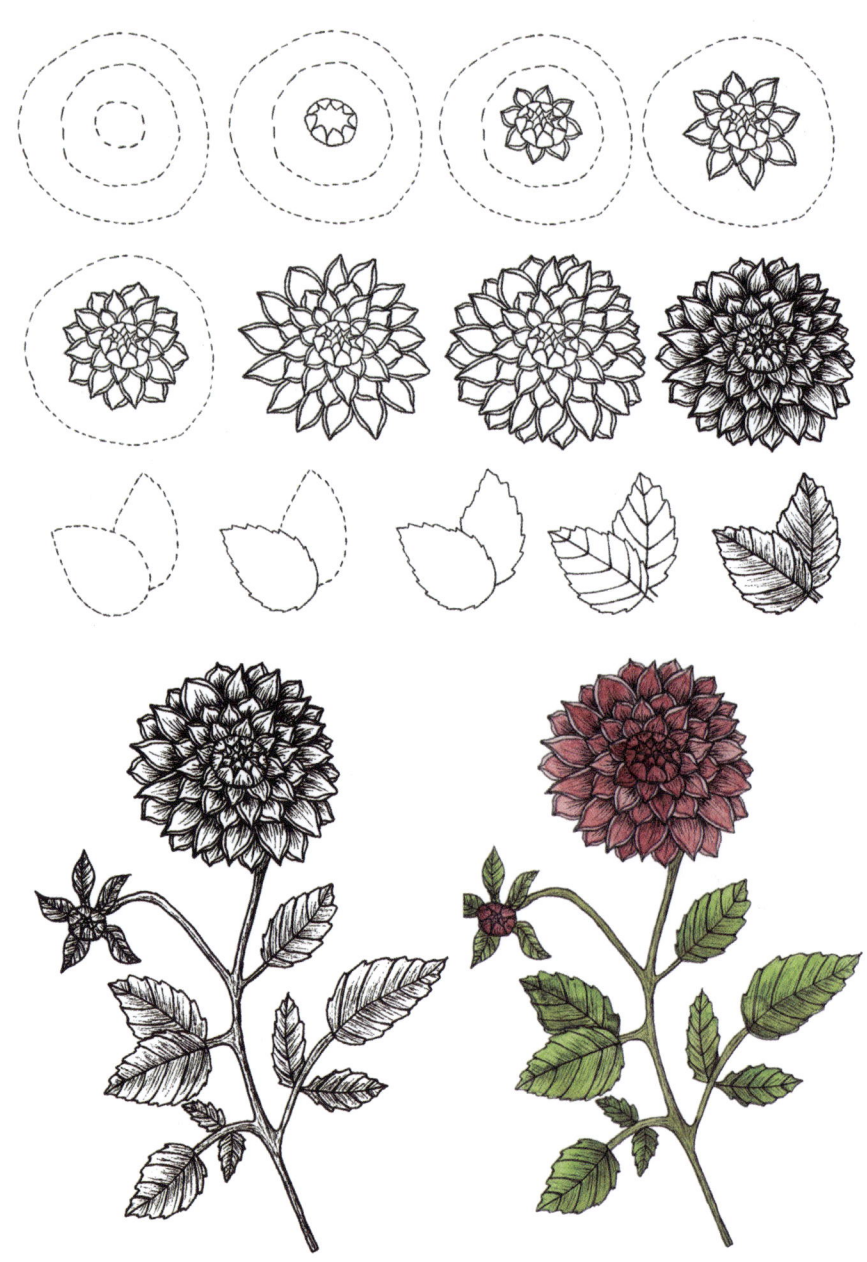

Rose

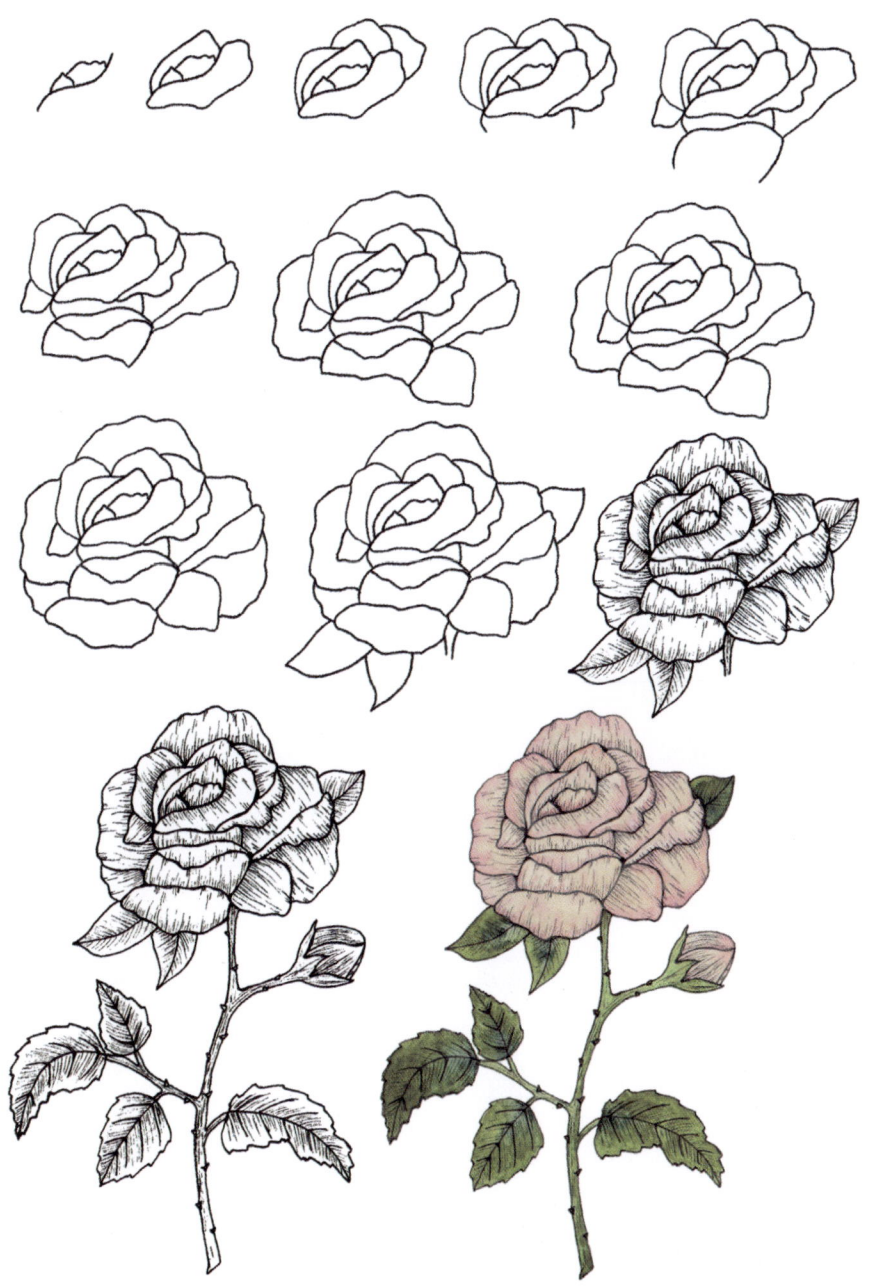

Crocus

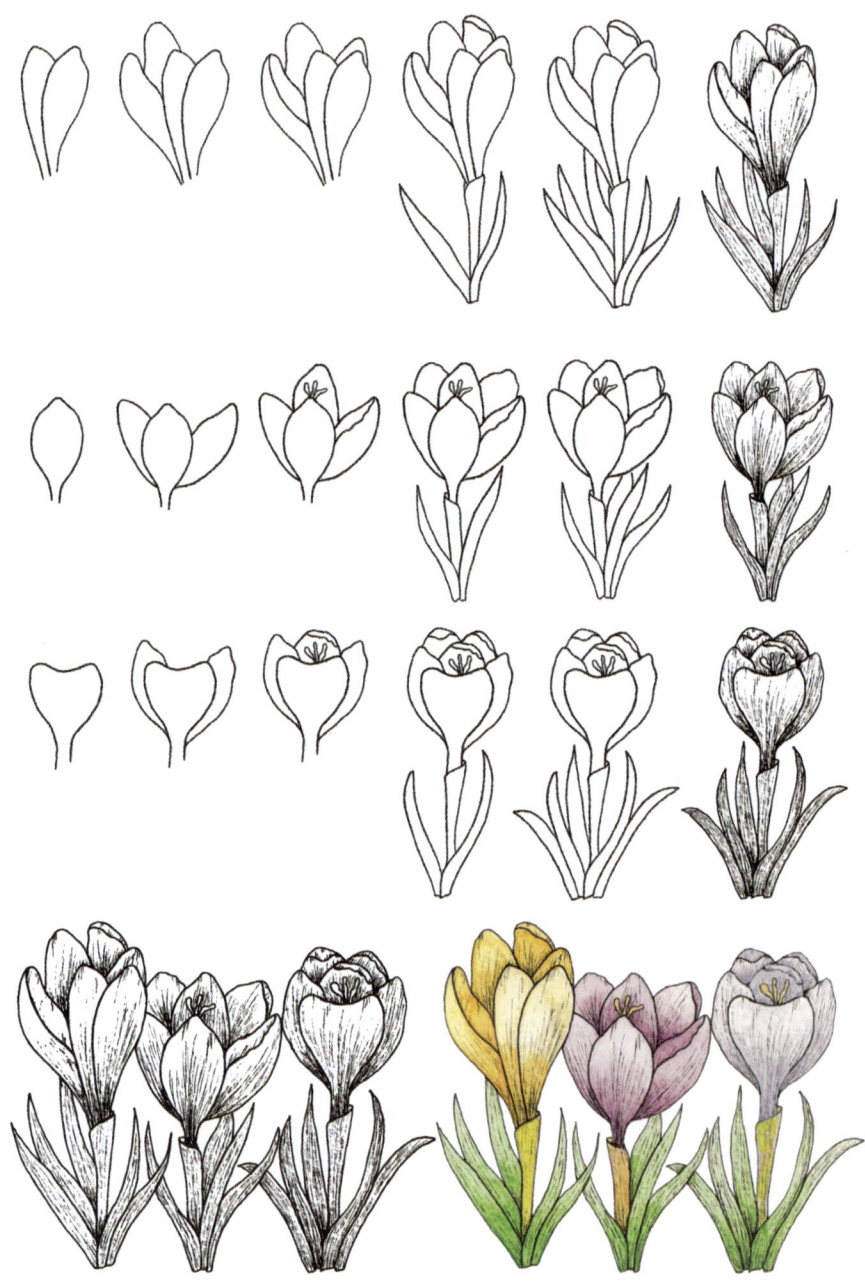

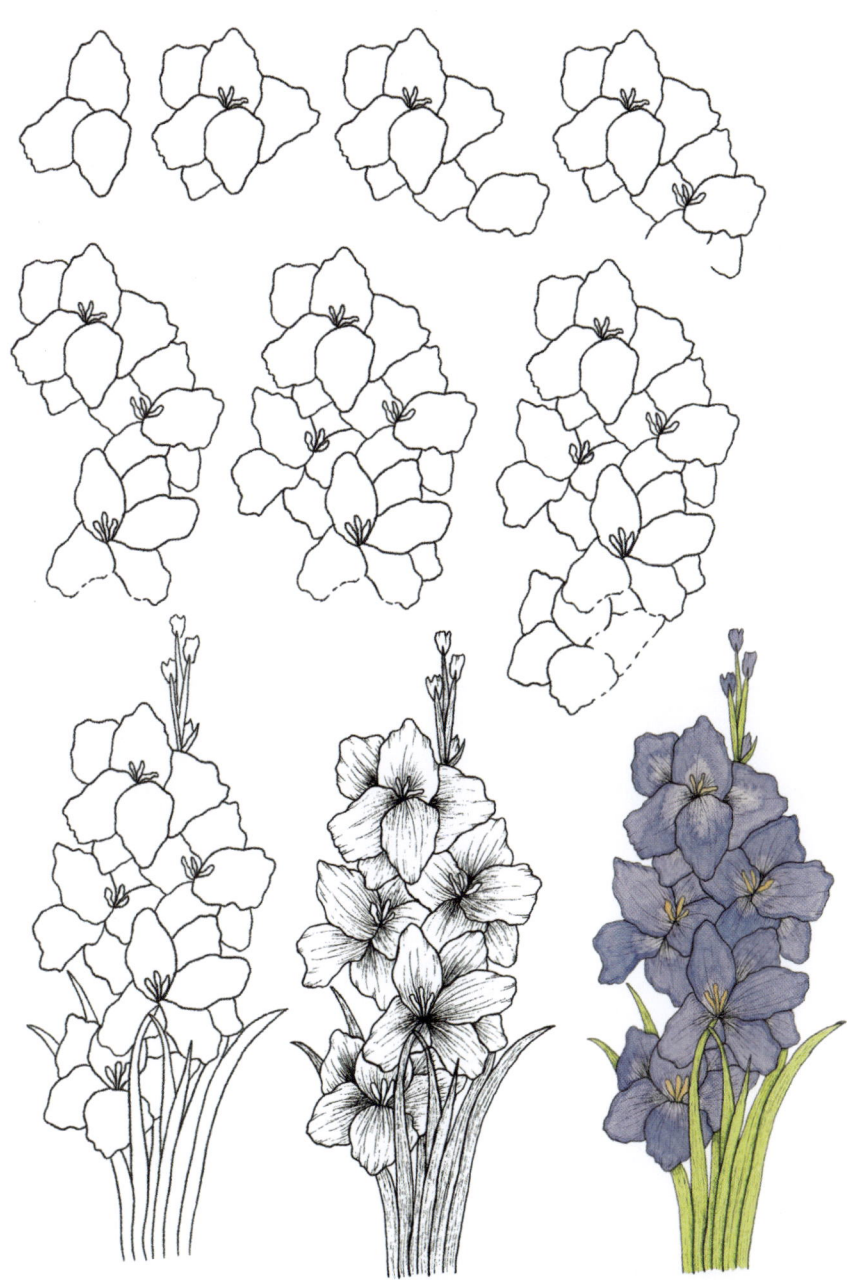

Foxglove

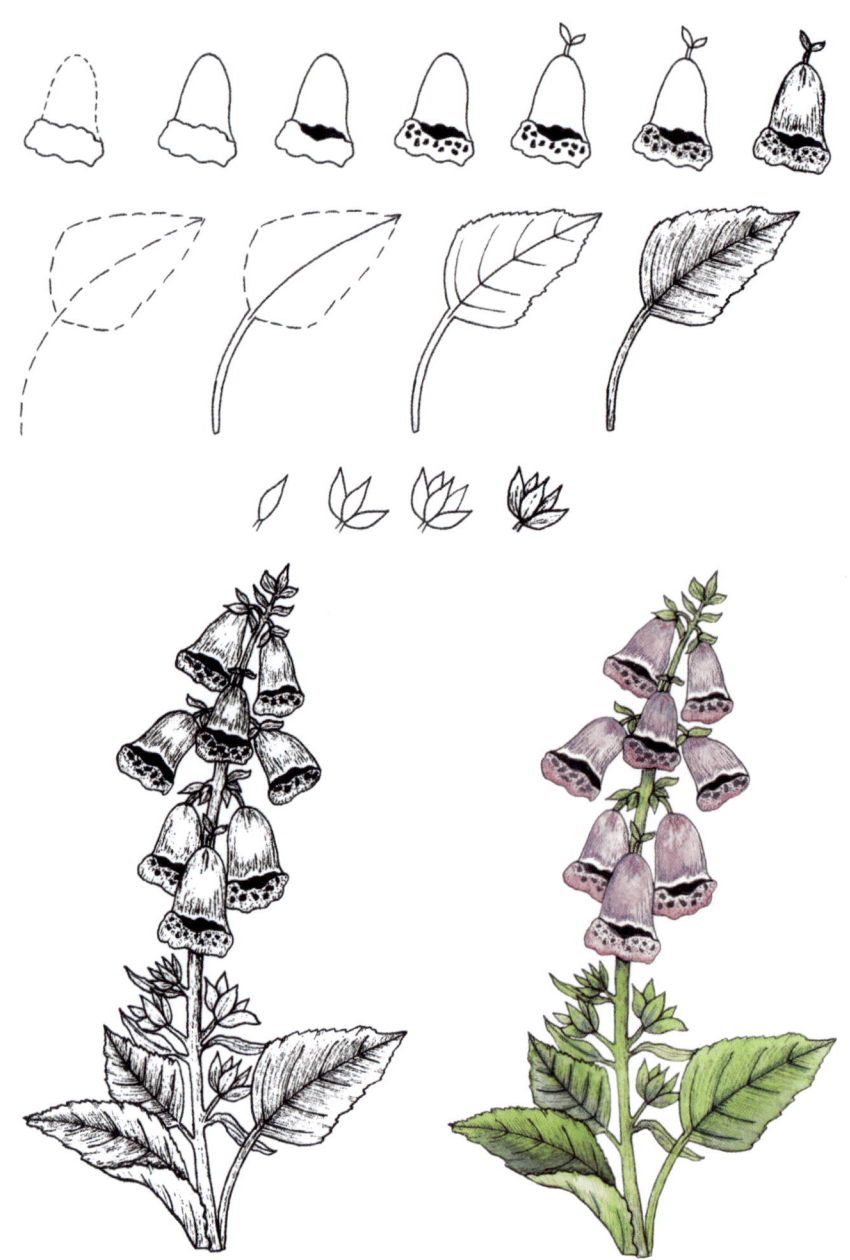

Buddleja

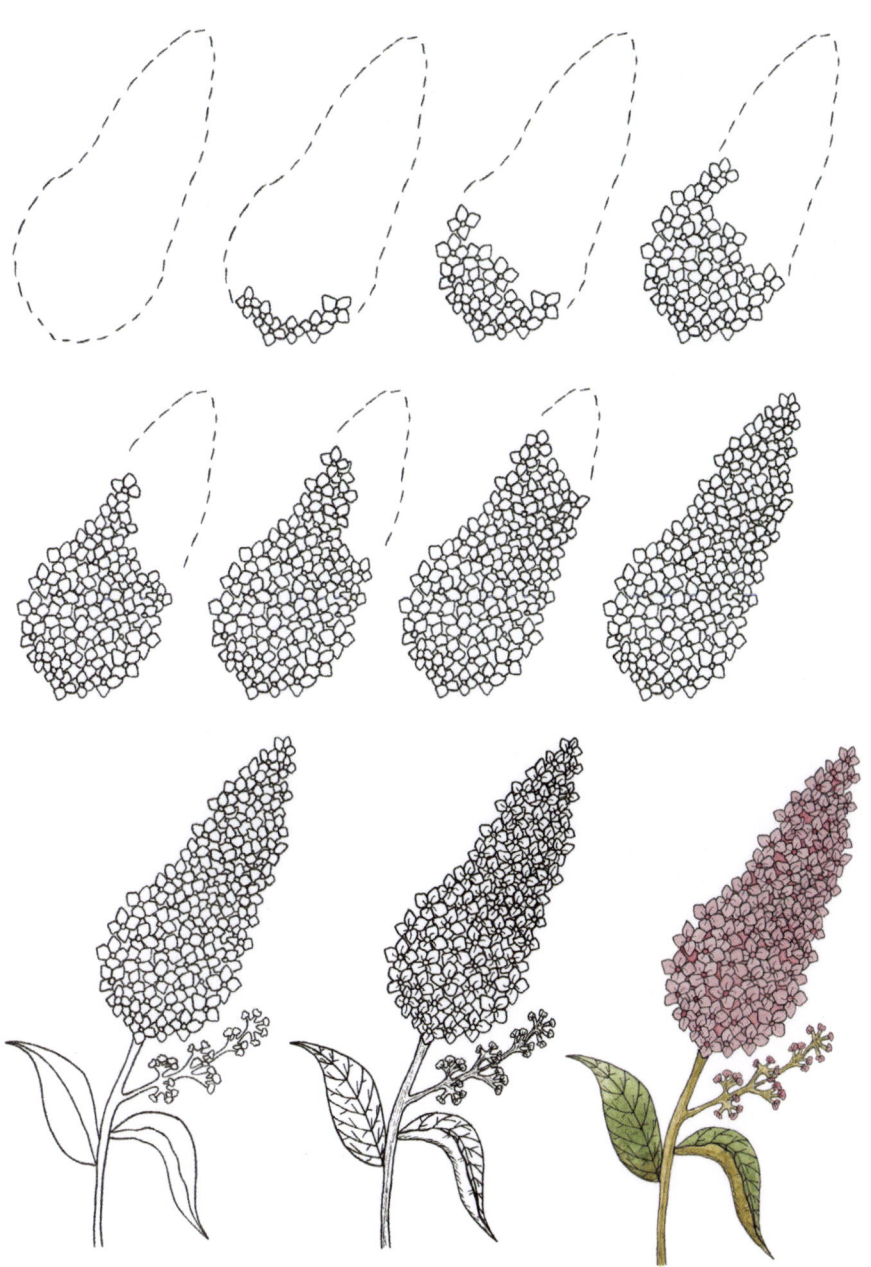

Mint

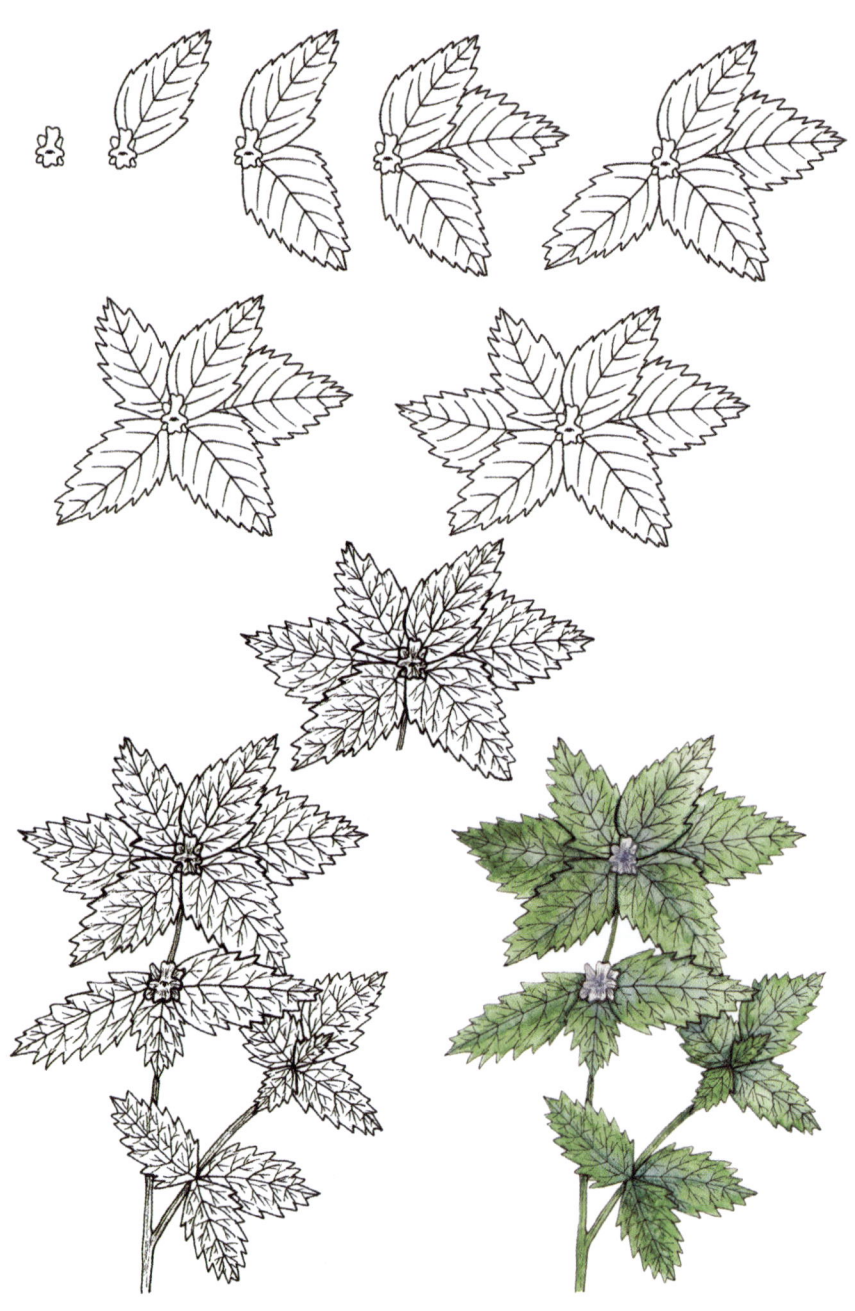

Lavender

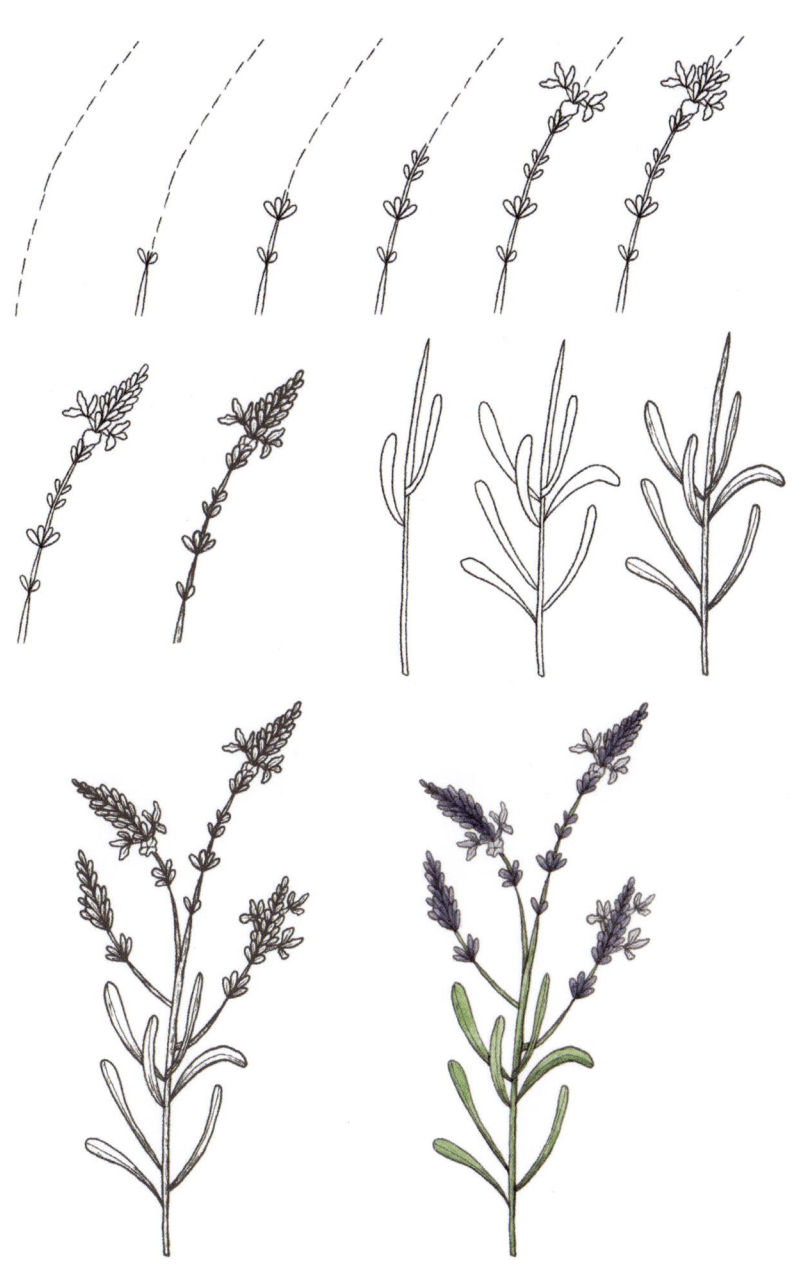

Basil

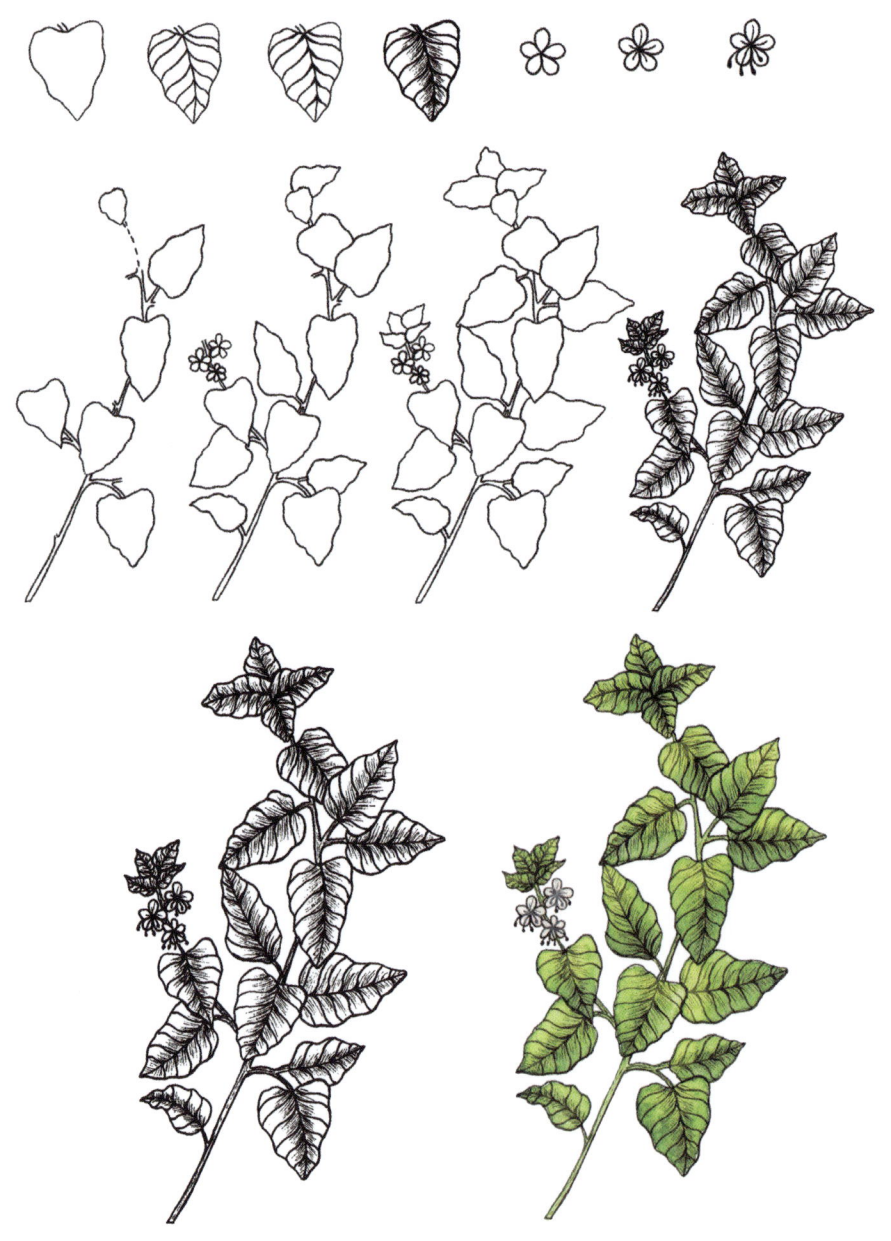

Thyme

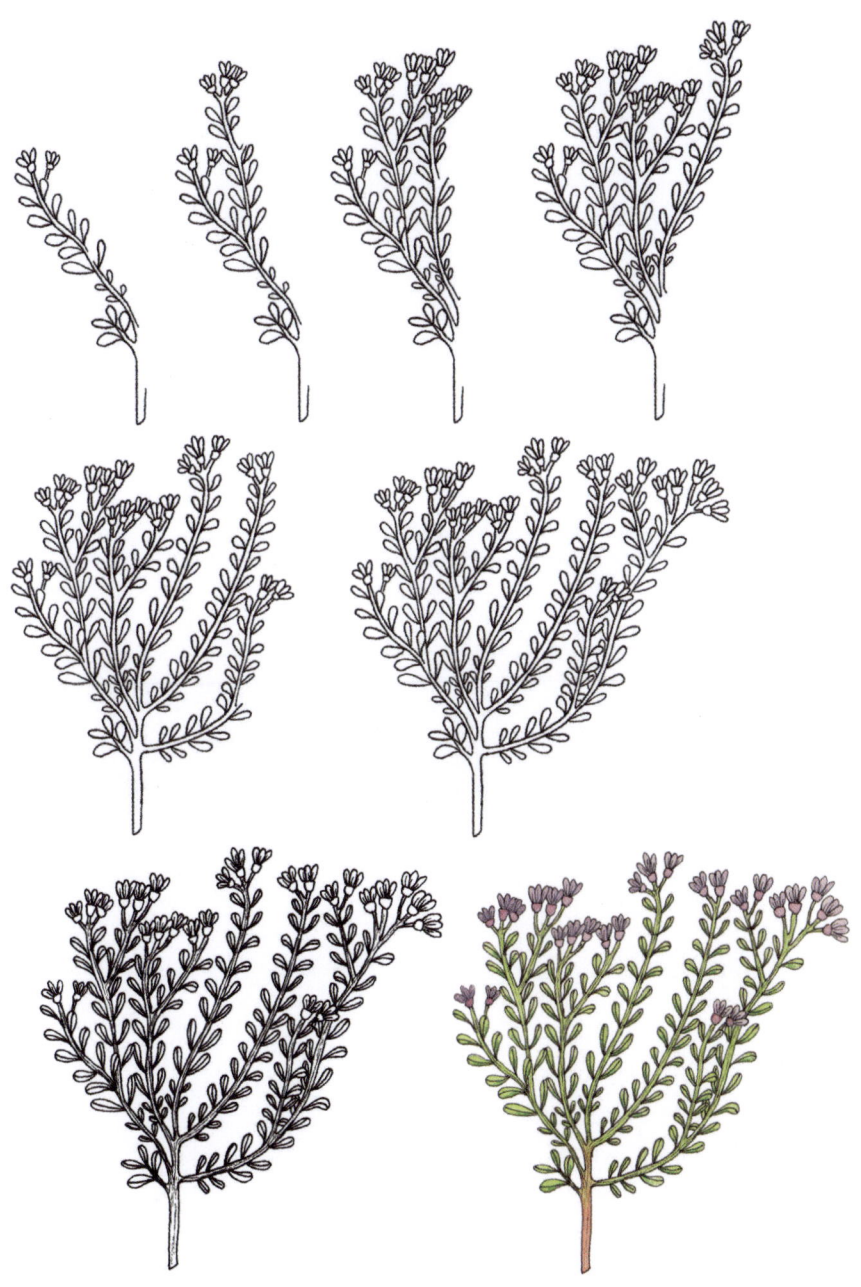

Calla Lily

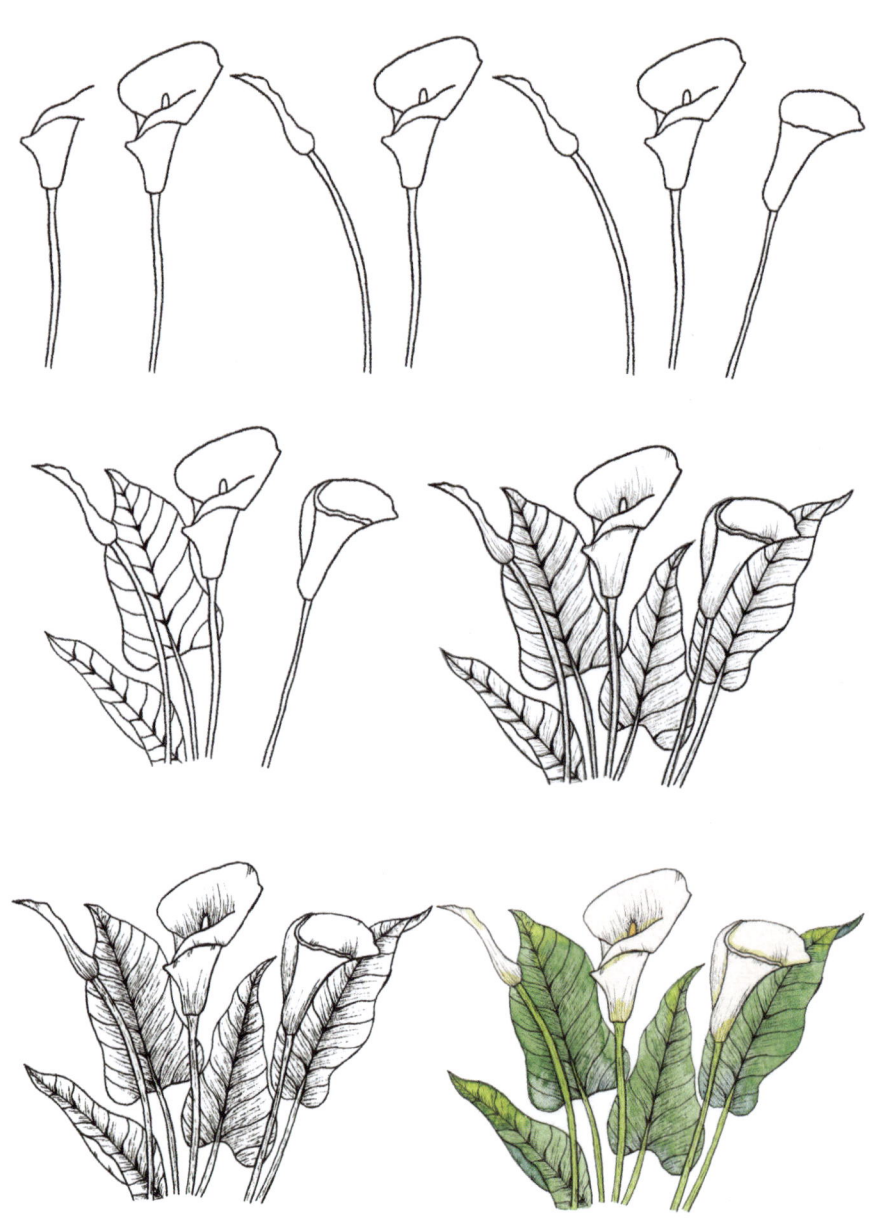

Buttercup

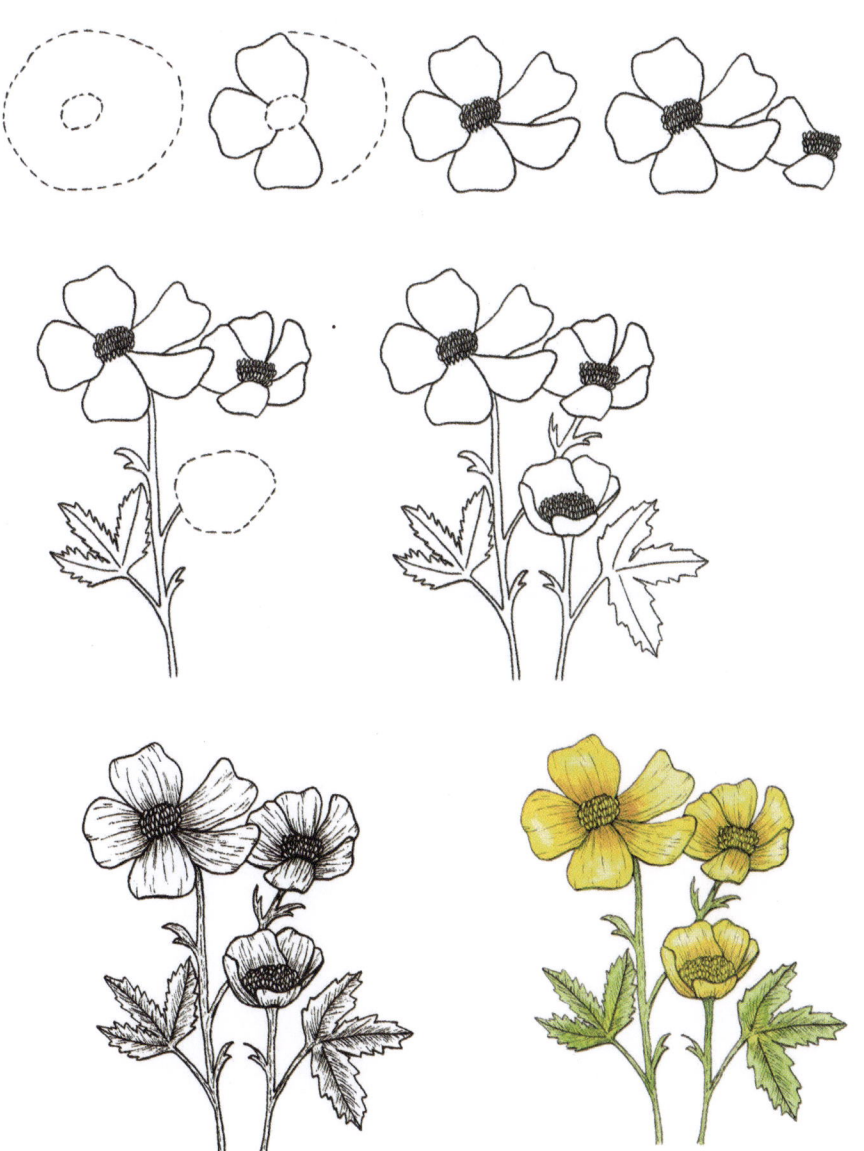

Clematis

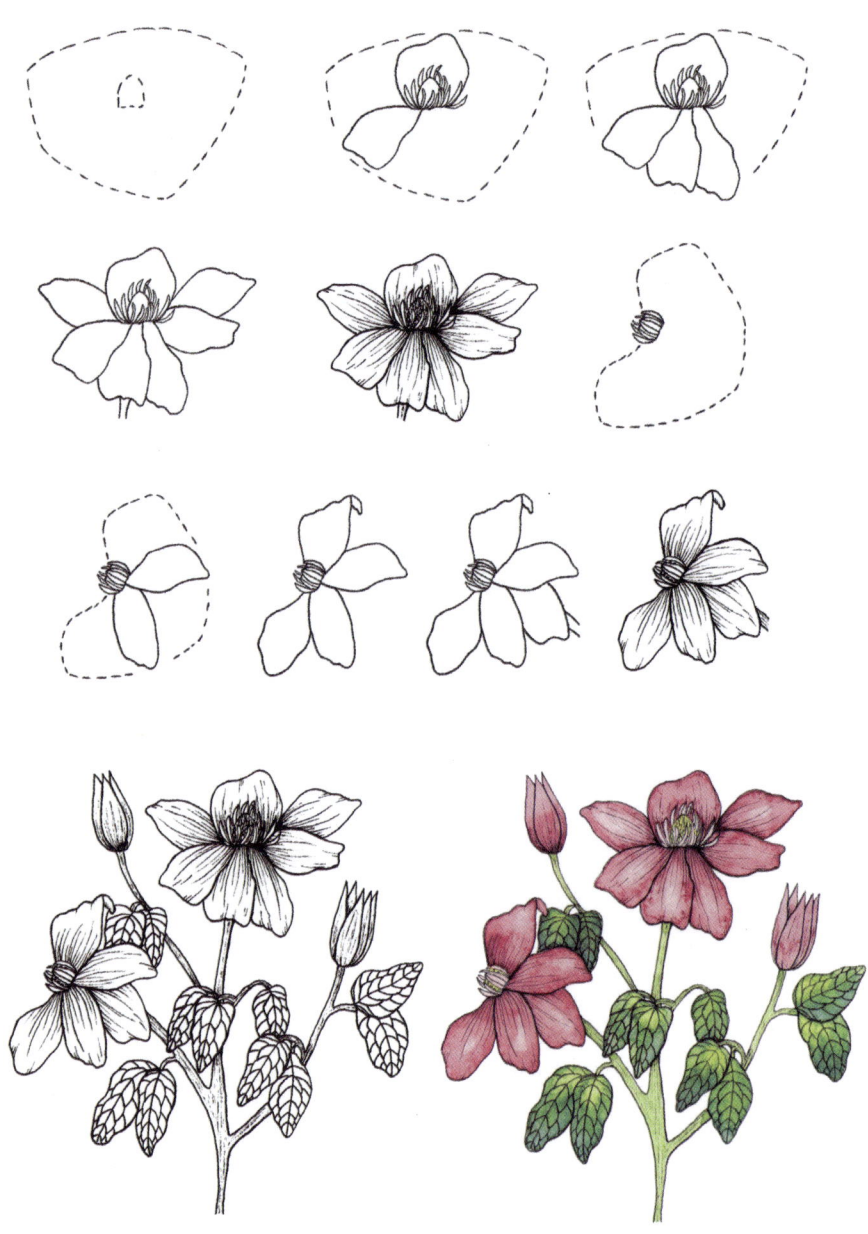

Delphinium

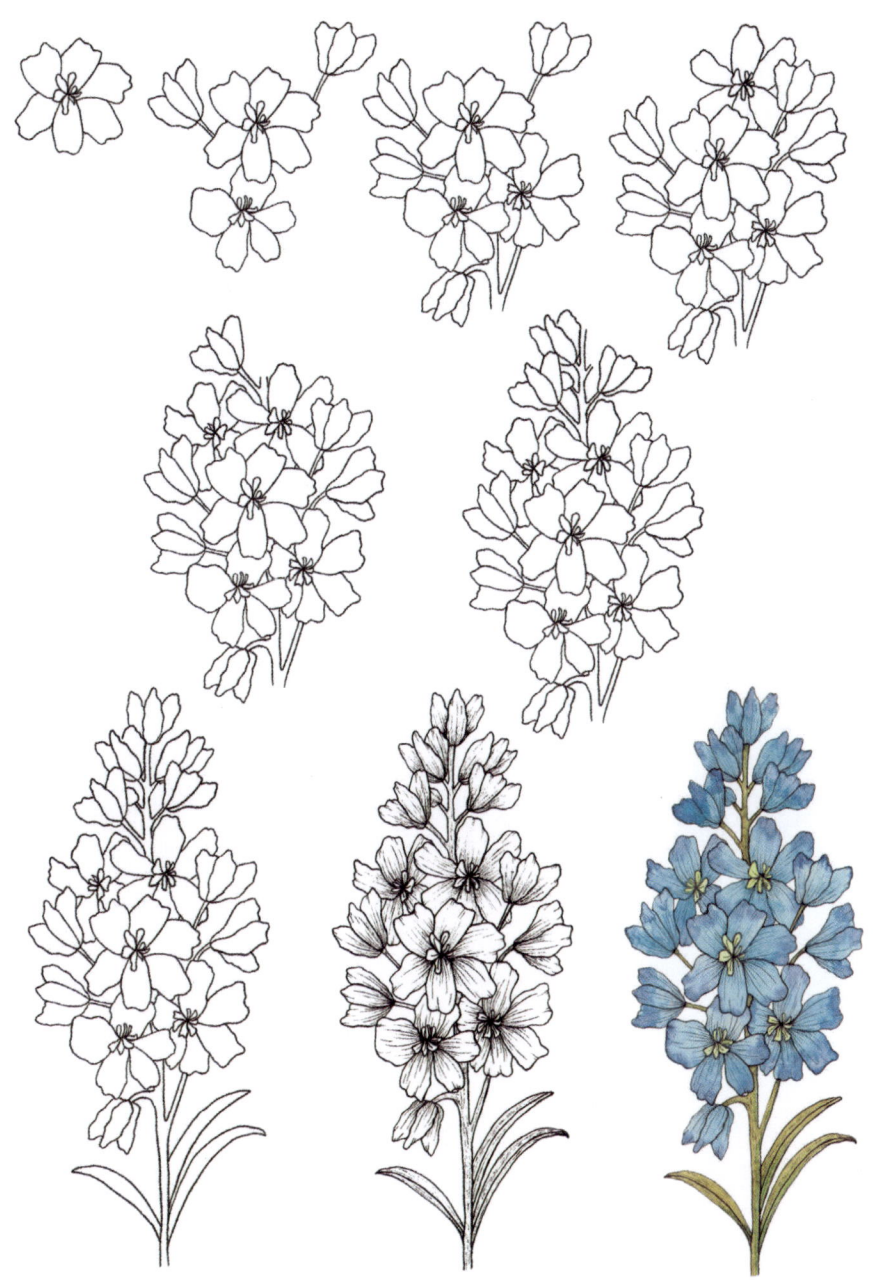

Peony

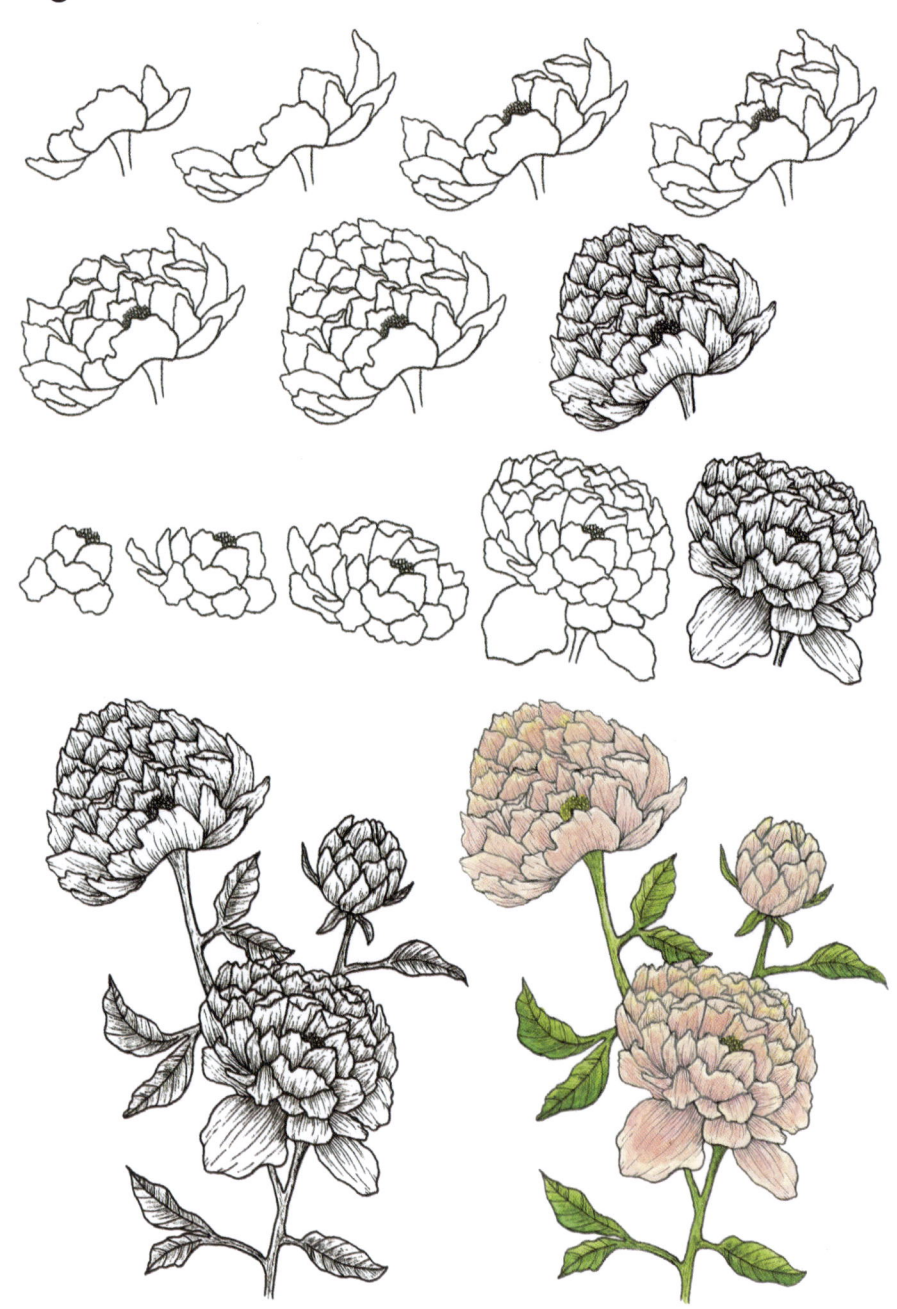

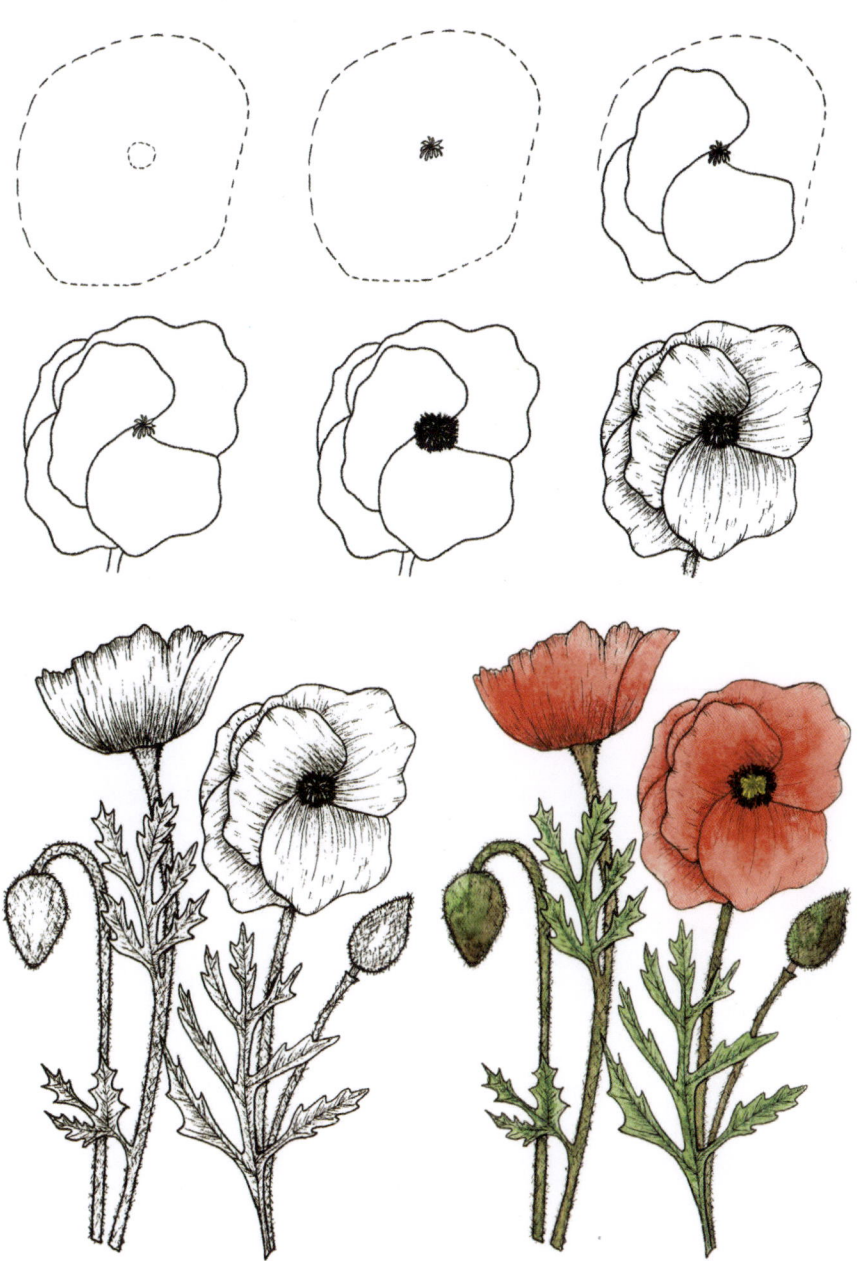

Camellia

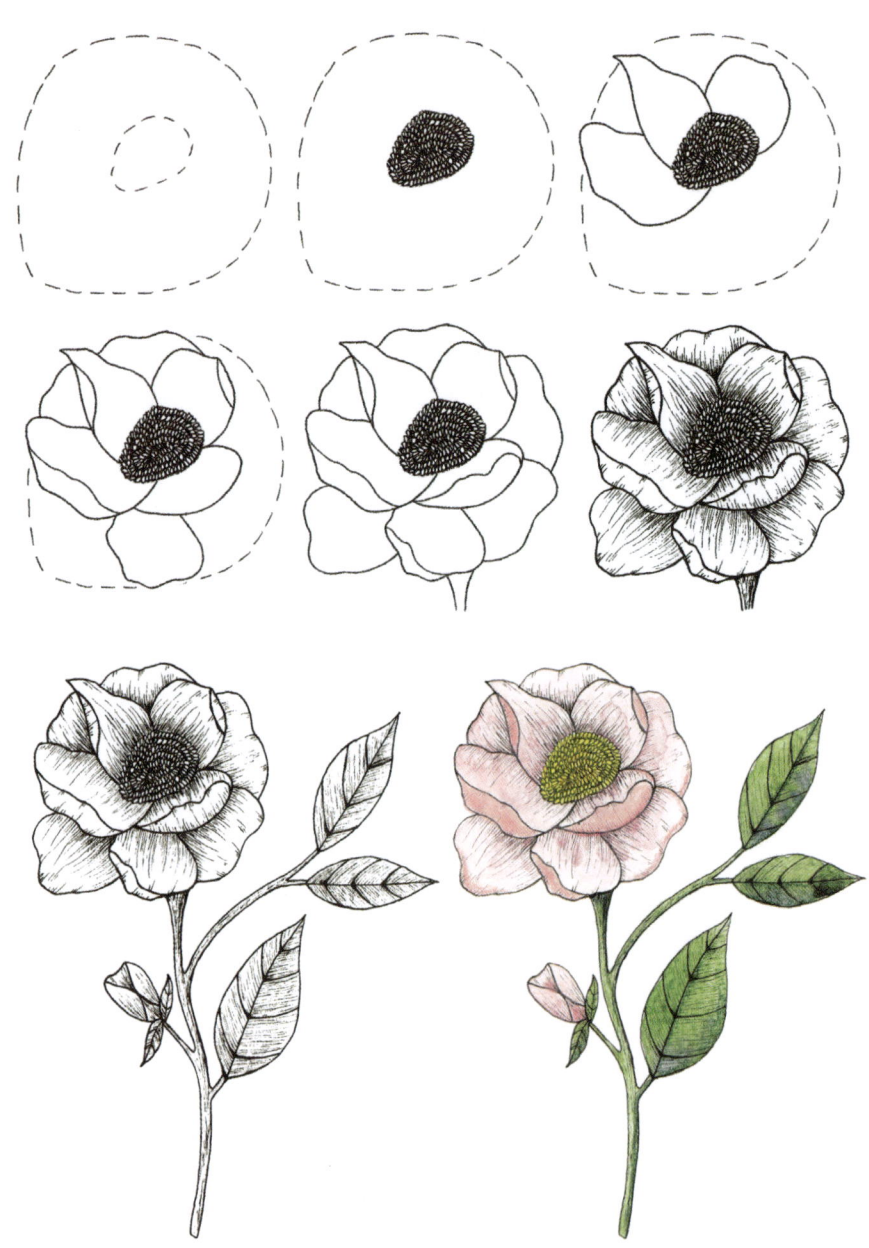

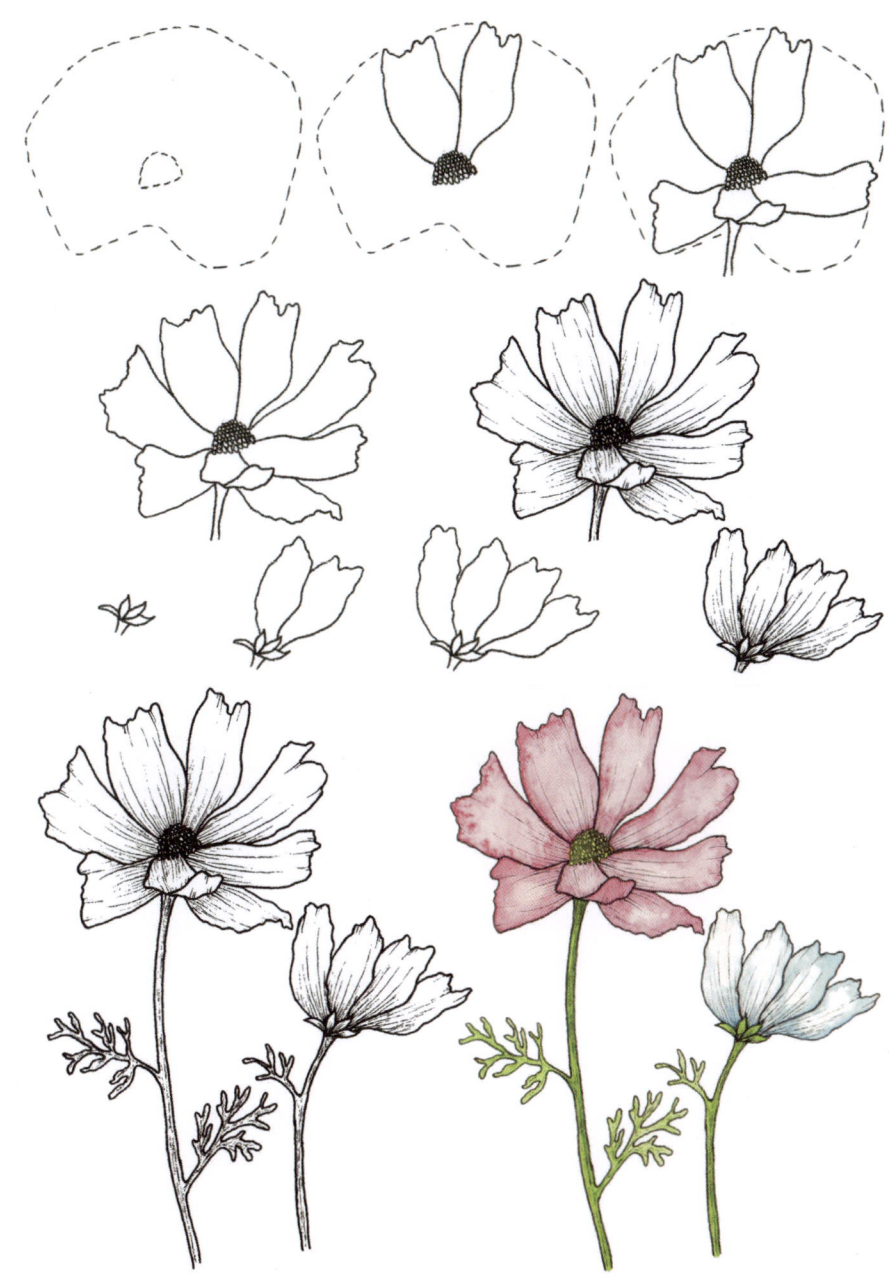

Carnation

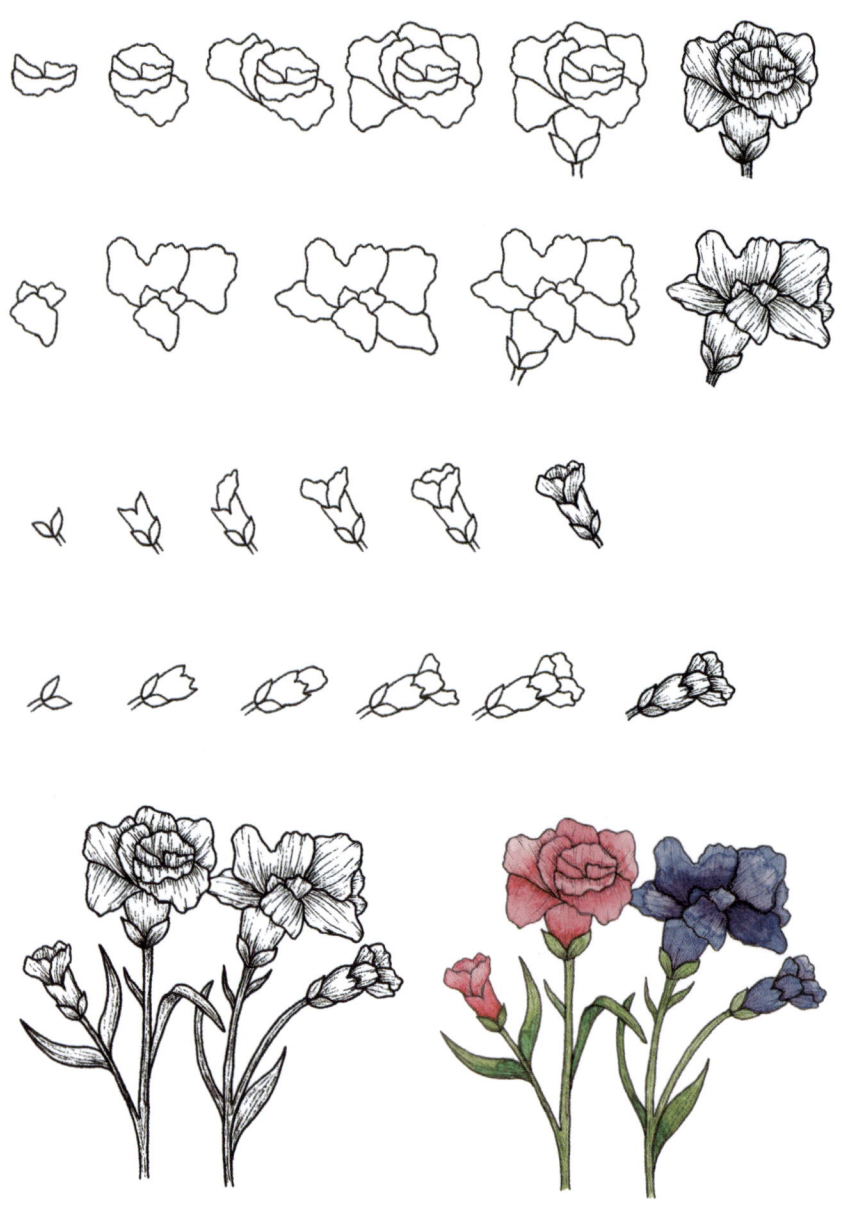

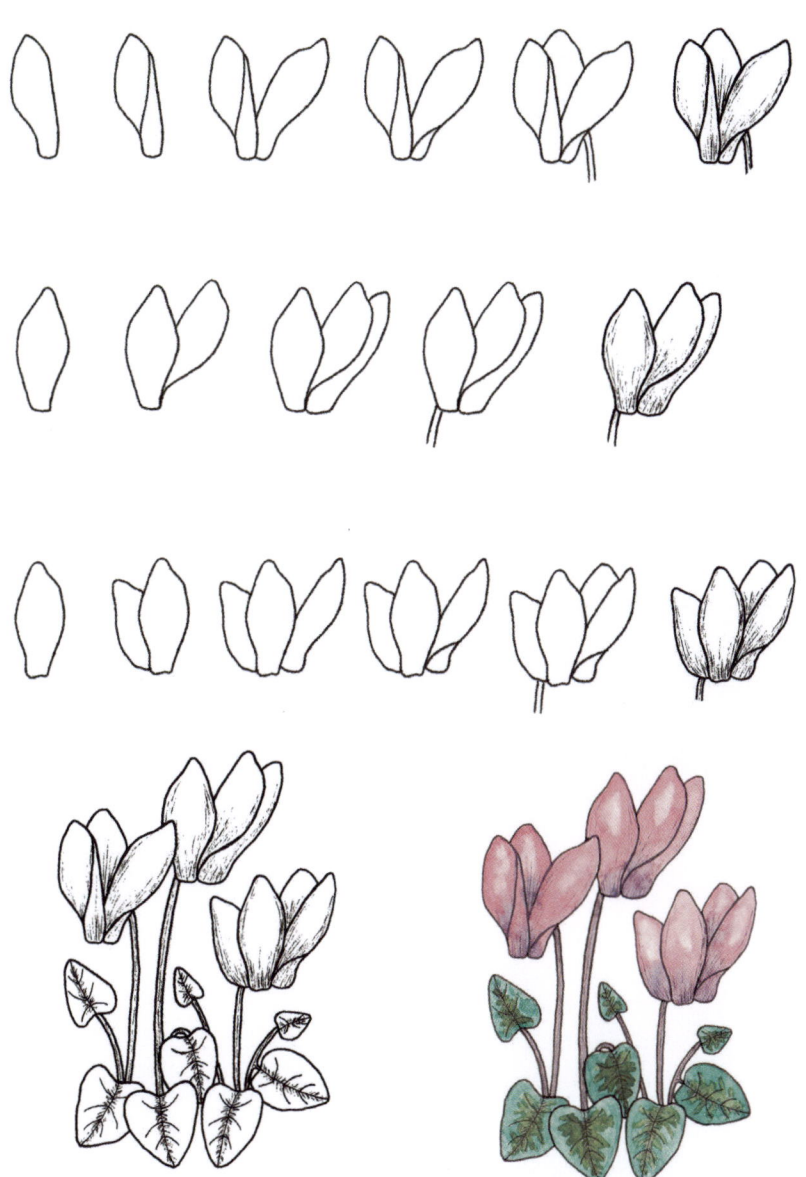

Anemone

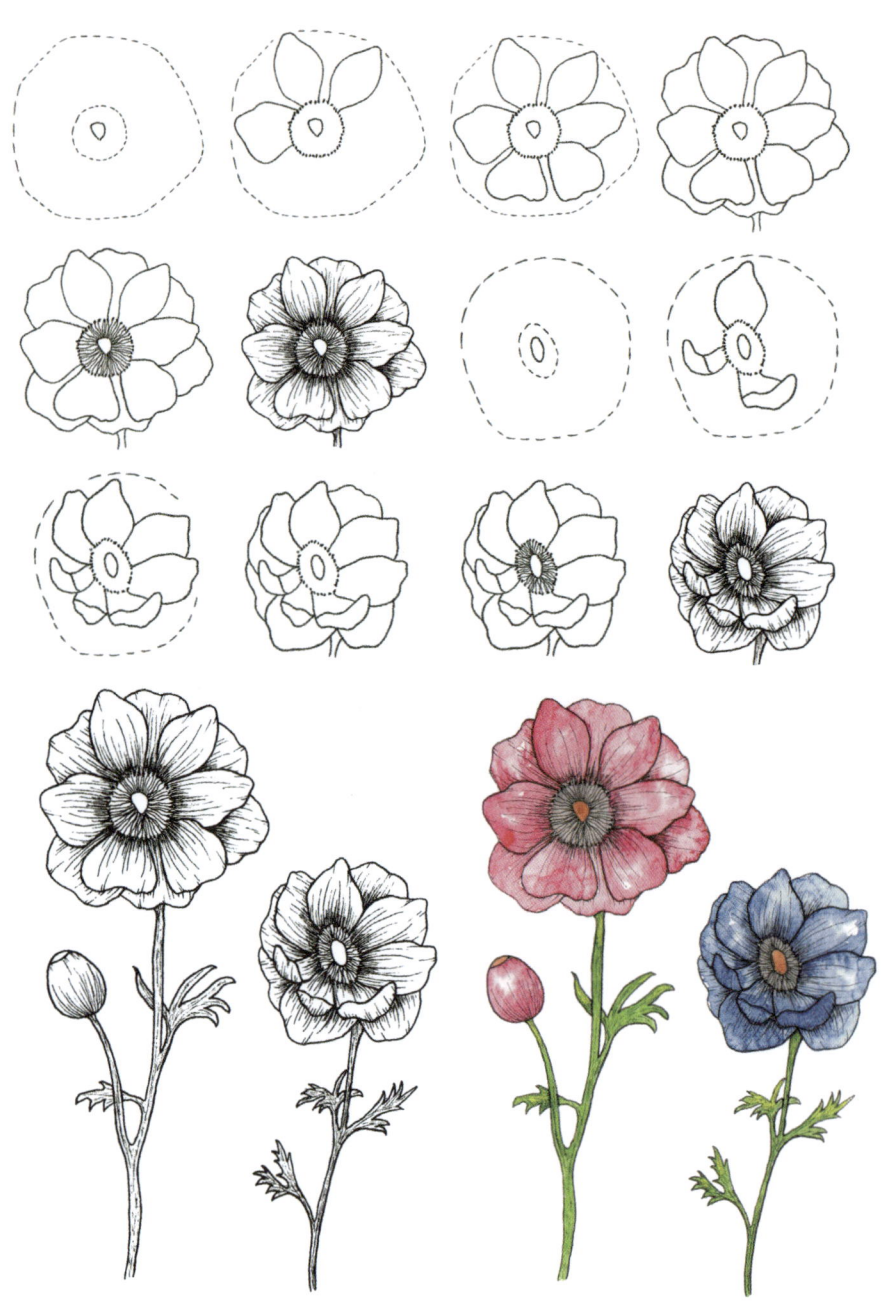

Primrose

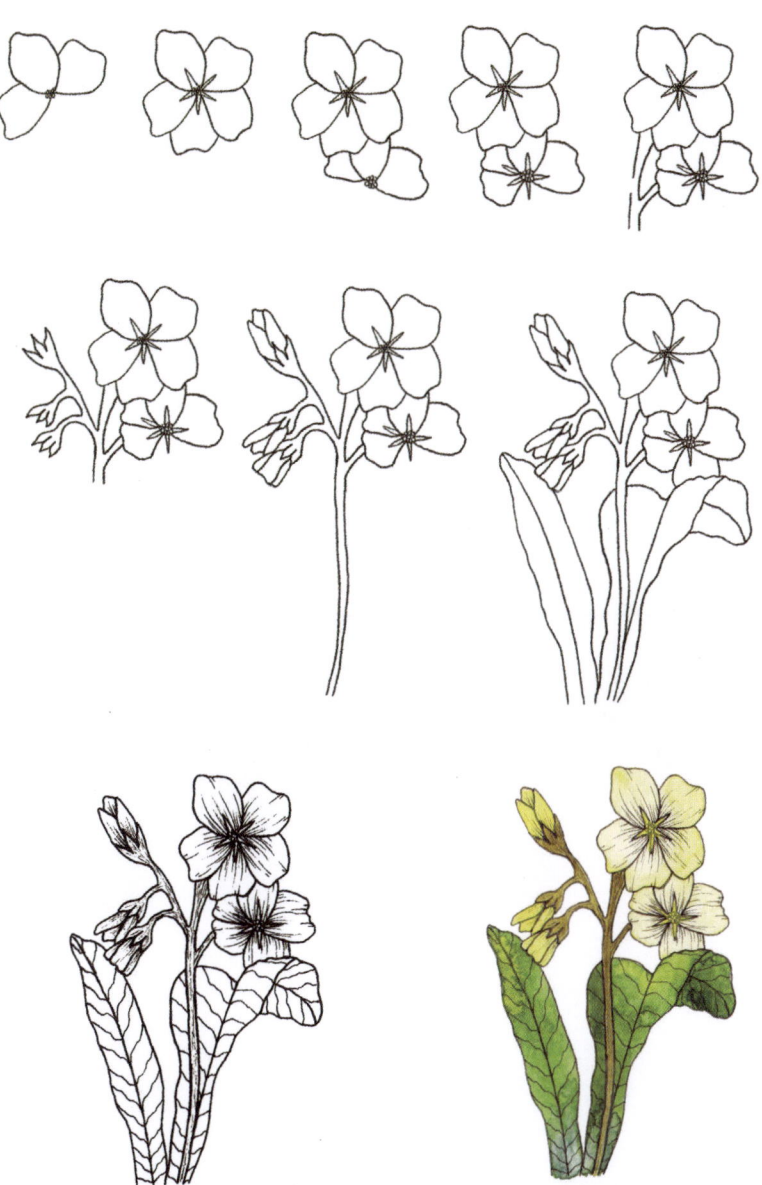

Bluebell

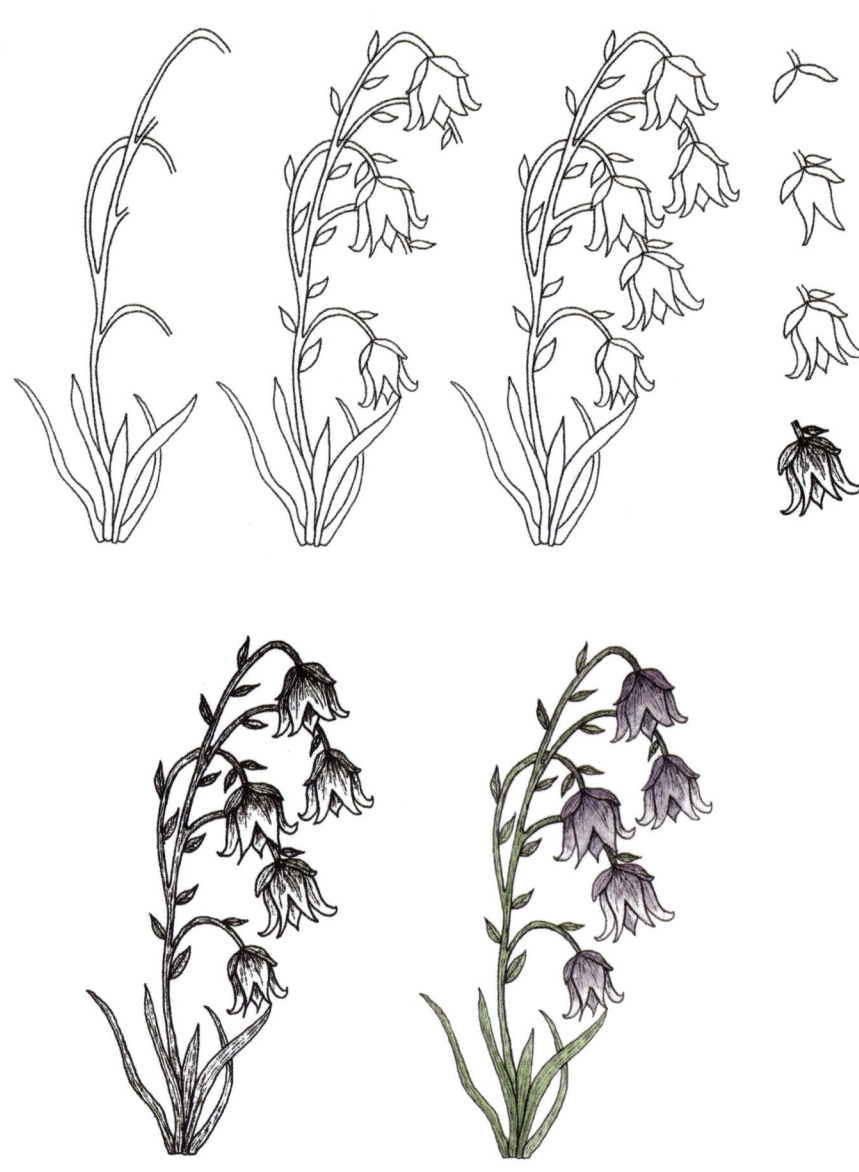

Helenium

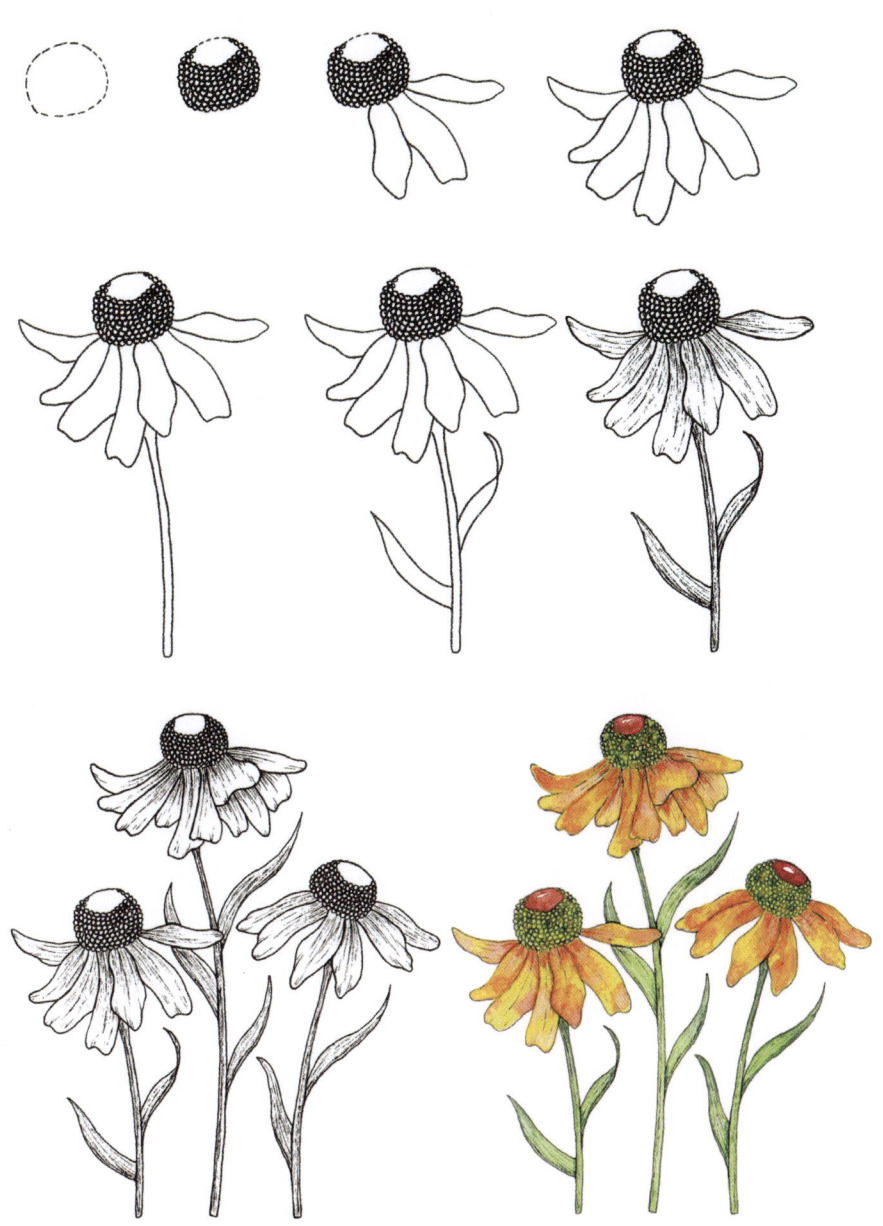

Cornflower

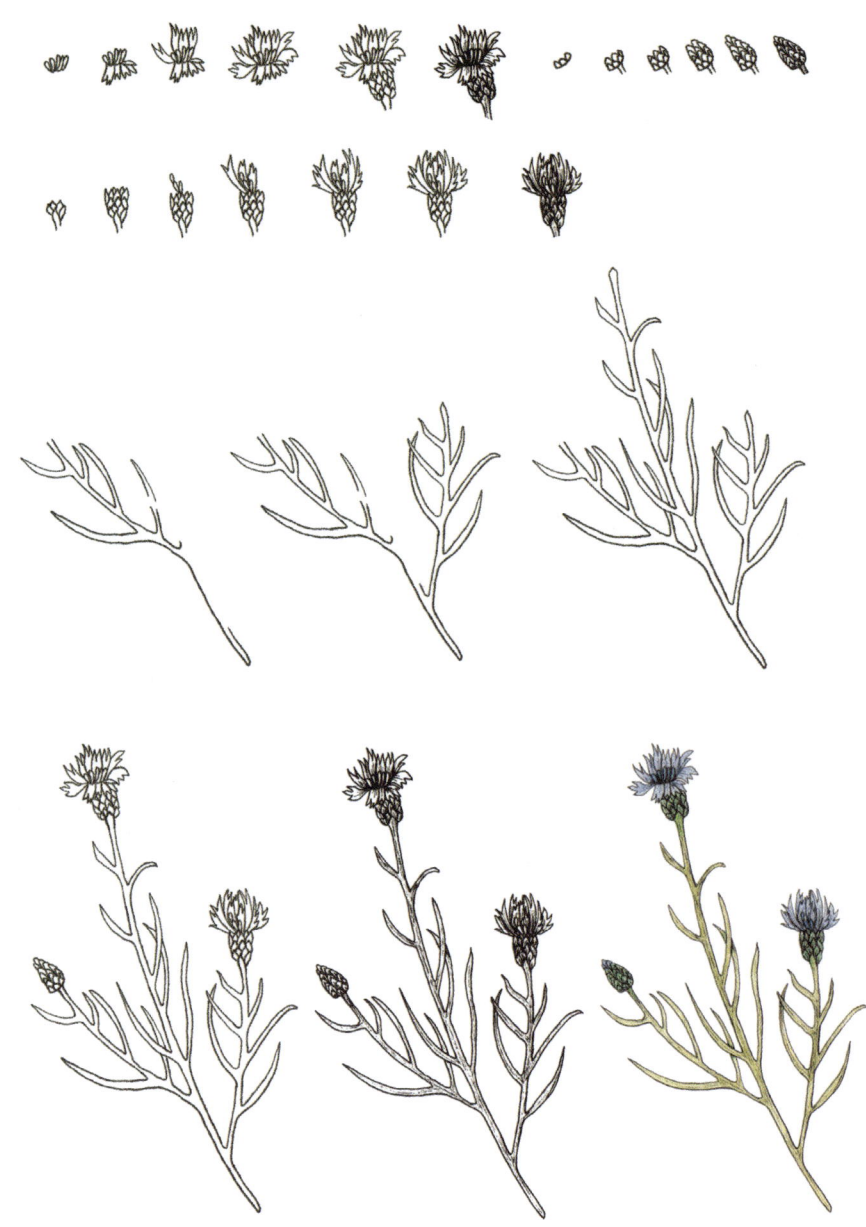

Aster

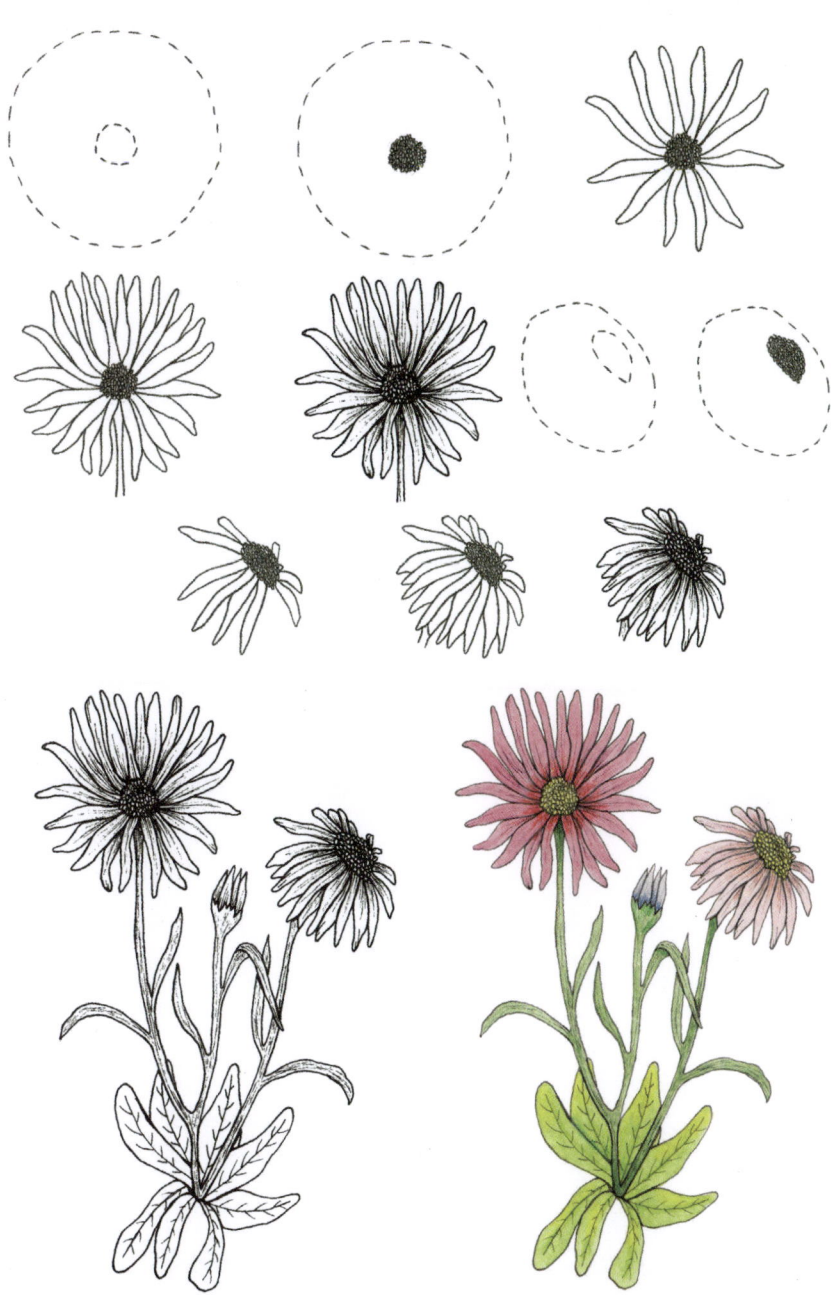

Hellebore

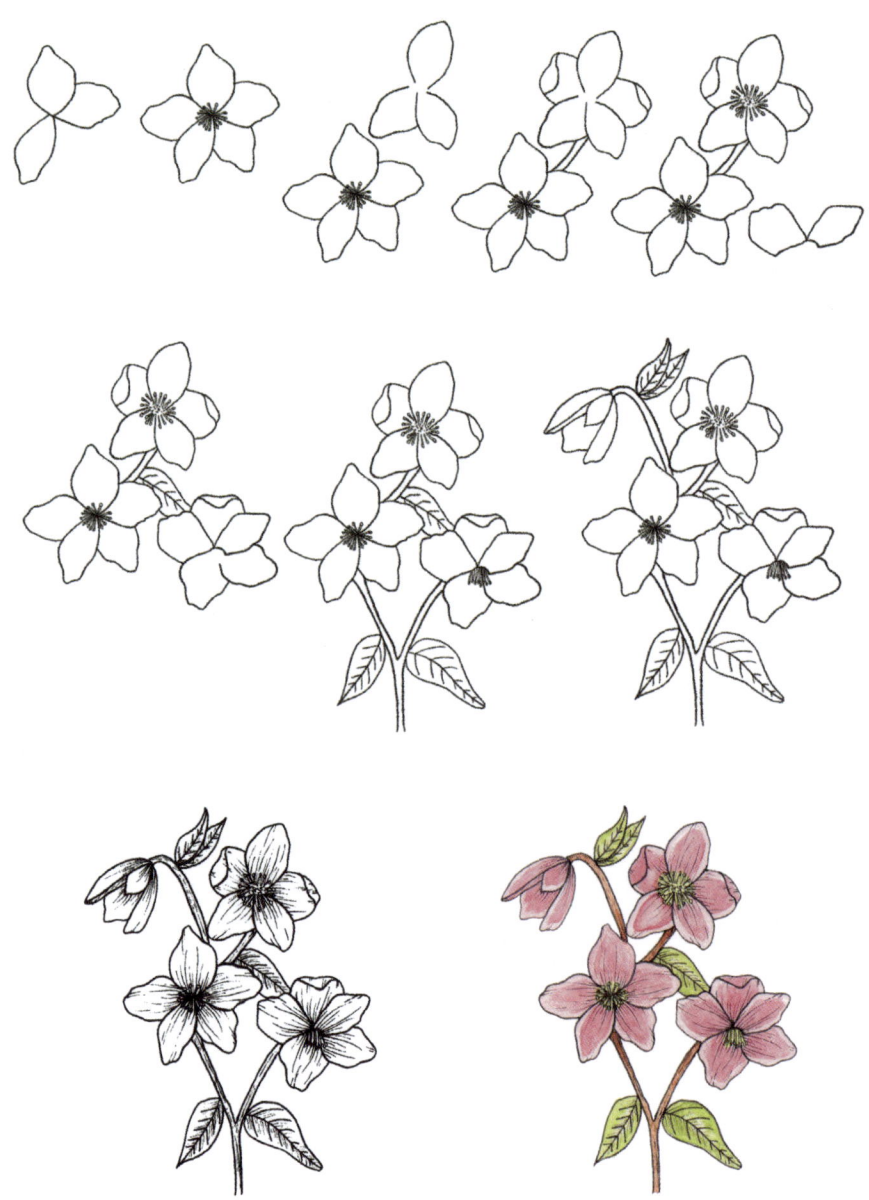

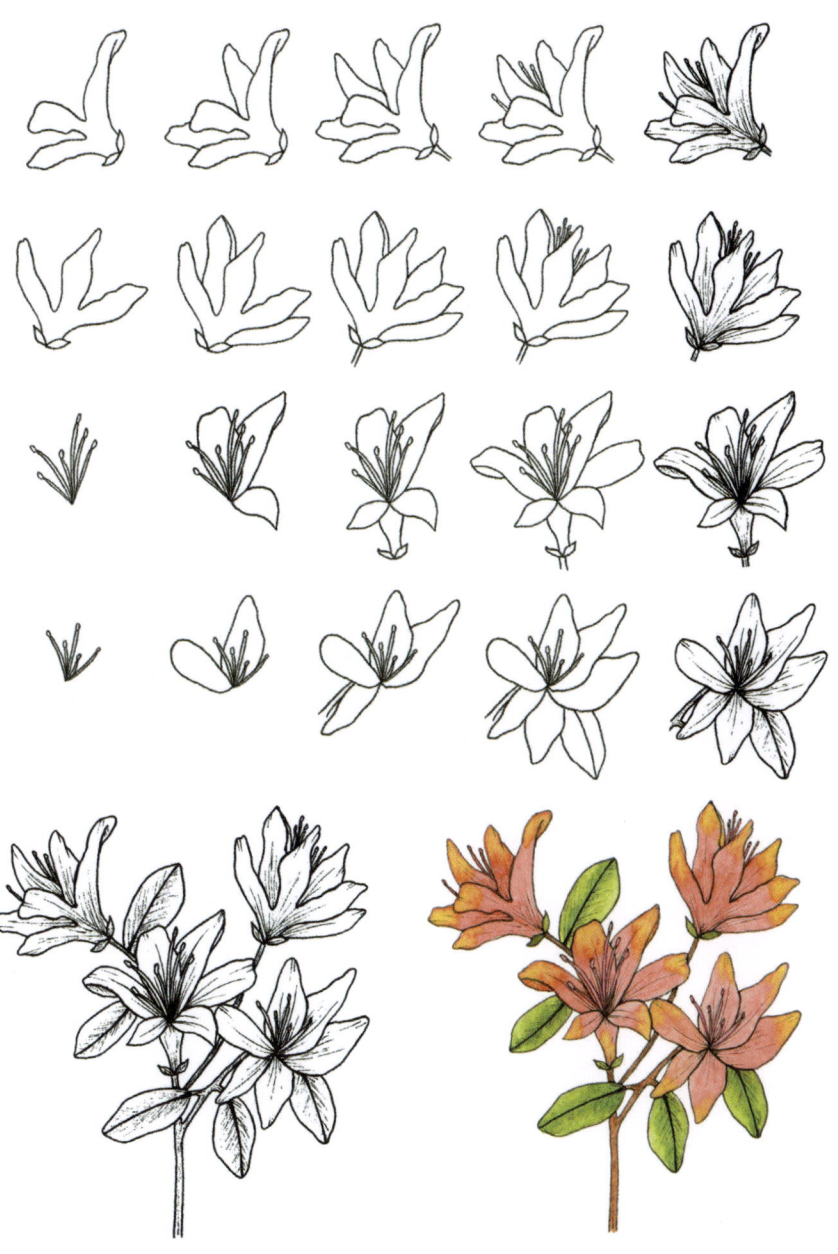

Bougainvillea

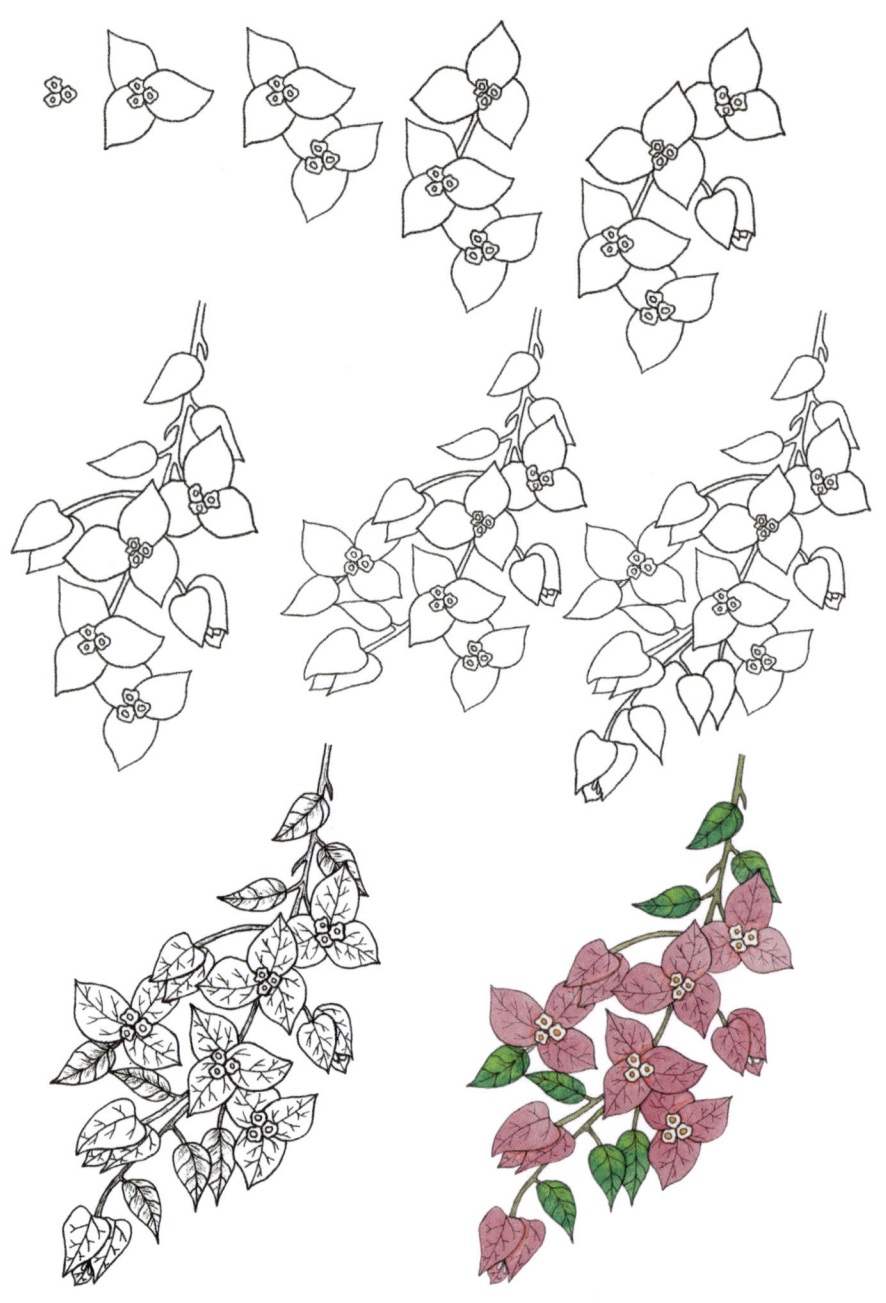

Lilac

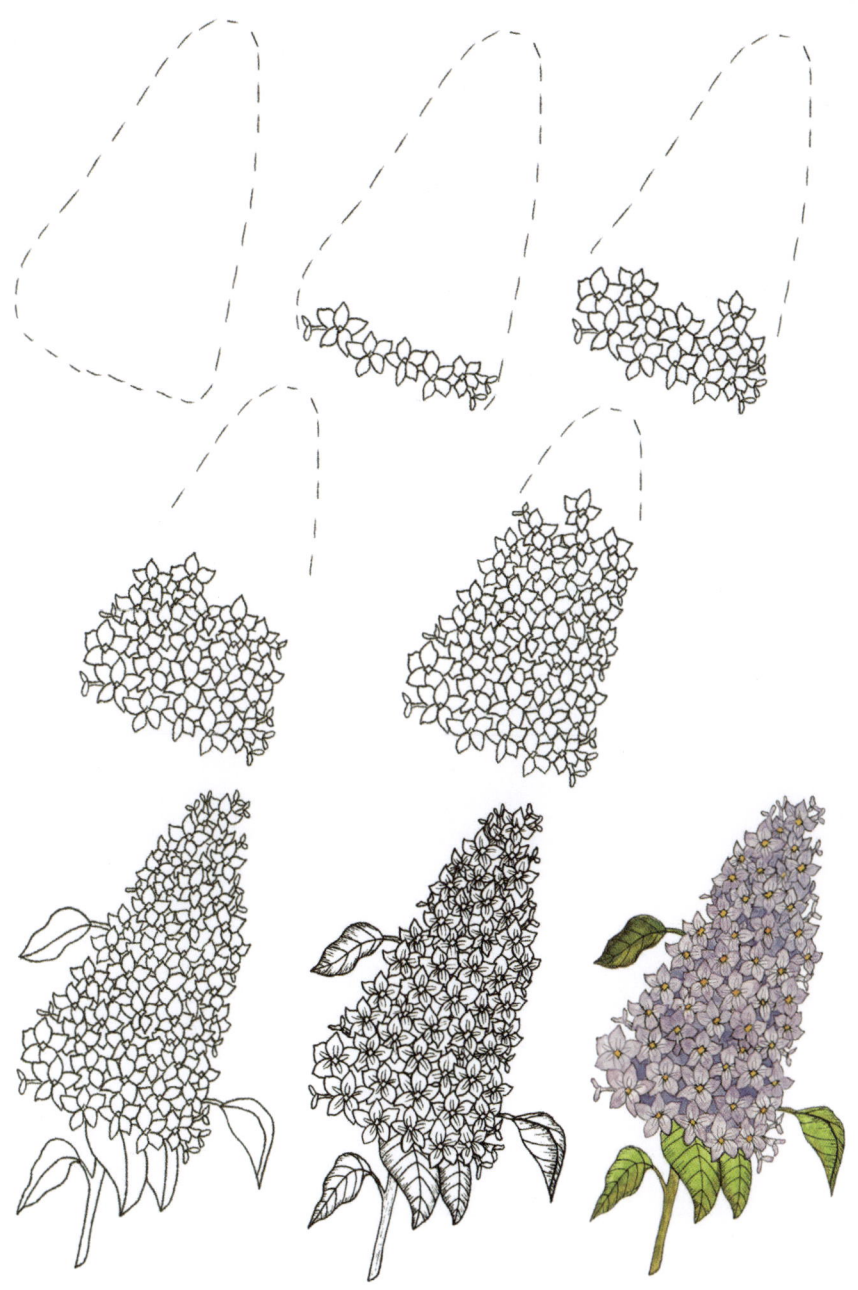

Lisianthus

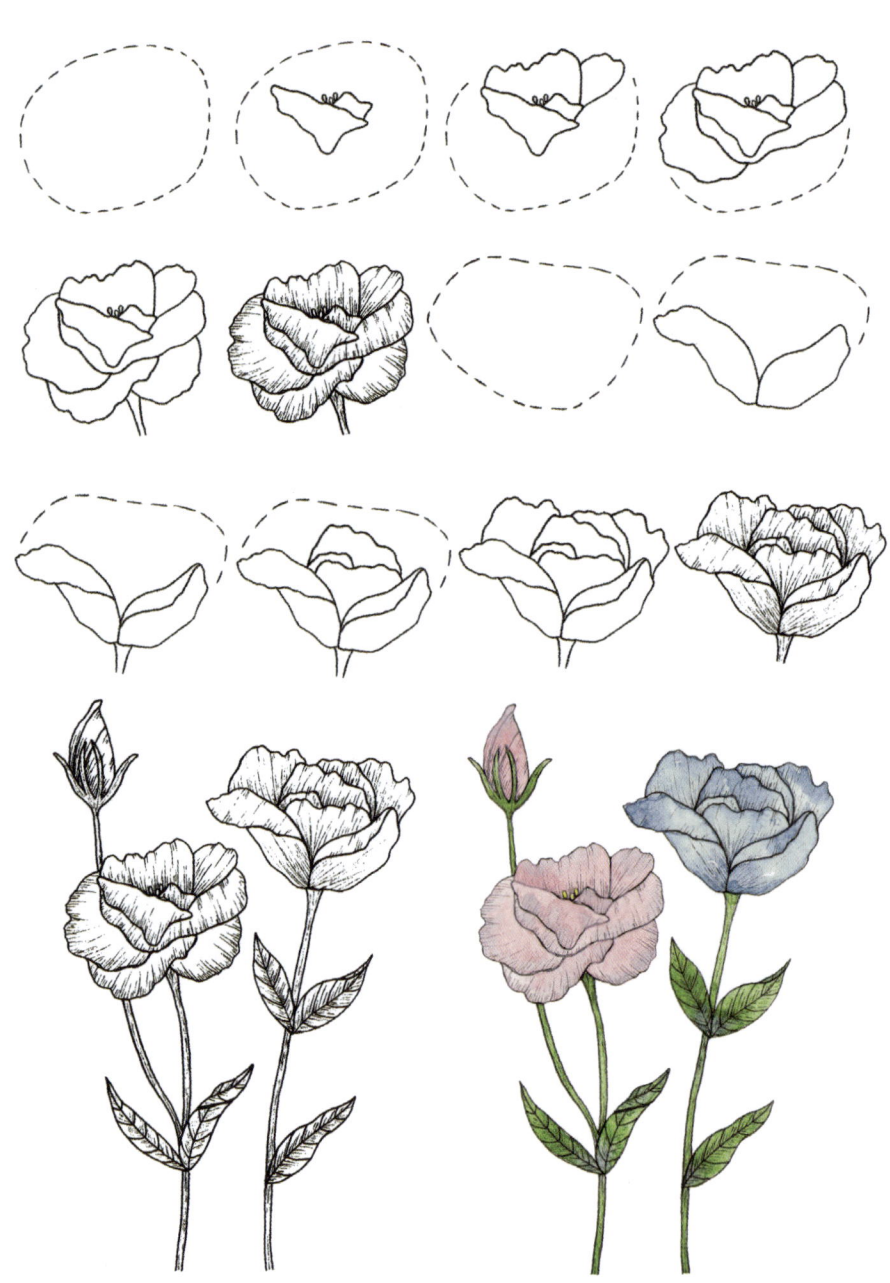

Morning Glory

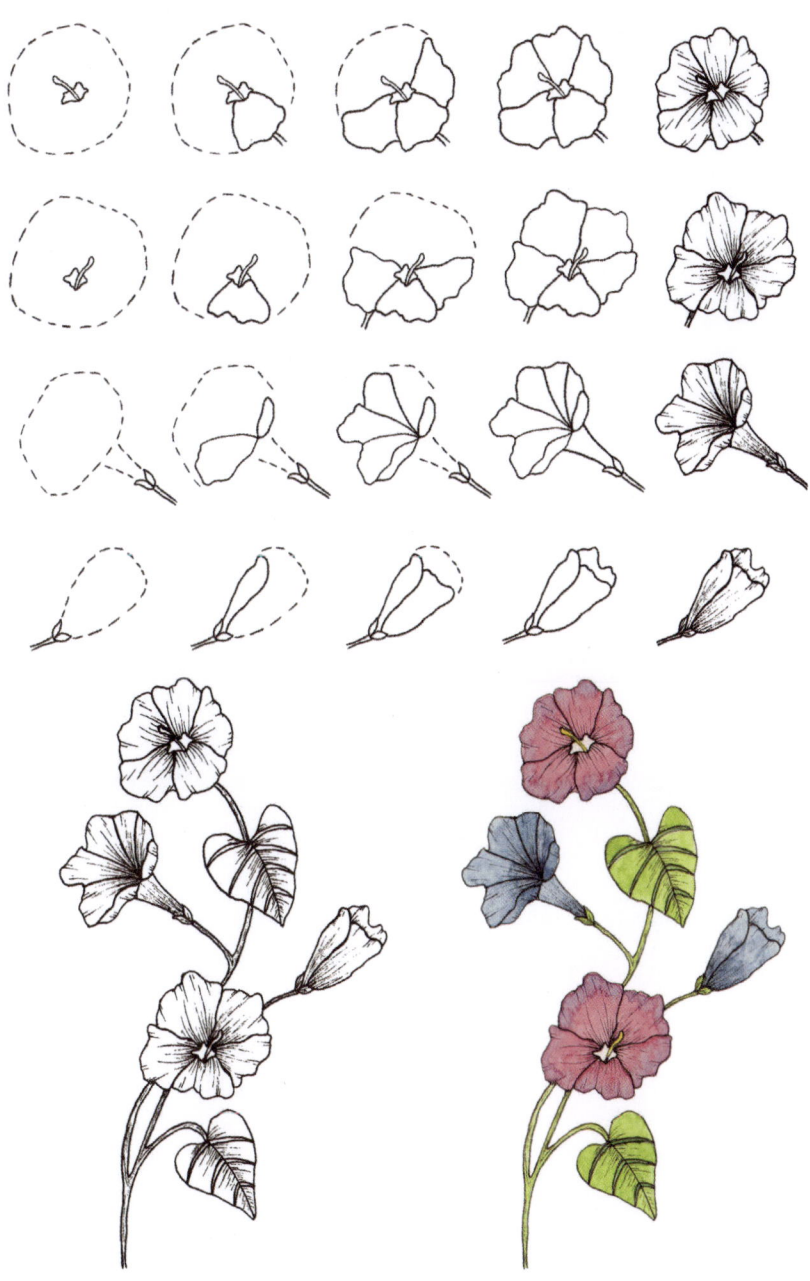

Chrysanthemum

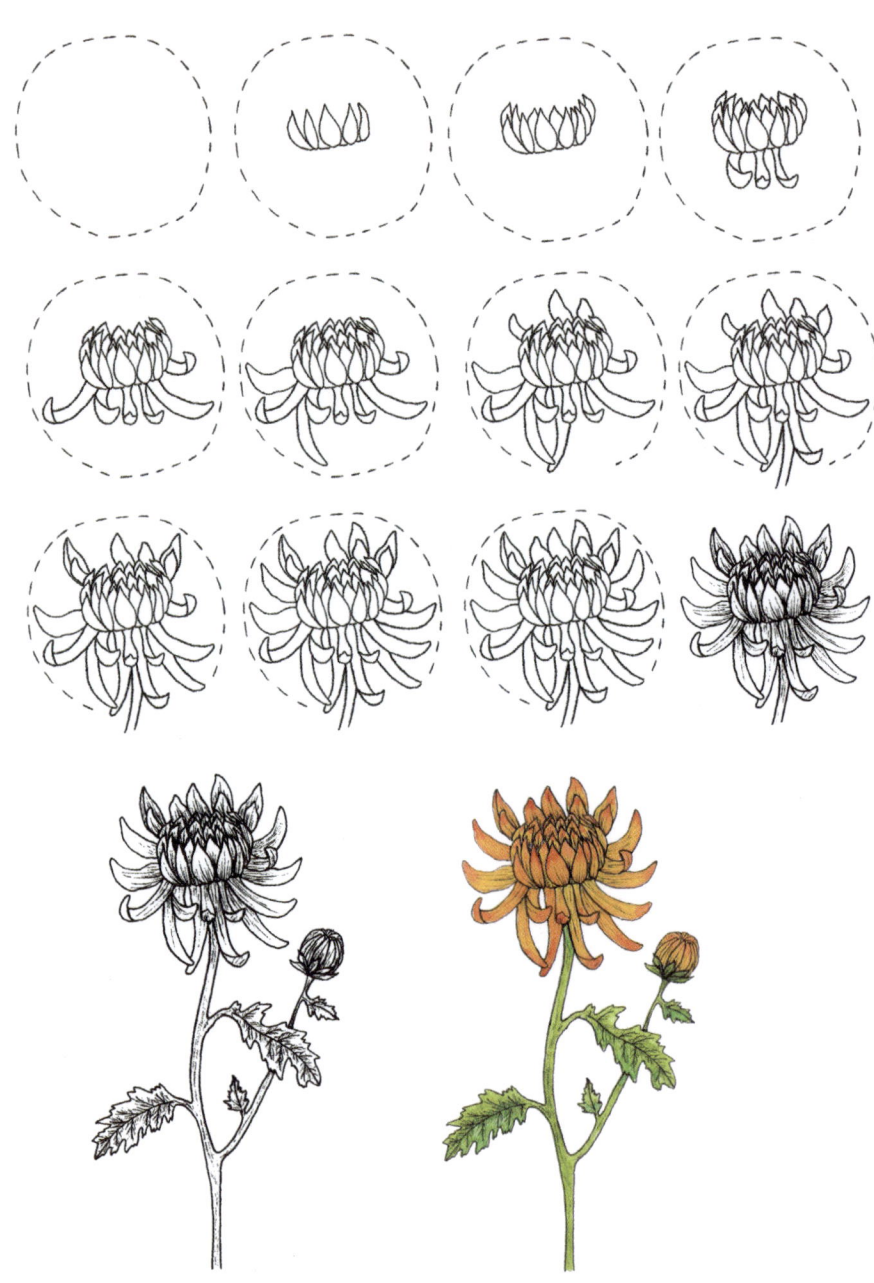

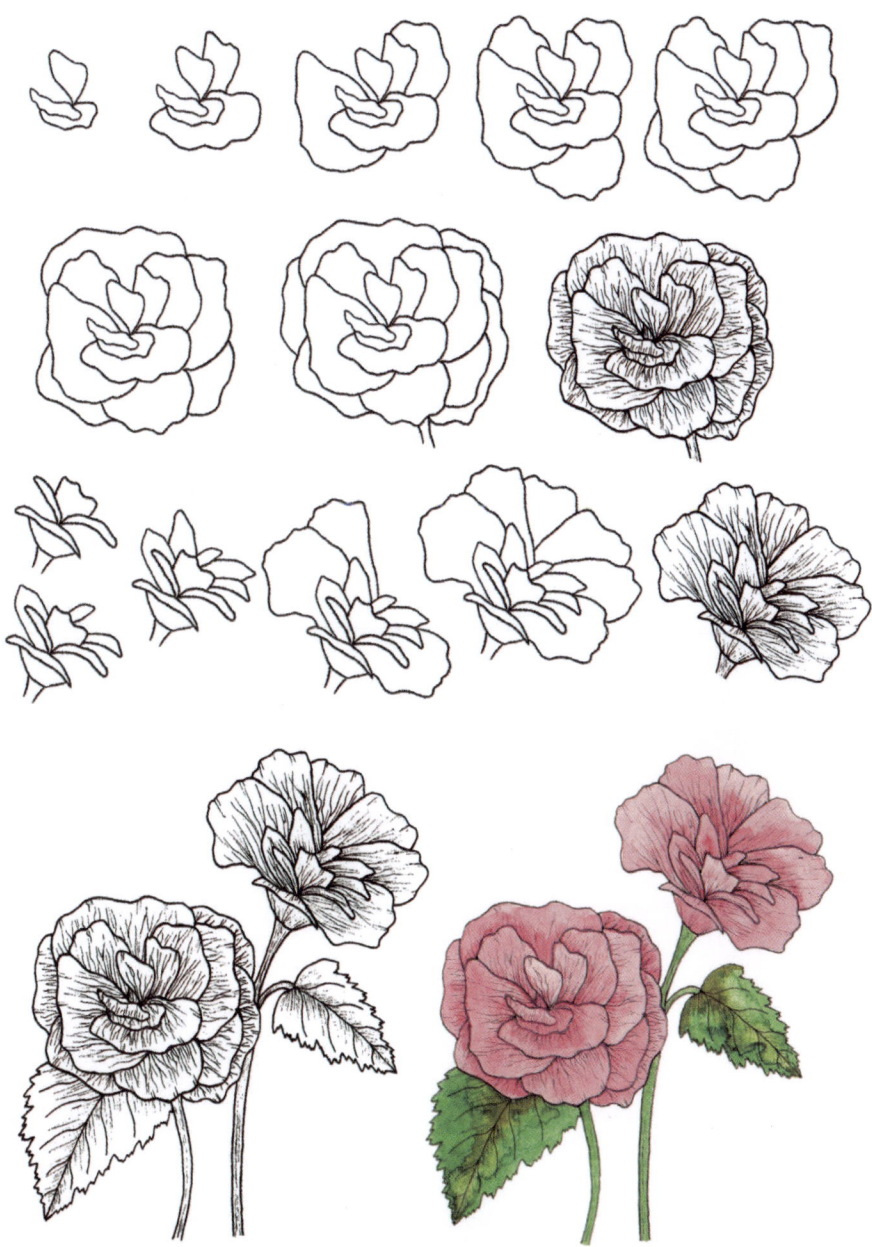

Orchid

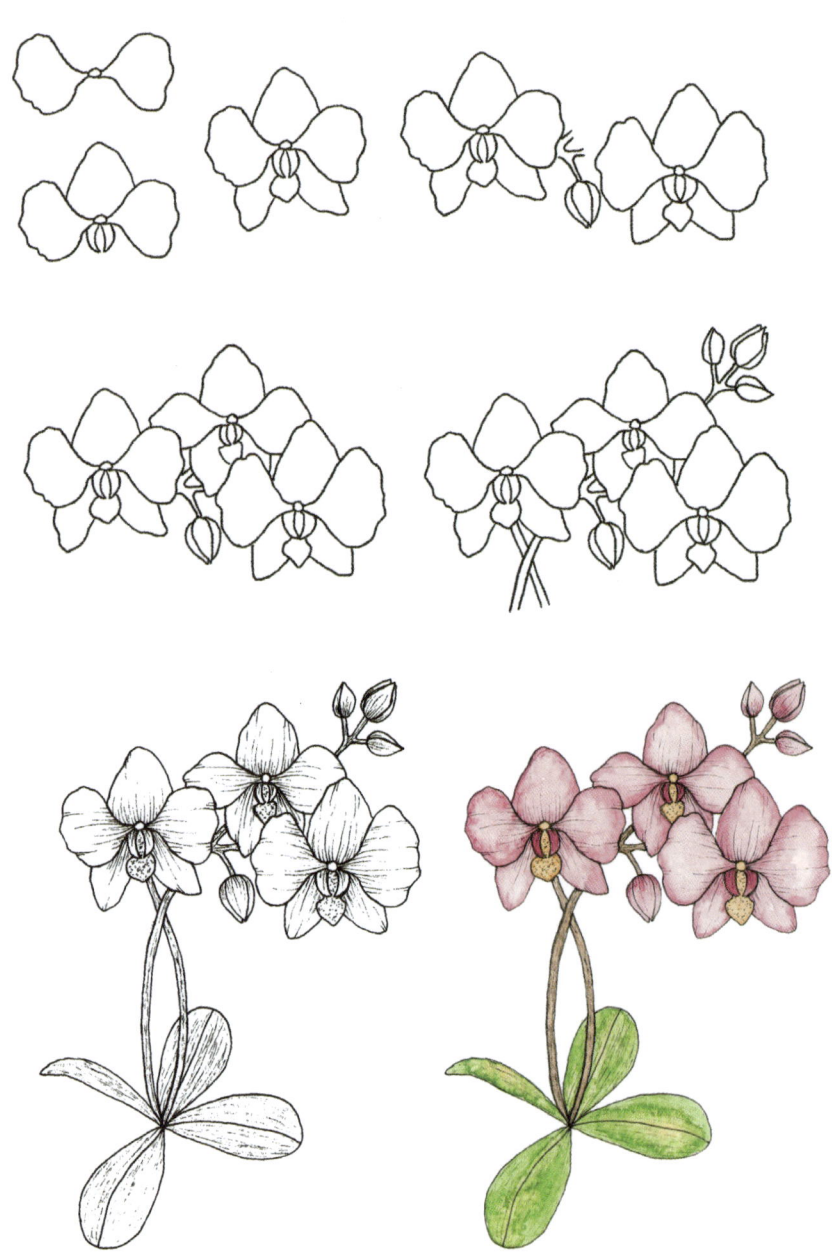

Hydrangea

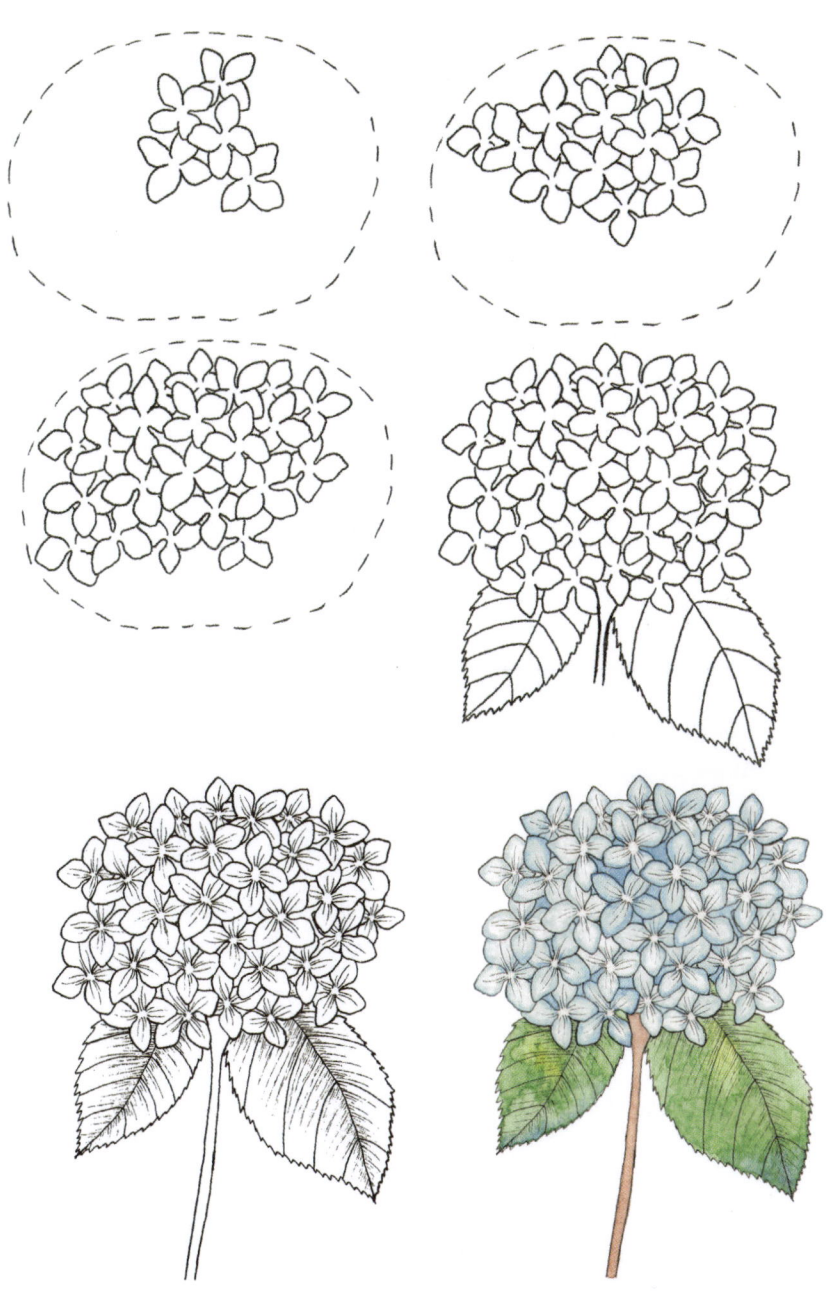

Marigold

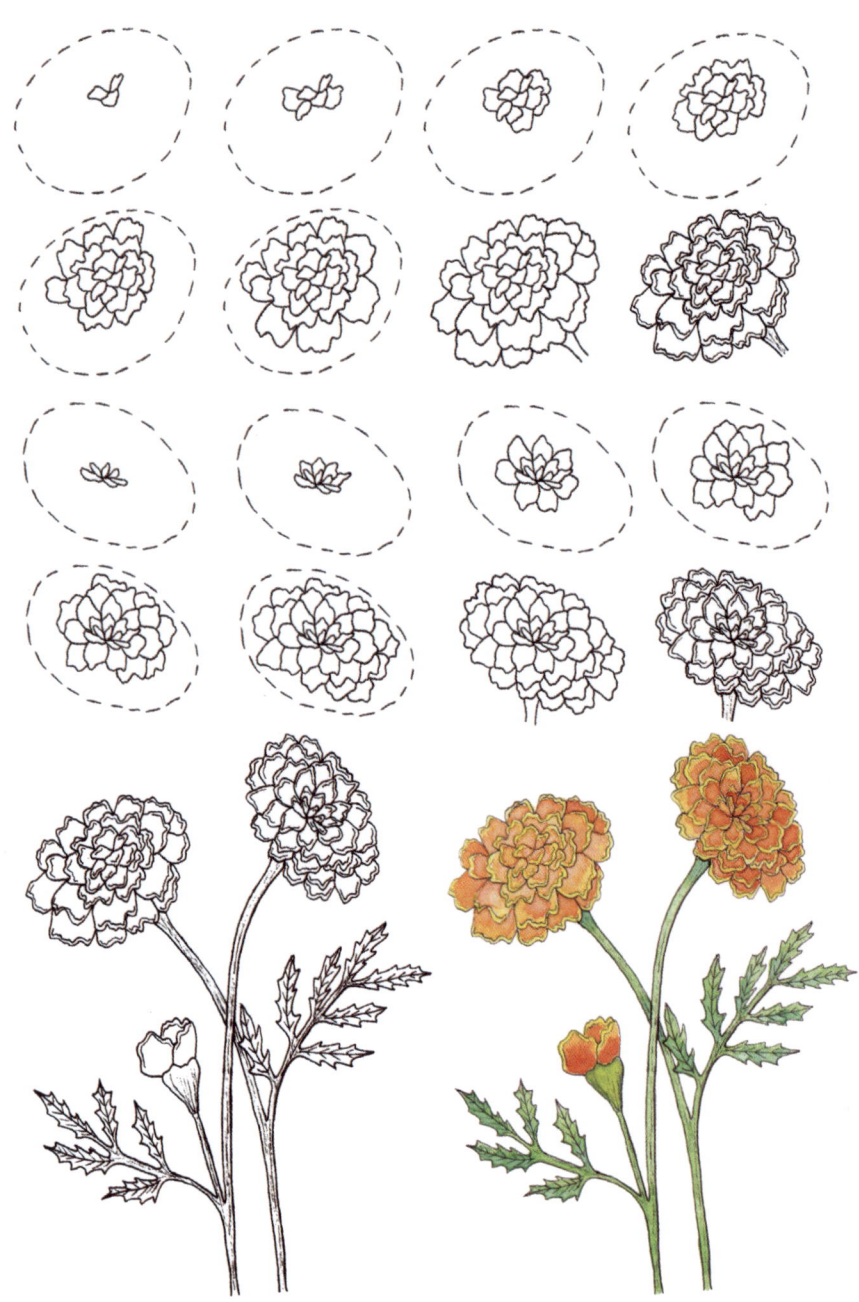

Craspedia

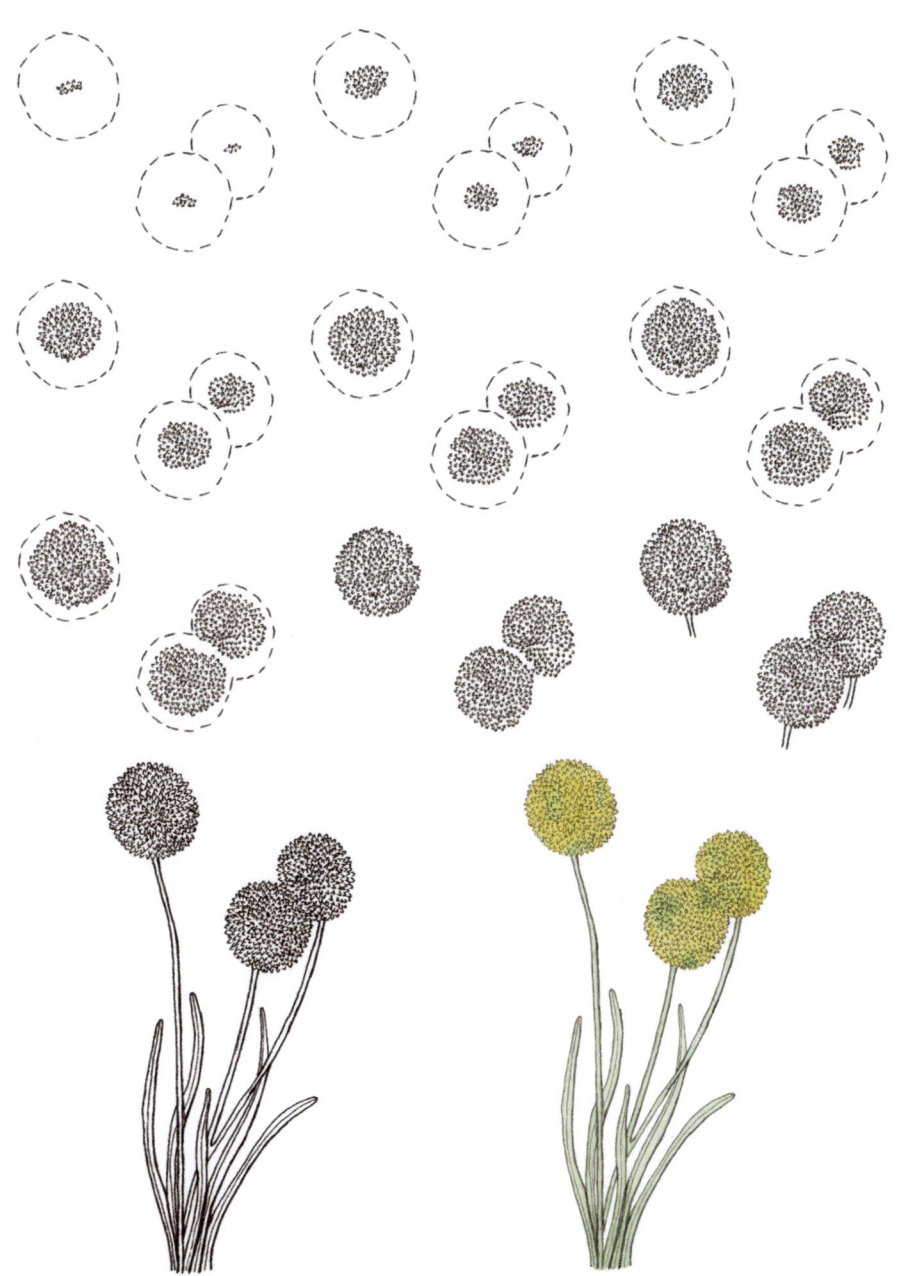

Forget-me-not

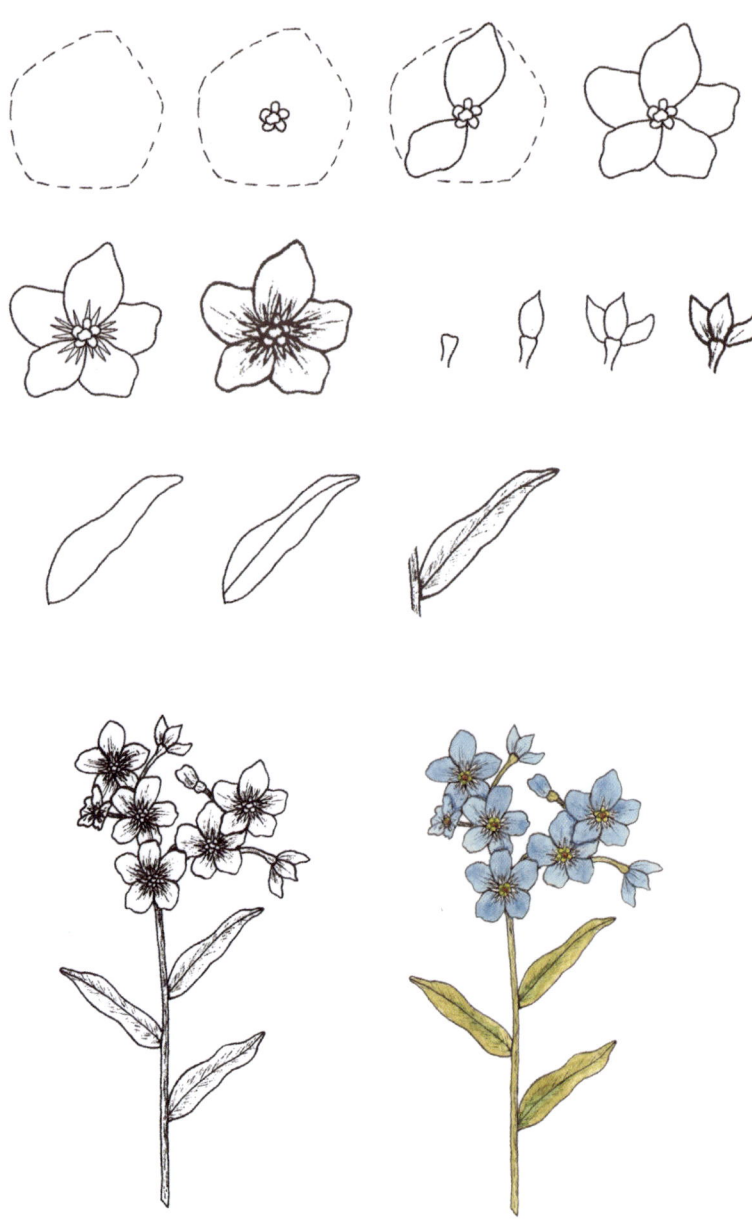

Freesia

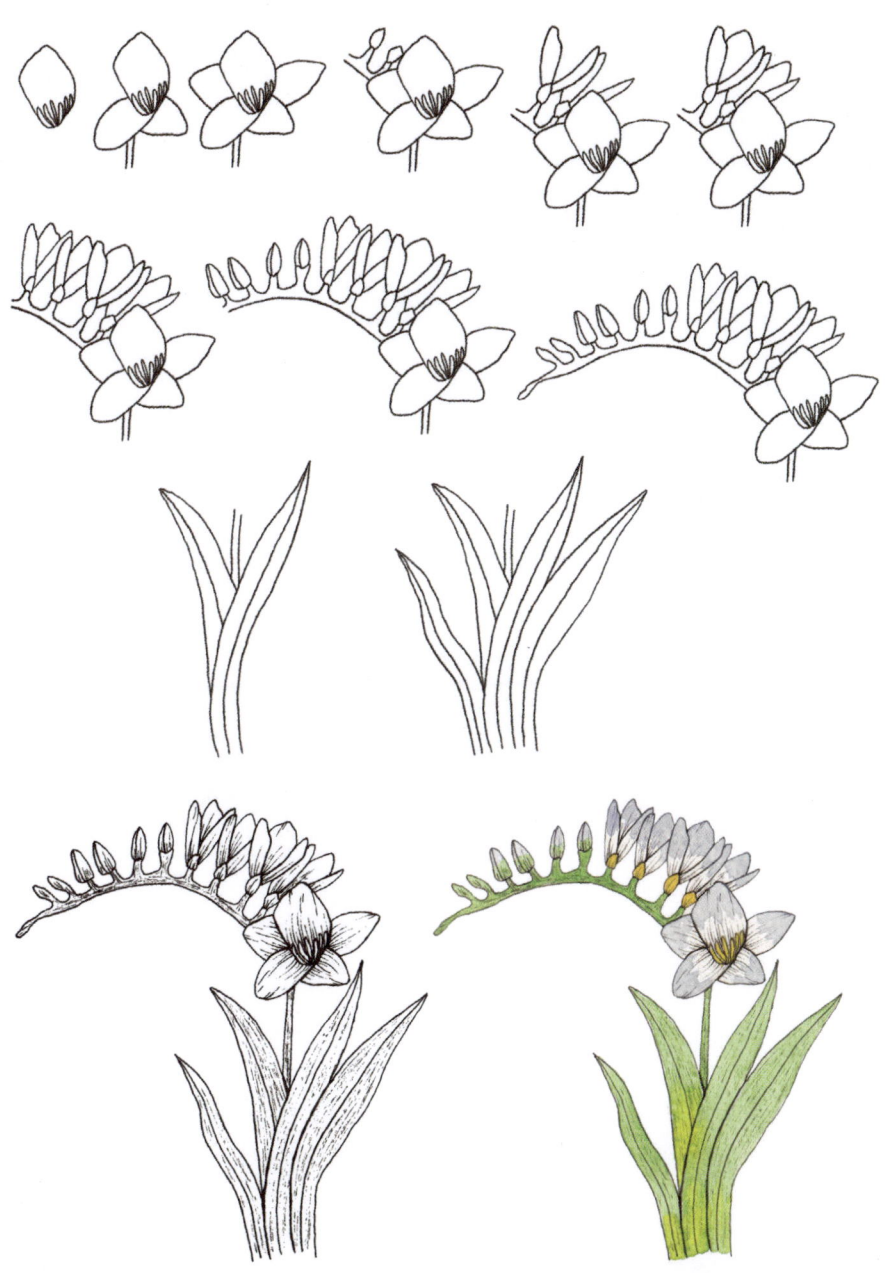

Gardenia

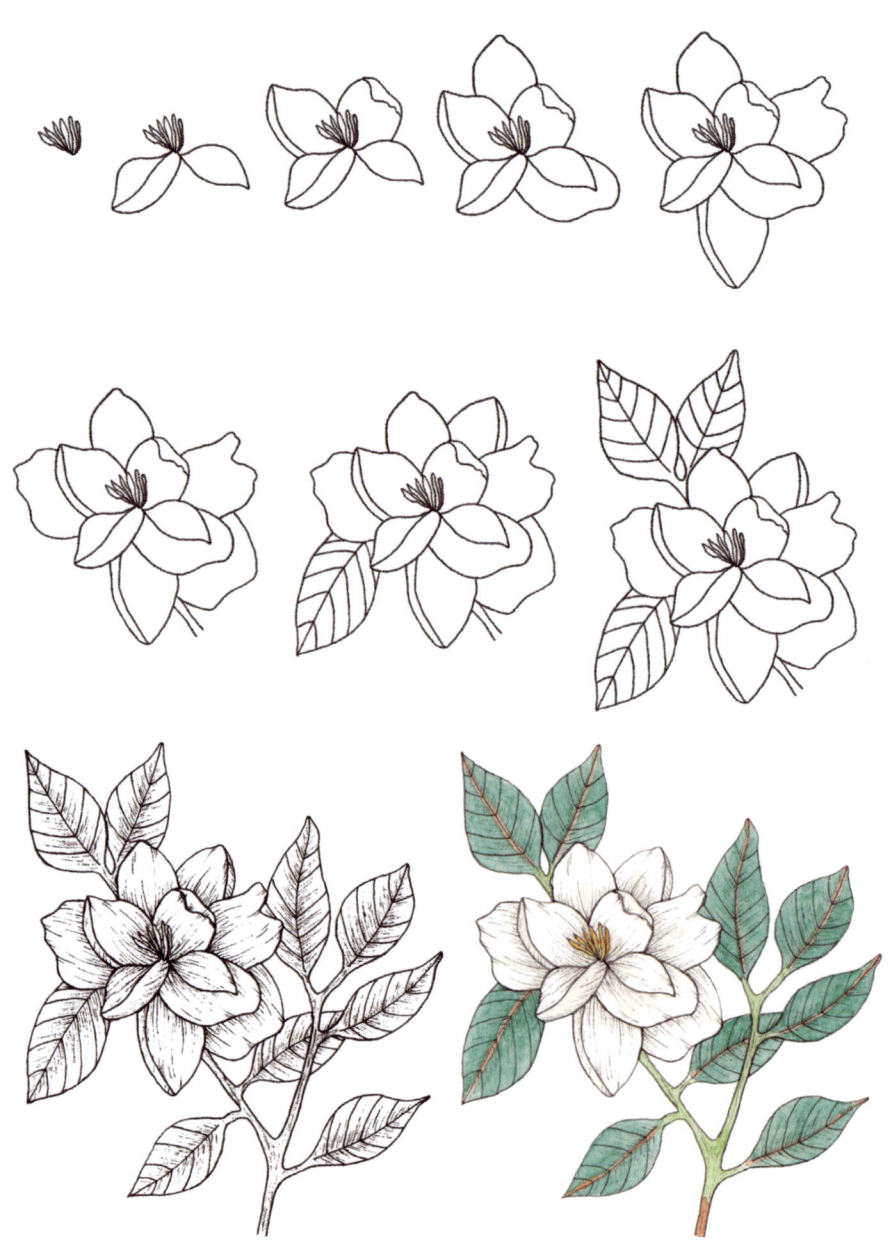

Gypsophila

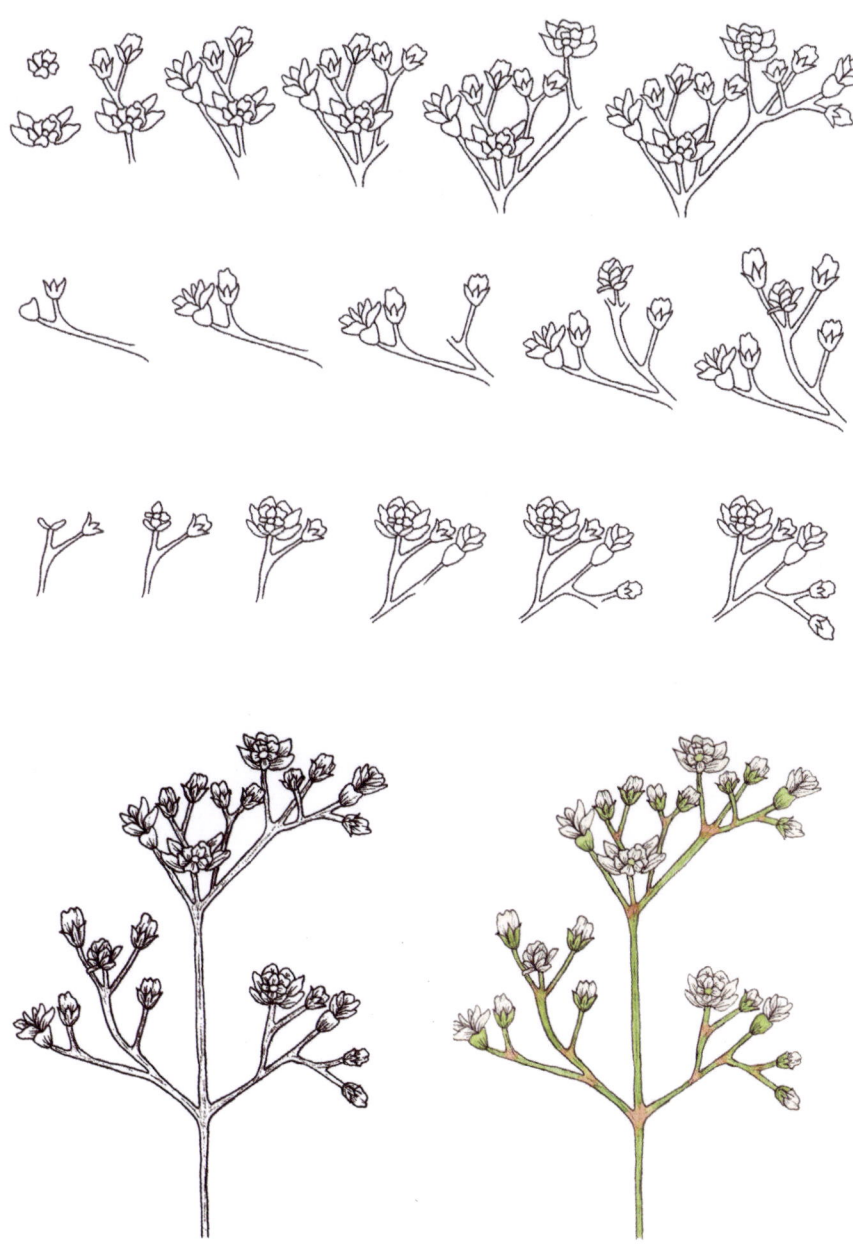

Honeysuckle

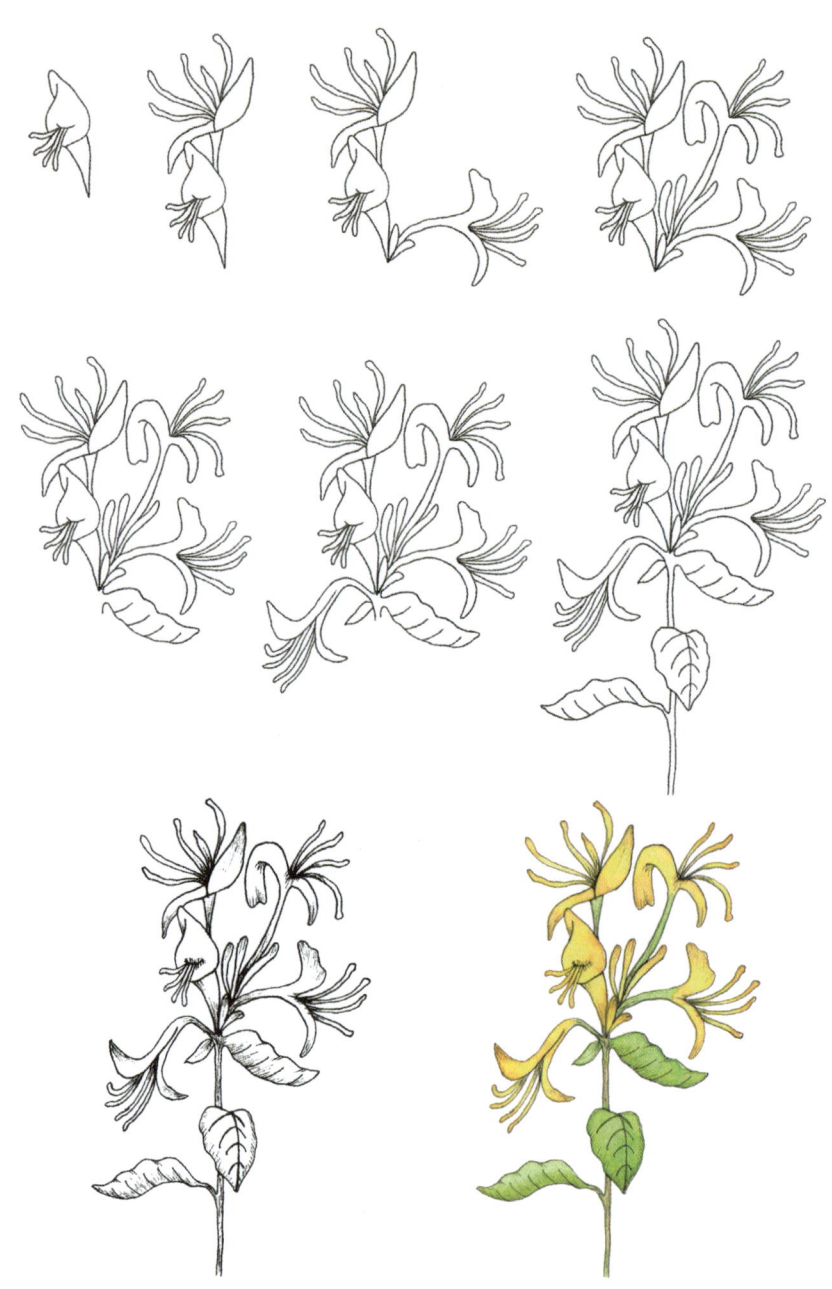

Jasmine

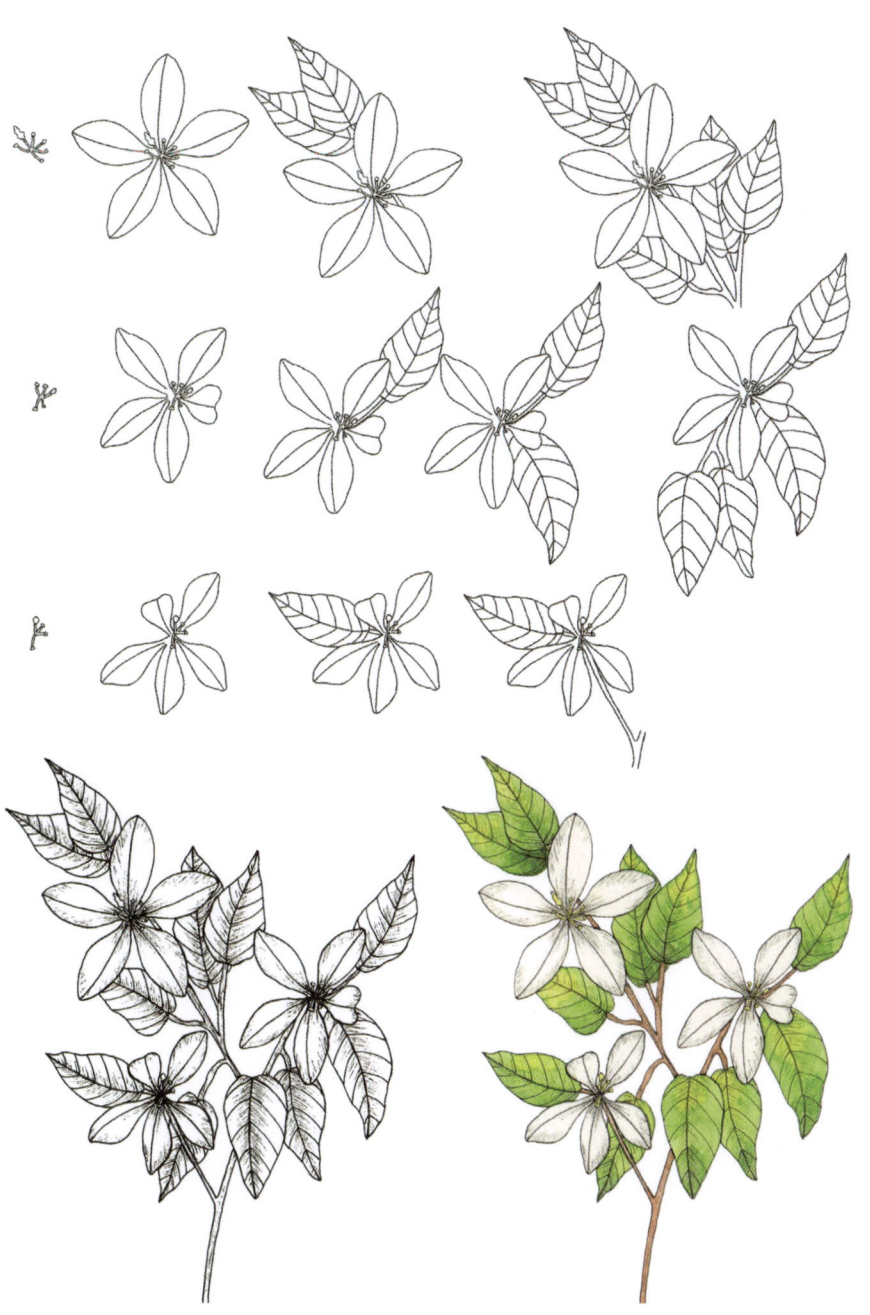

Poinsettia

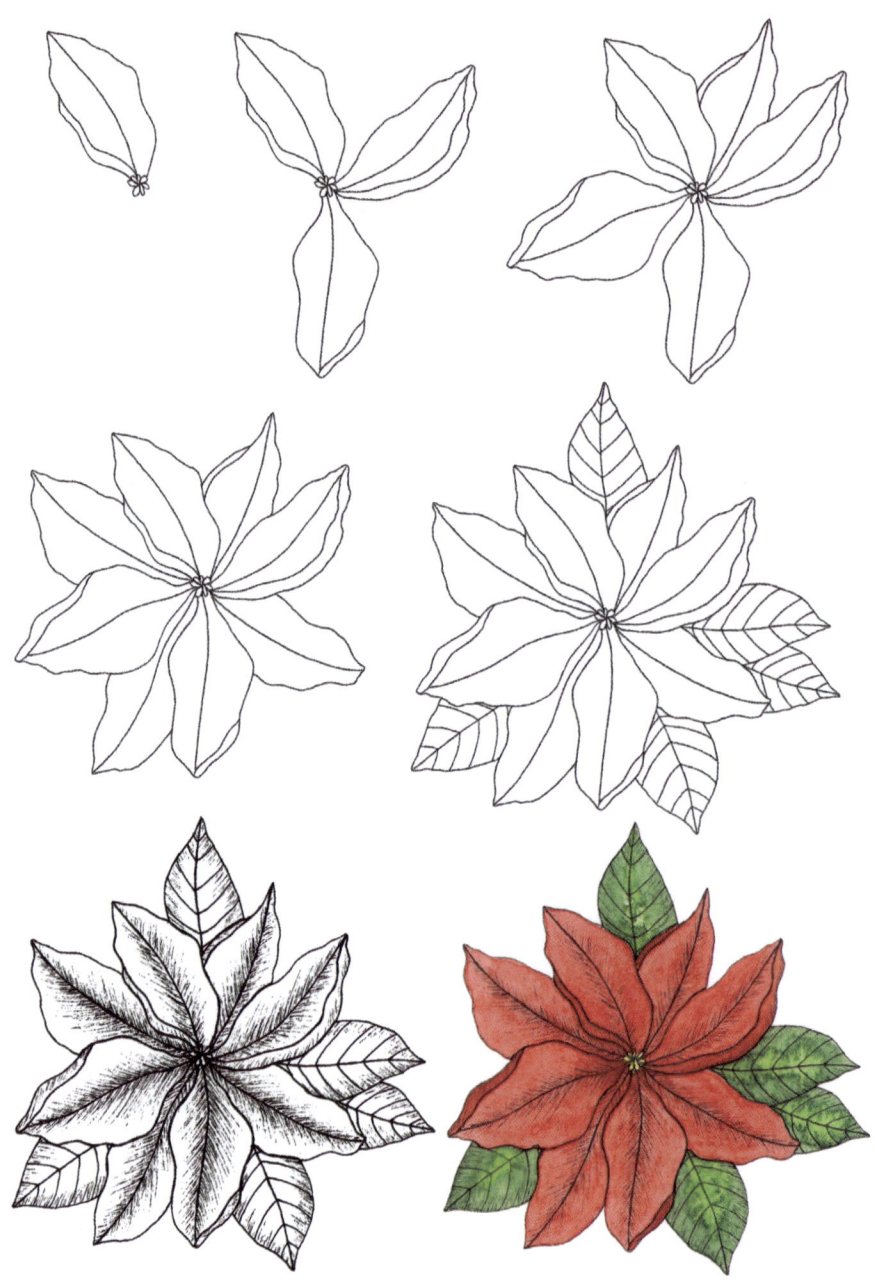

Verbena

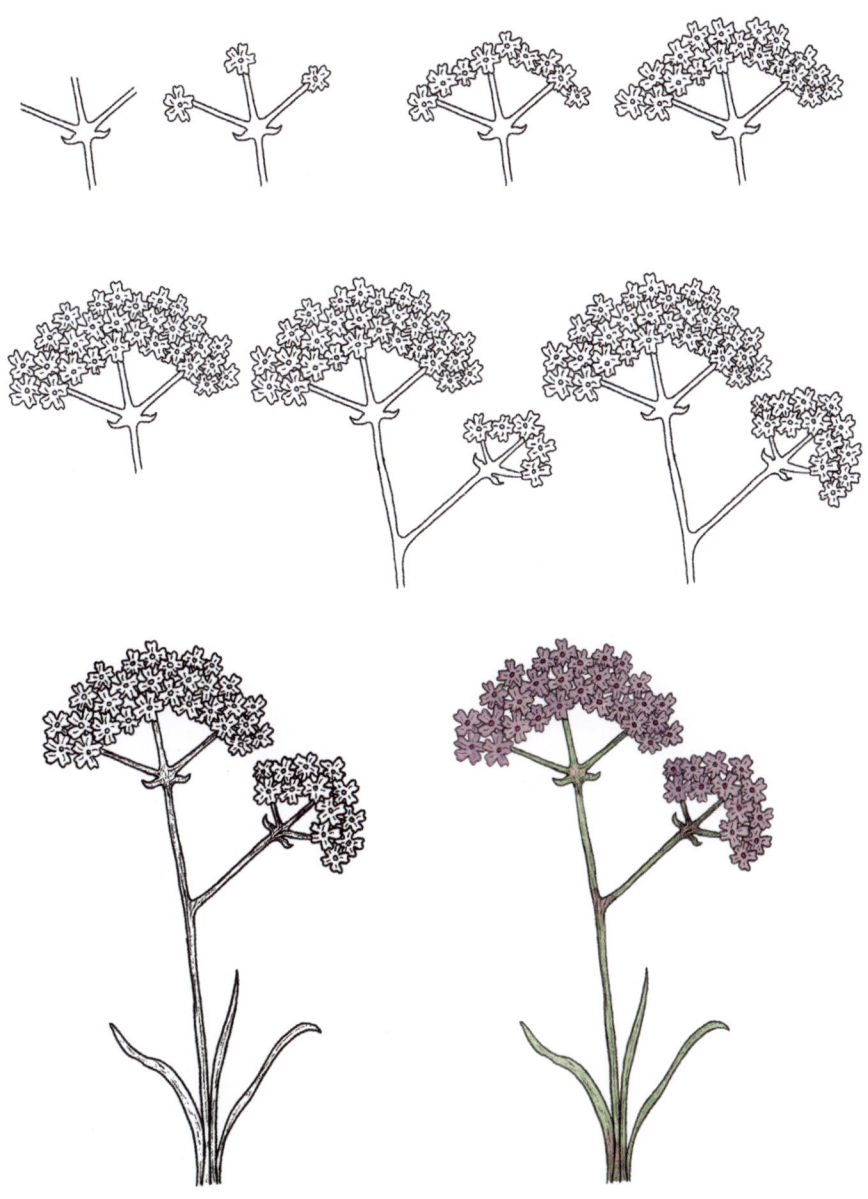

Lily of the Valley

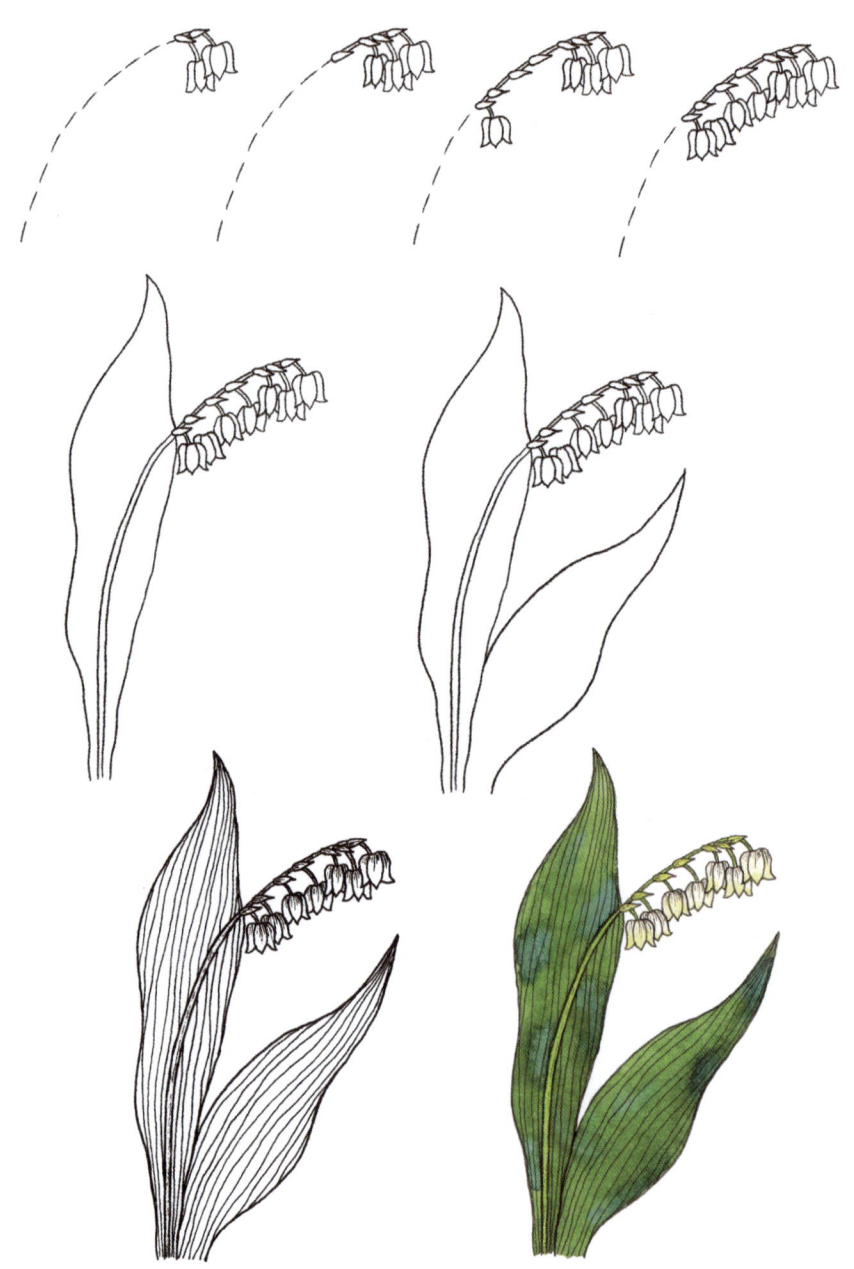

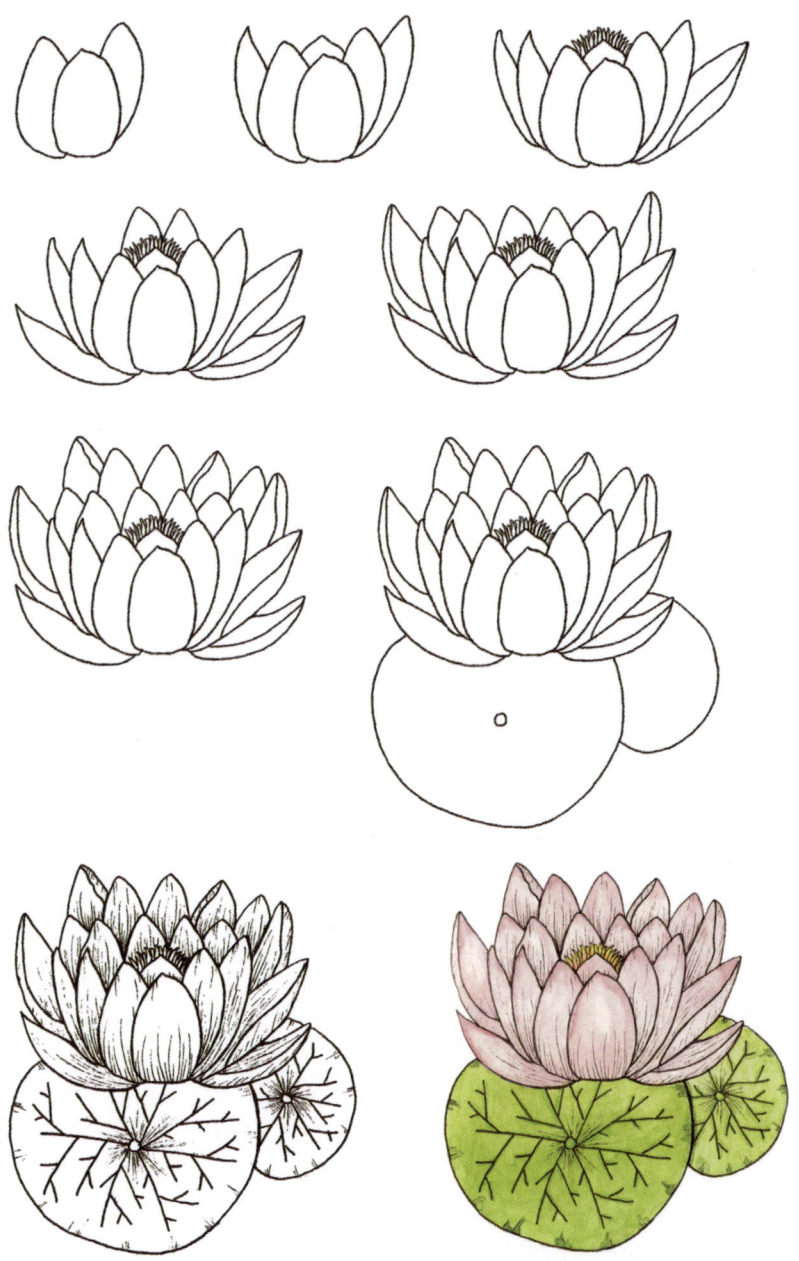

Lupin

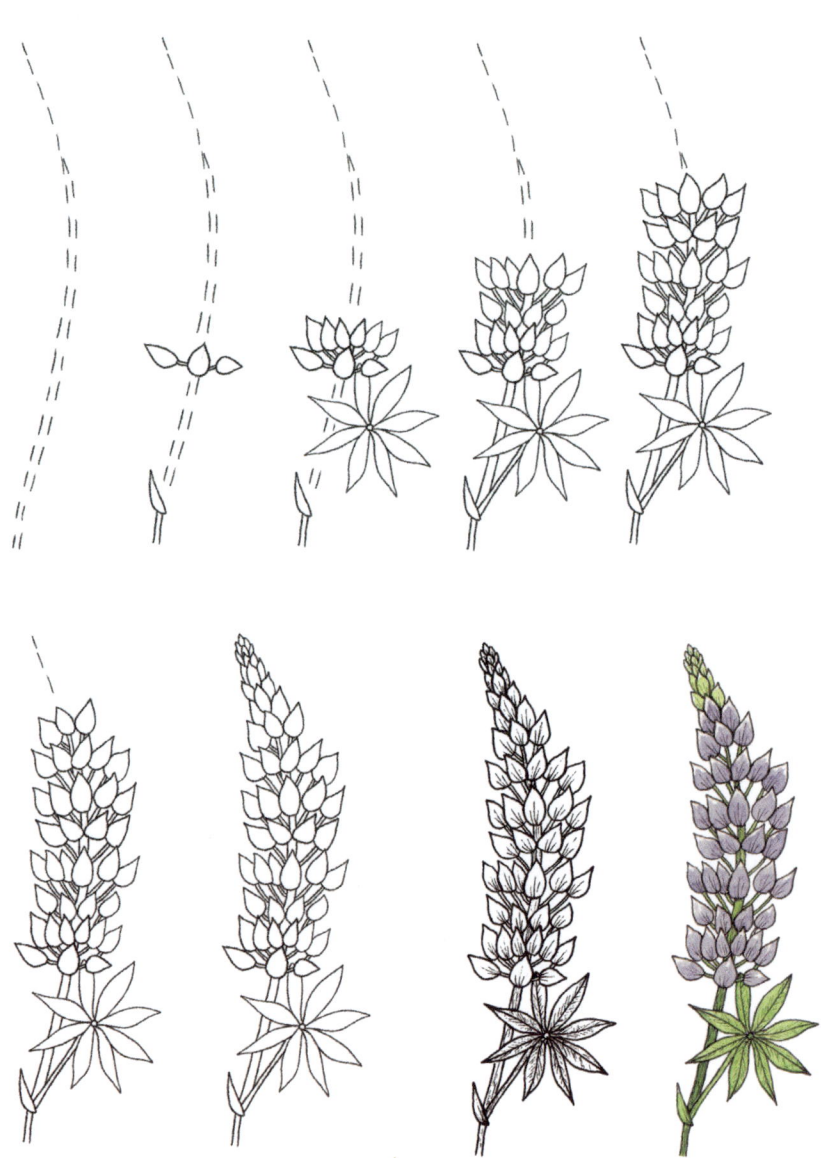

Magnolia

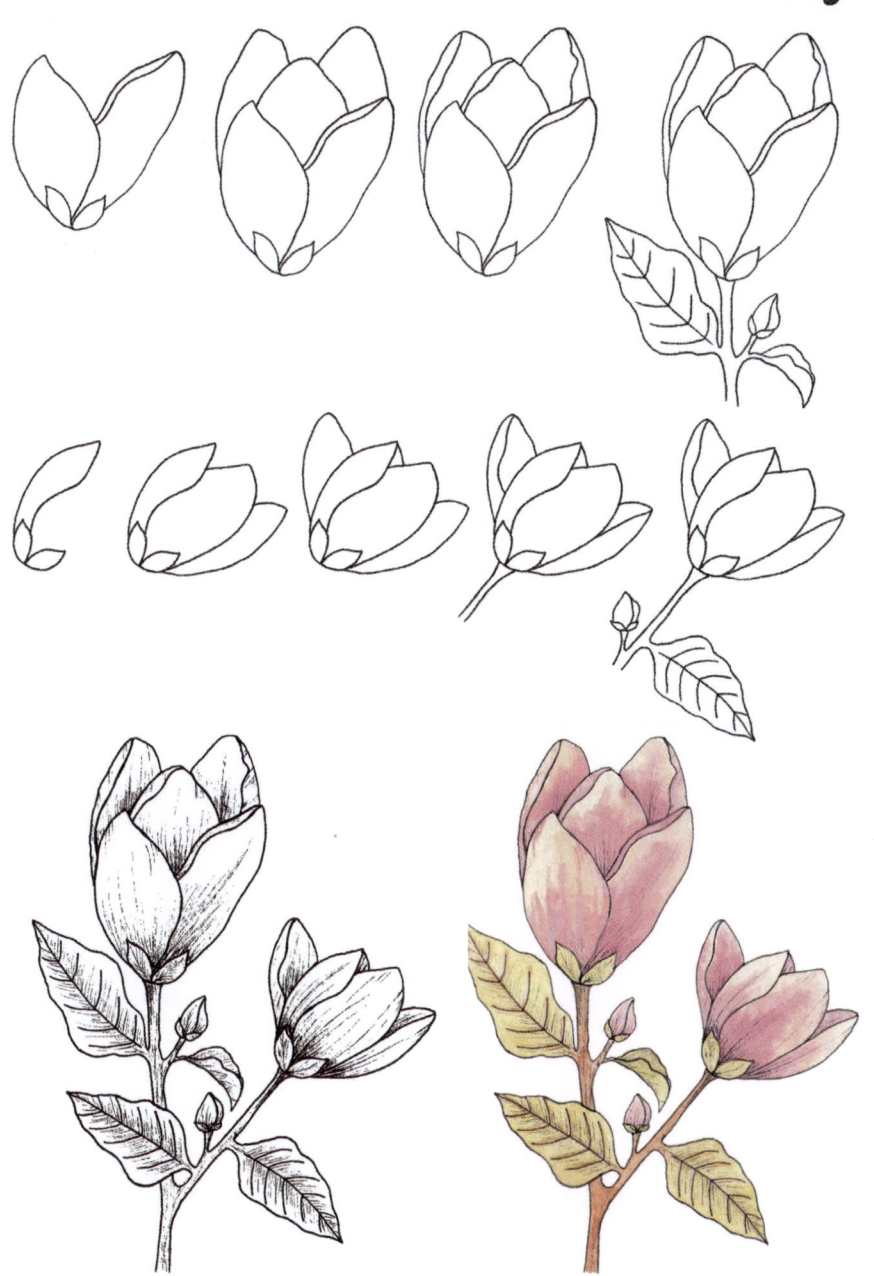

Monkshood

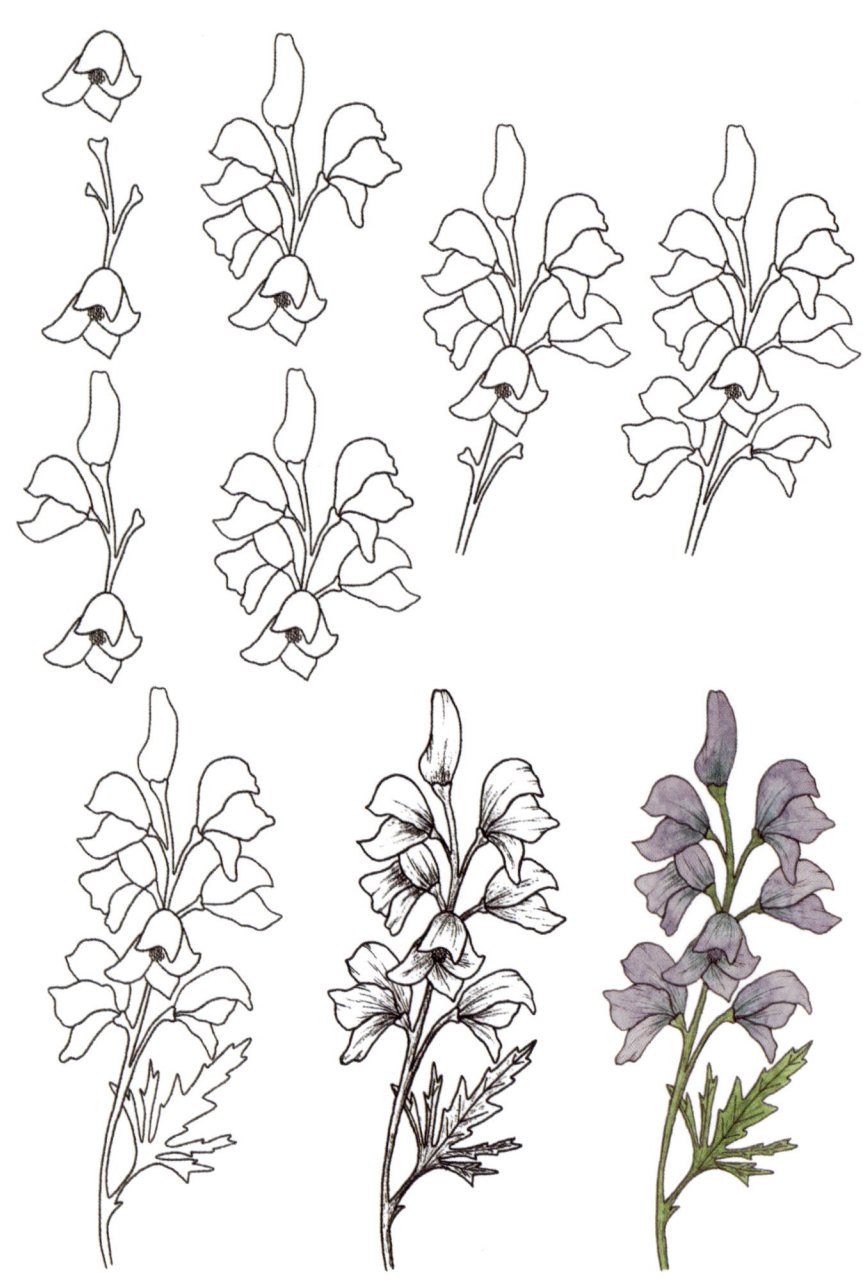

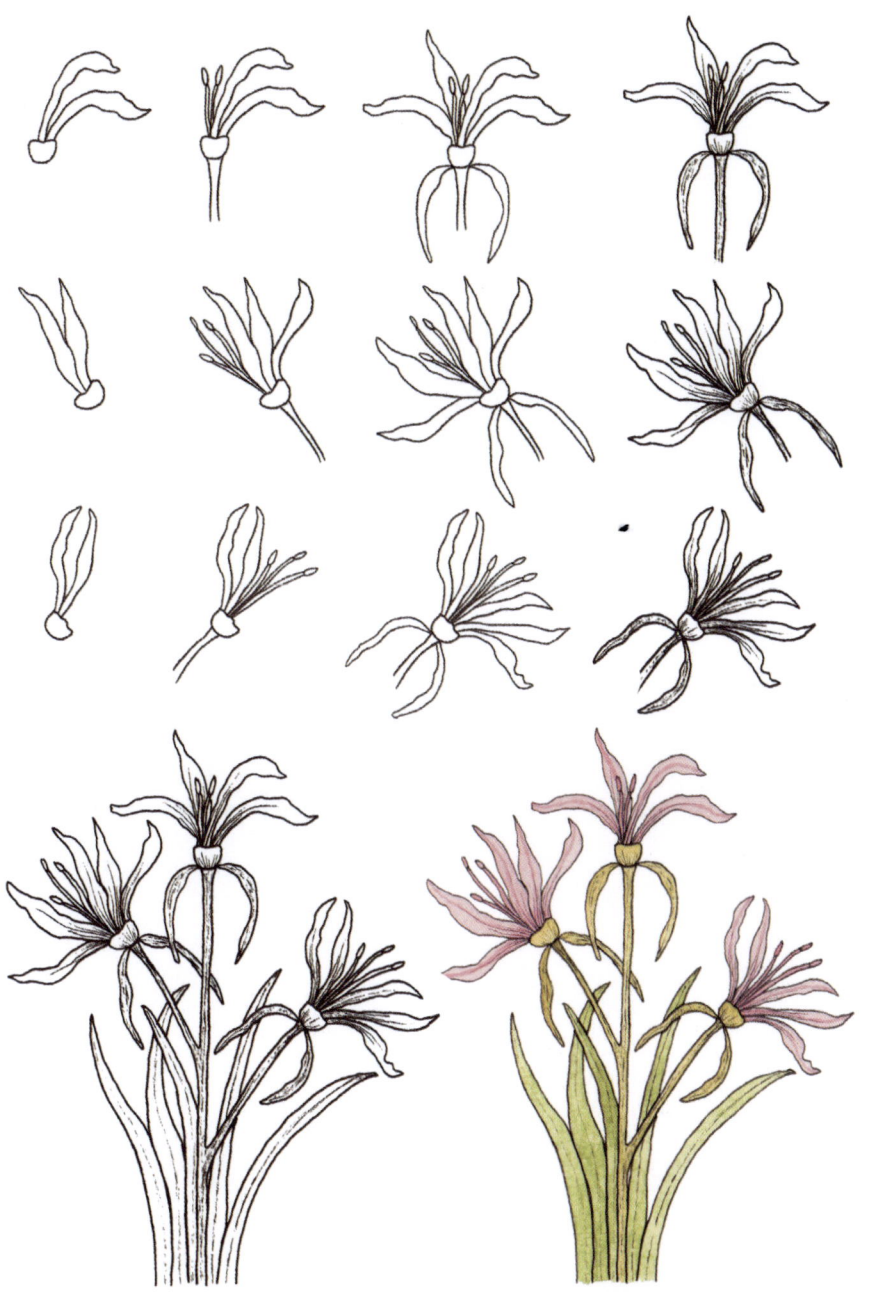

Nigella

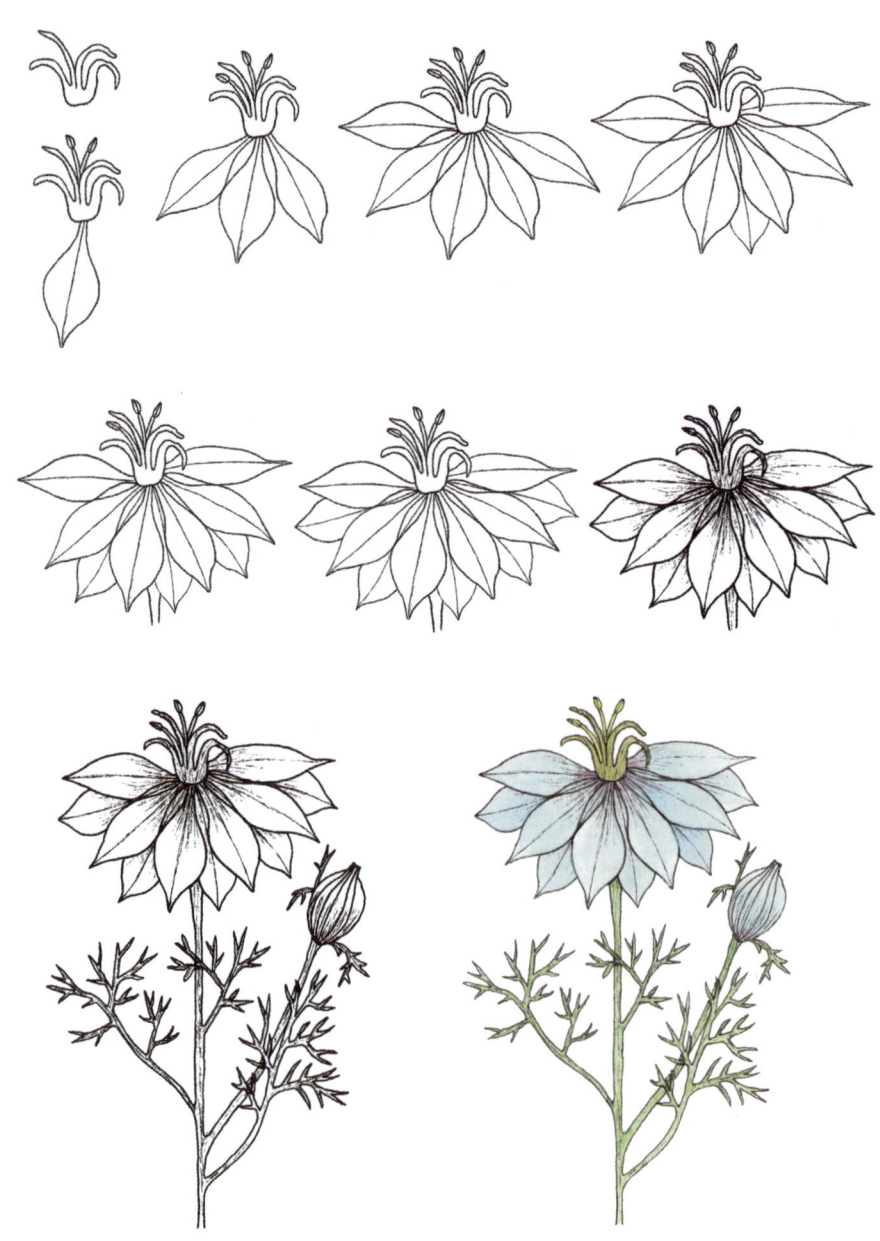

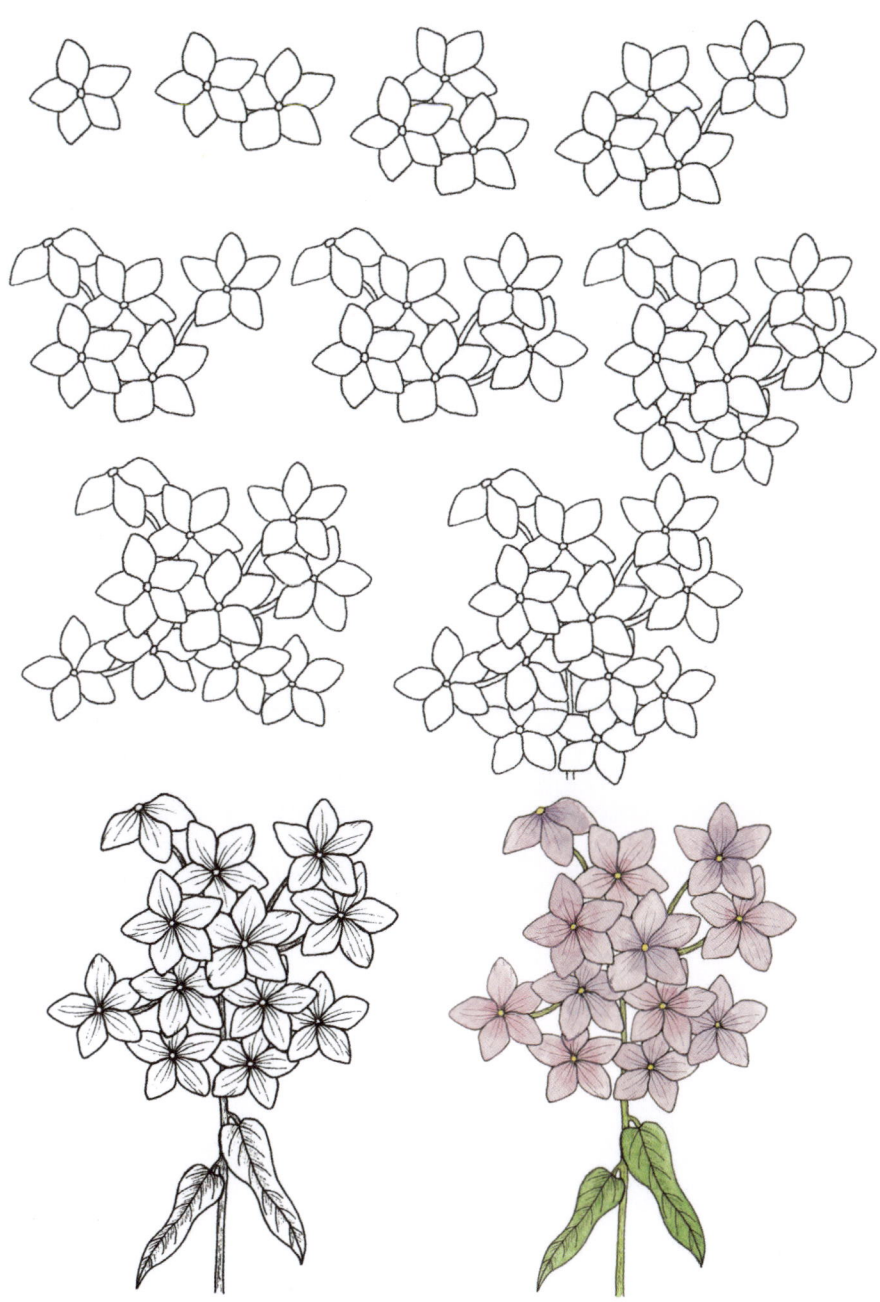

Queen Anne's Lace

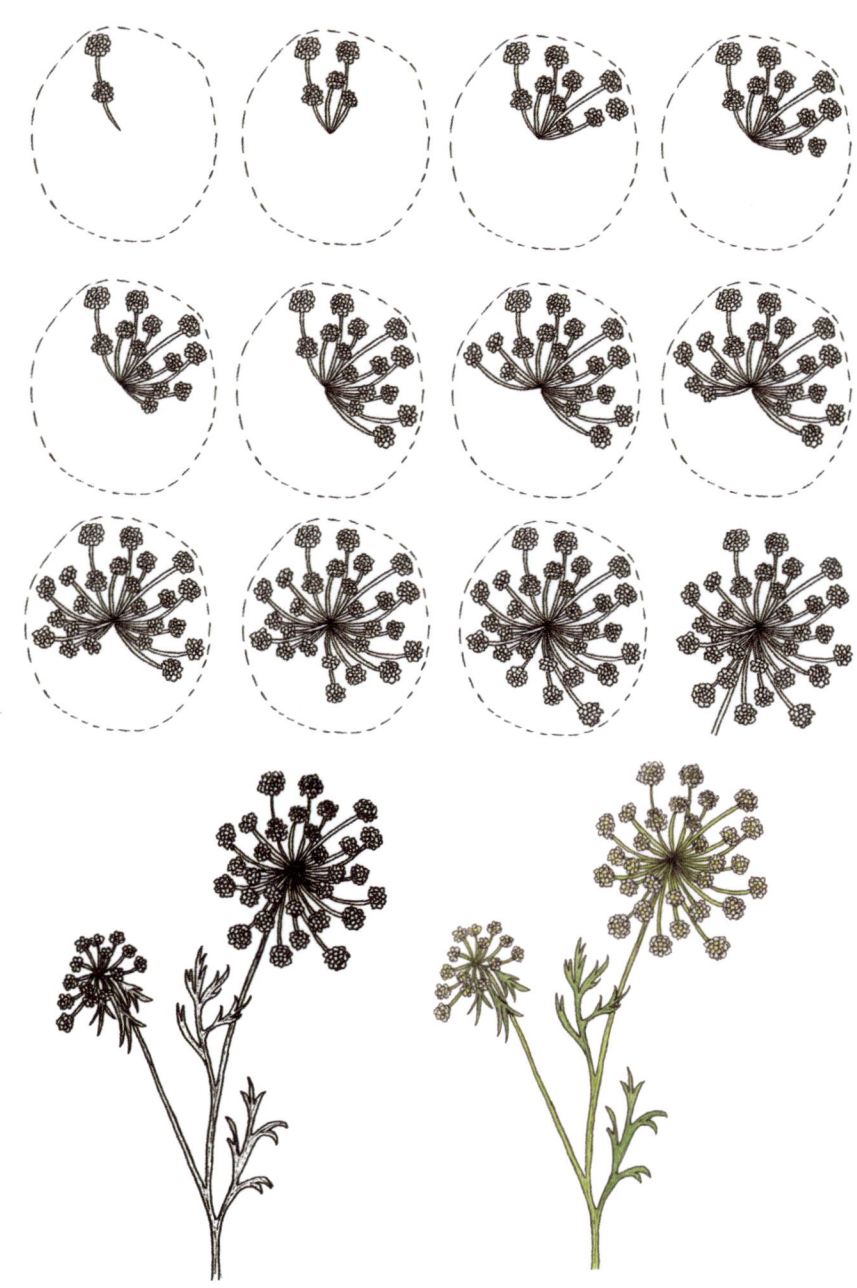

Rudbeckia

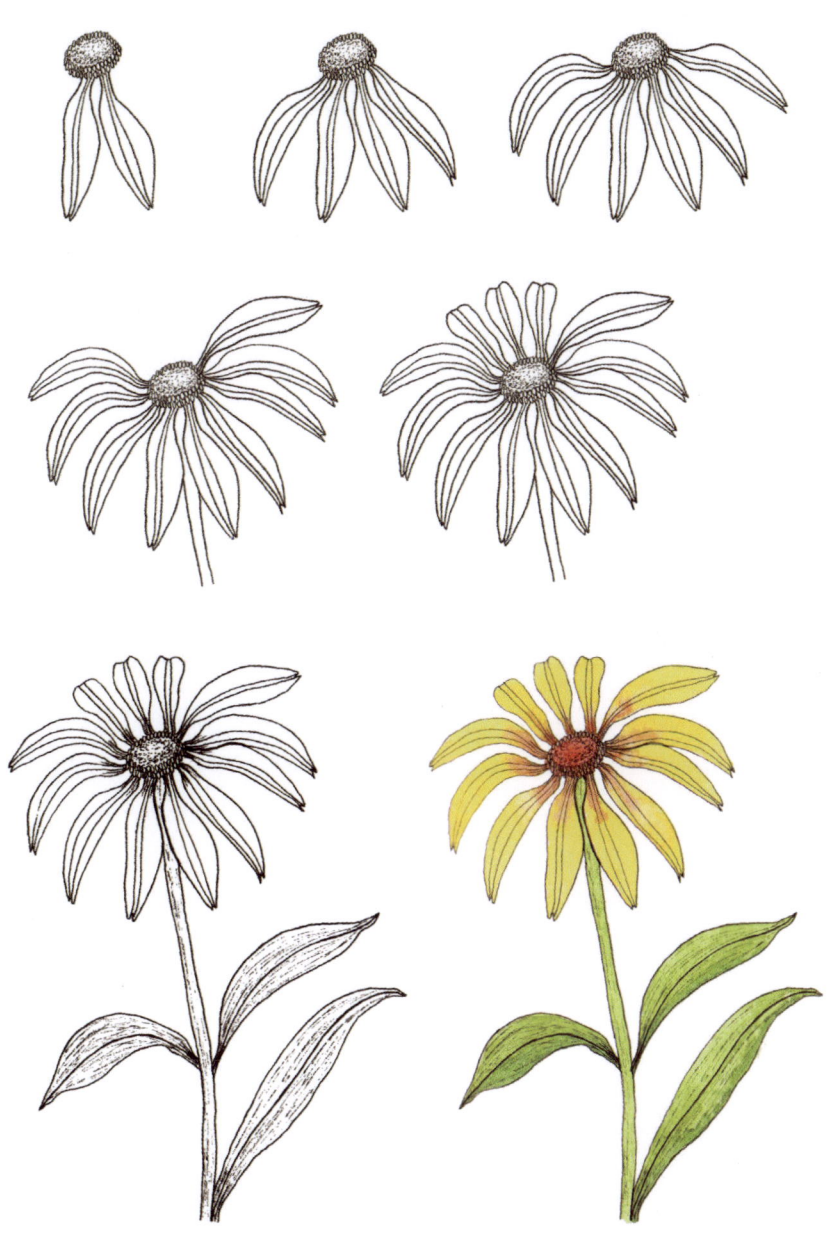

Peace Lily

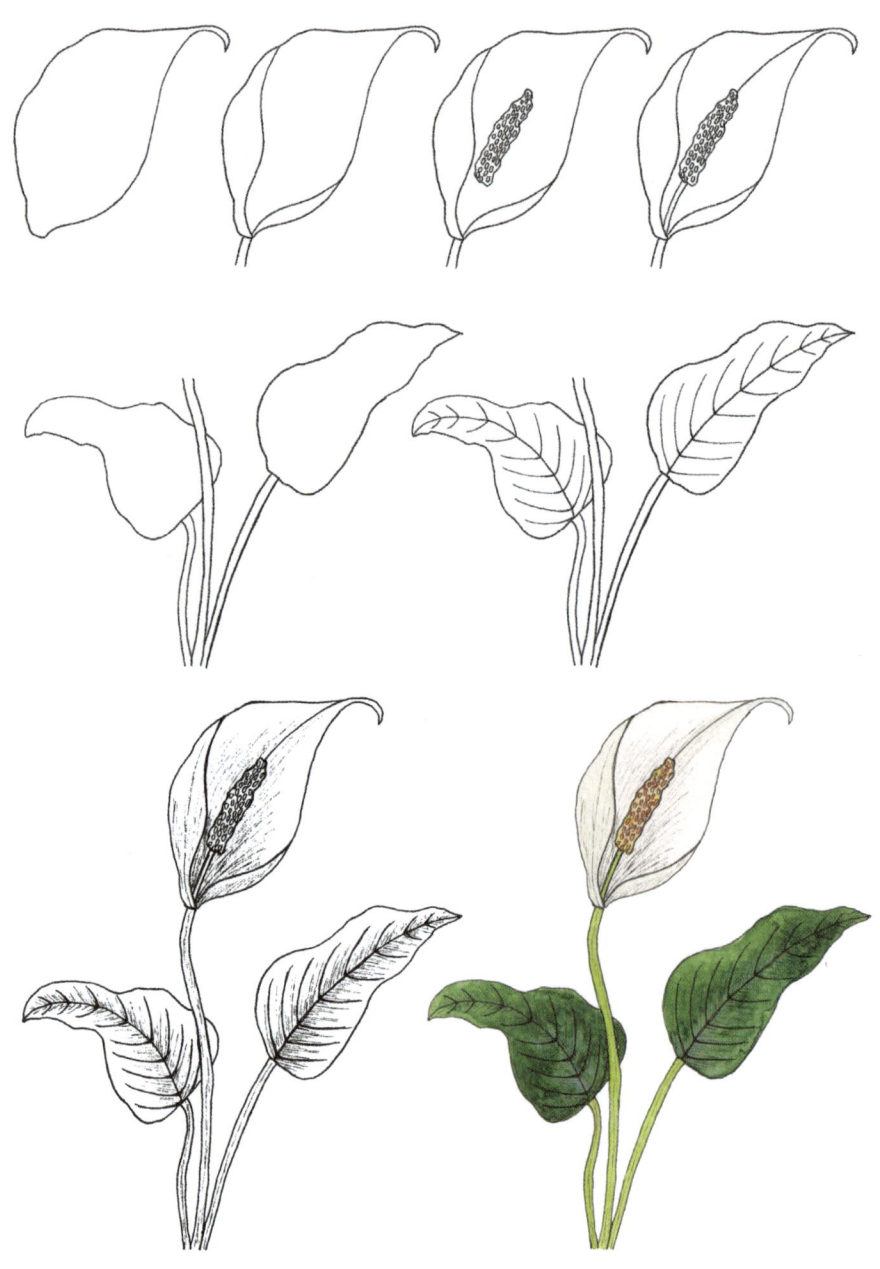

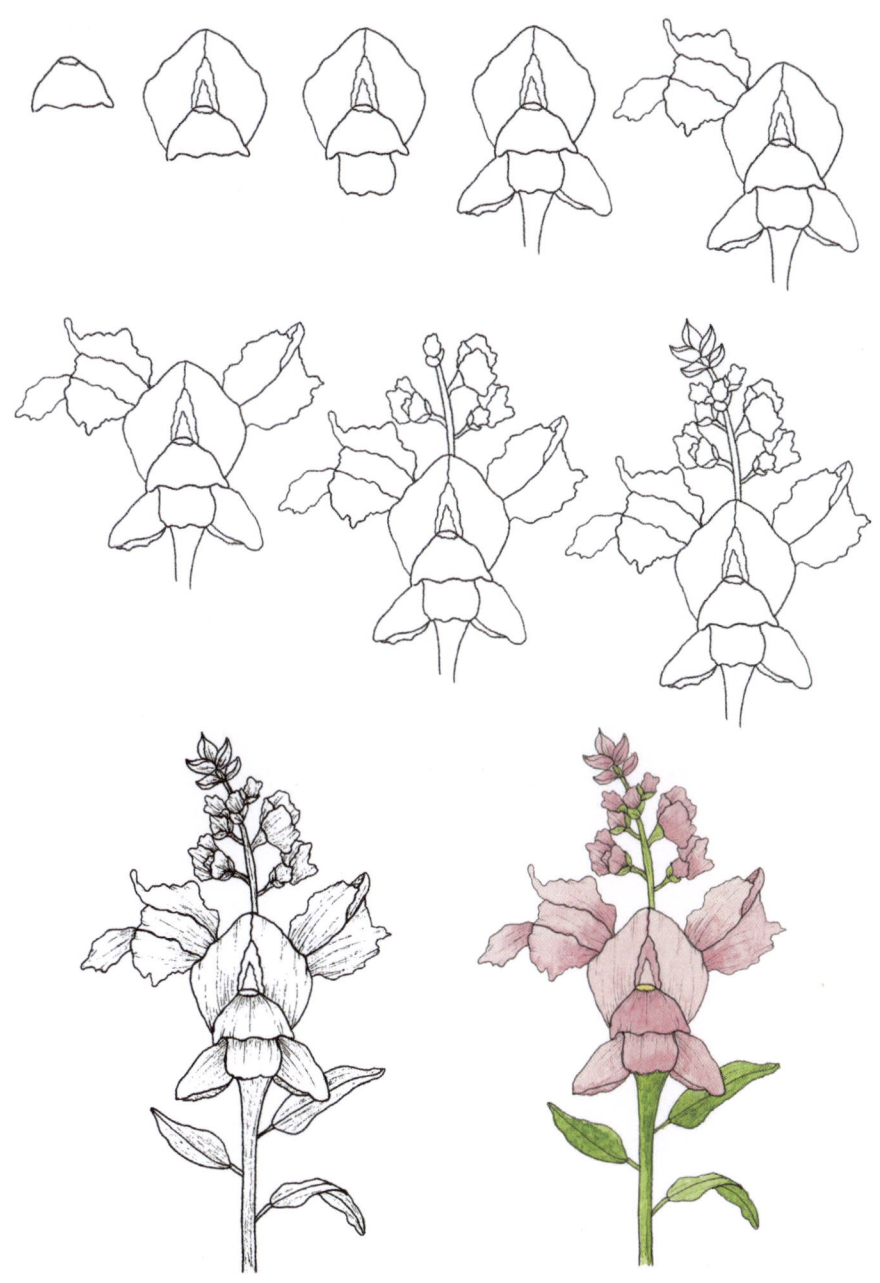

Sweet Pea

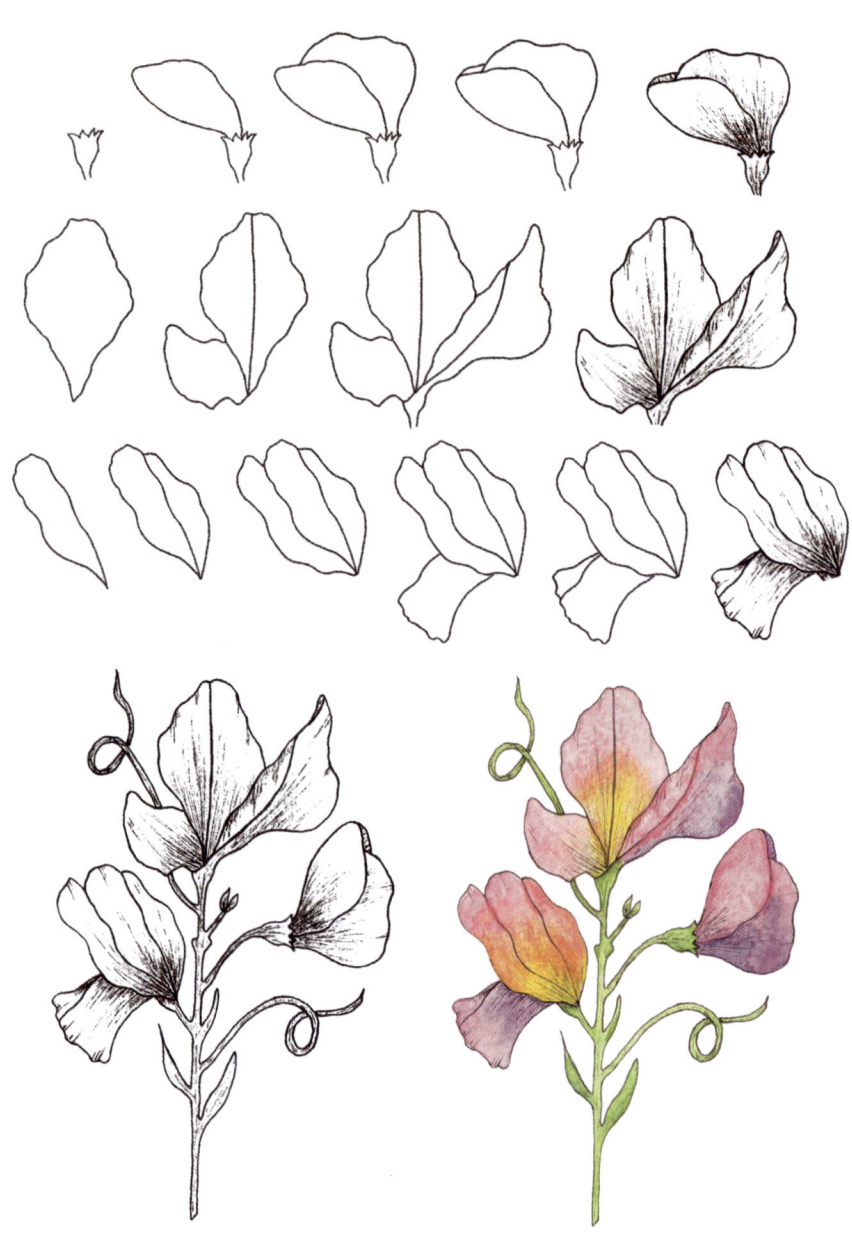

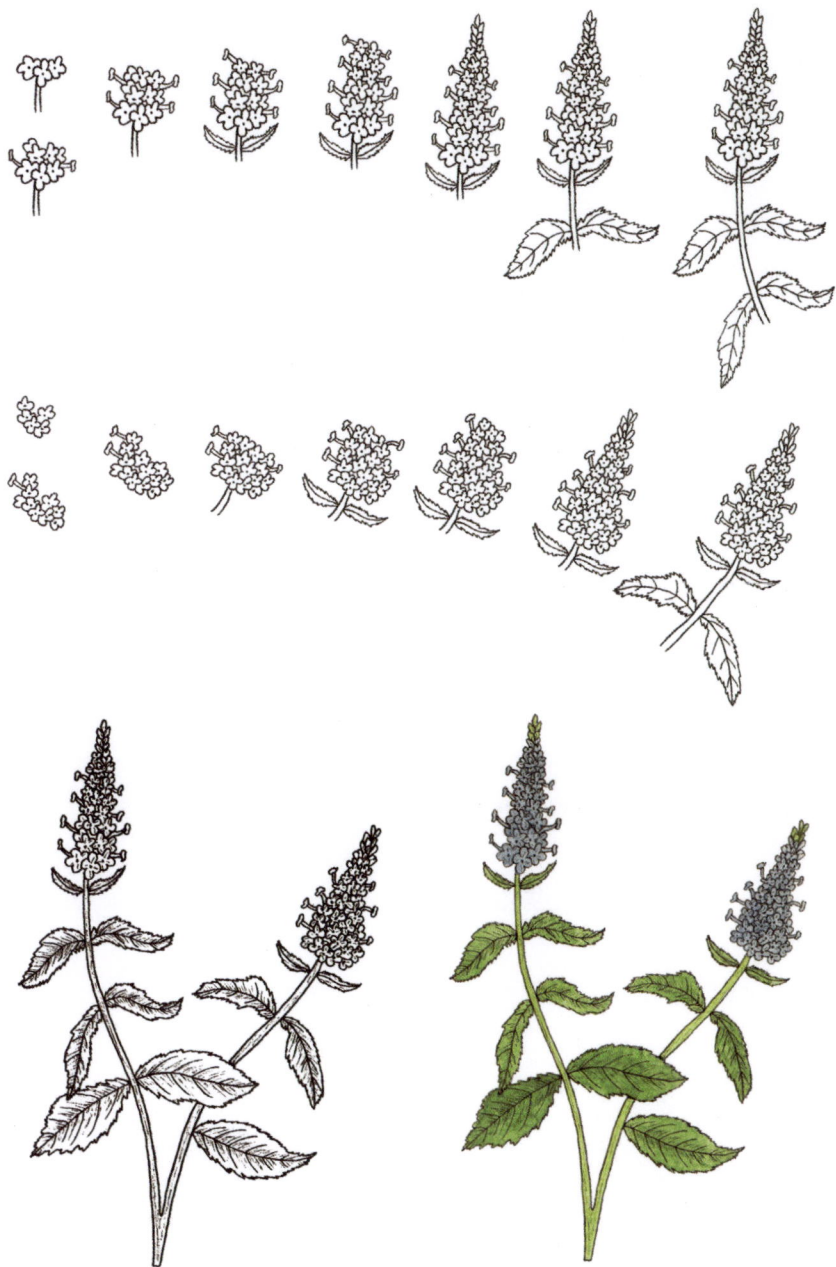

Waxflower

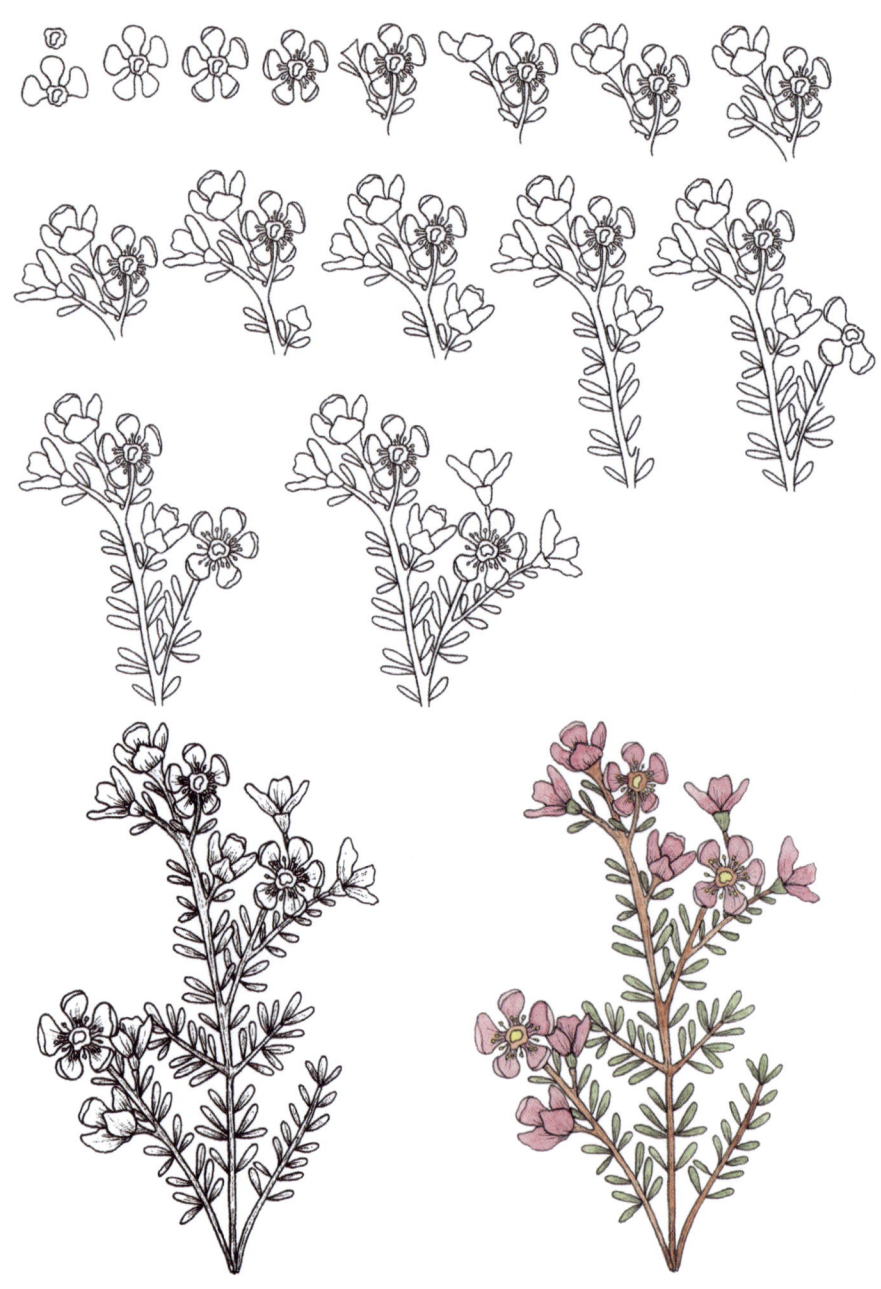

Wisteria

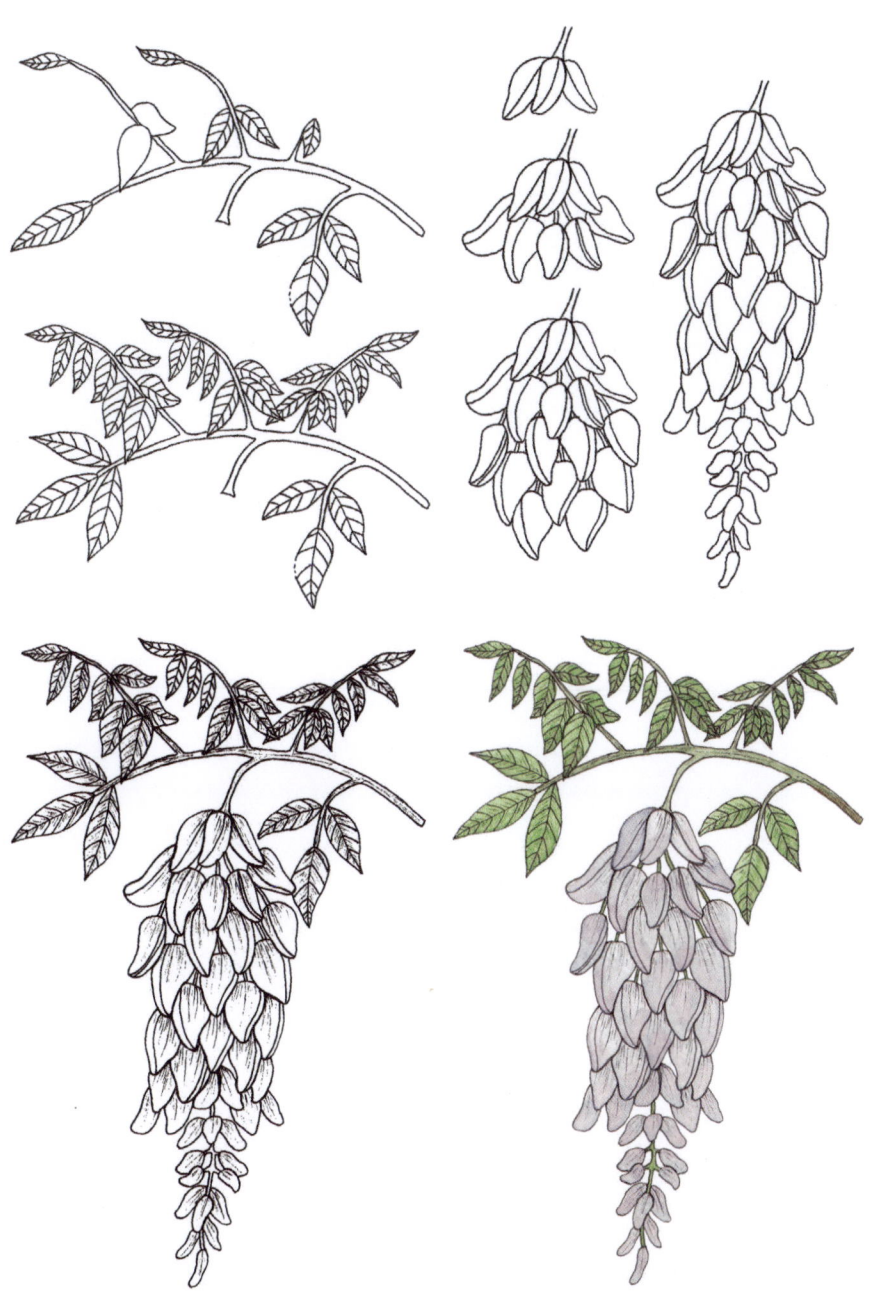

79

Bouvardia

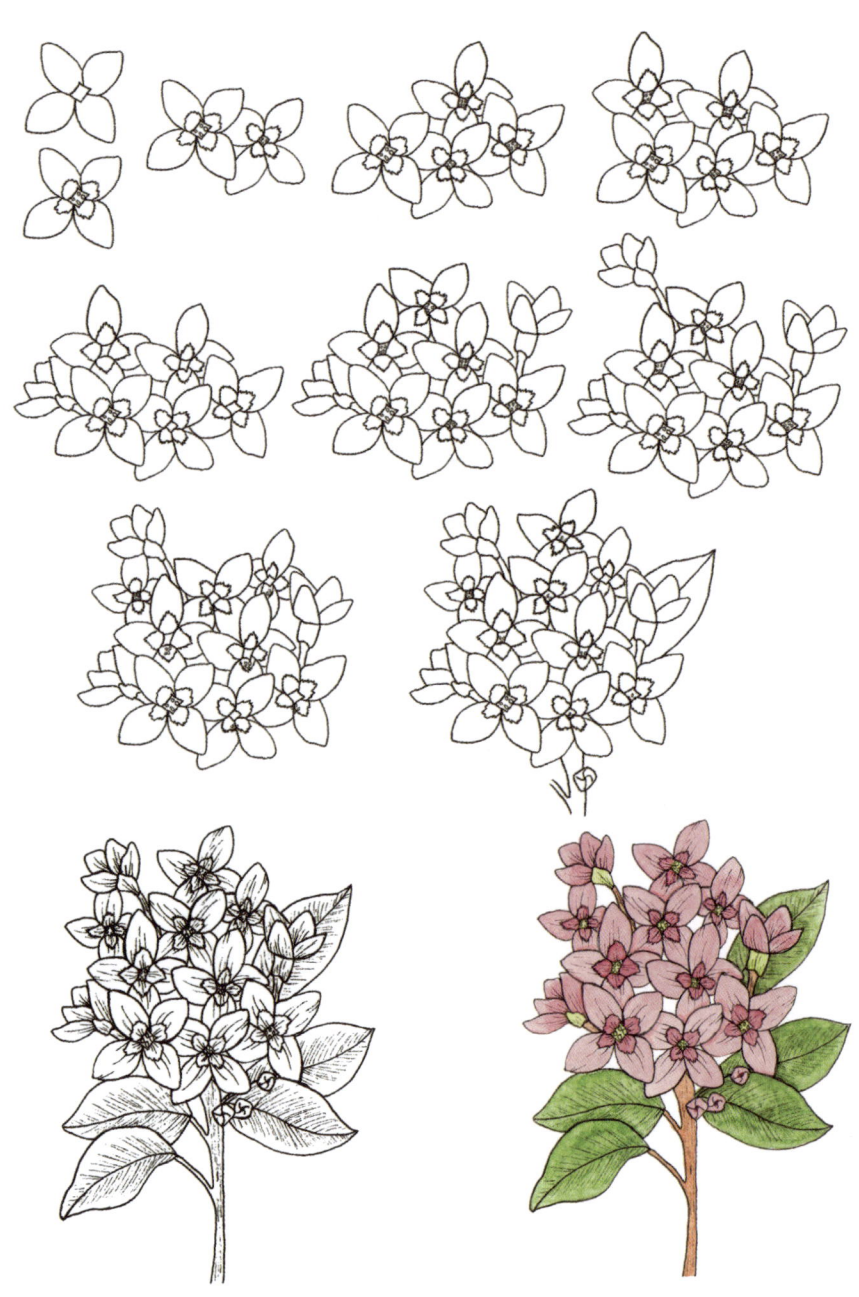

Zinnia

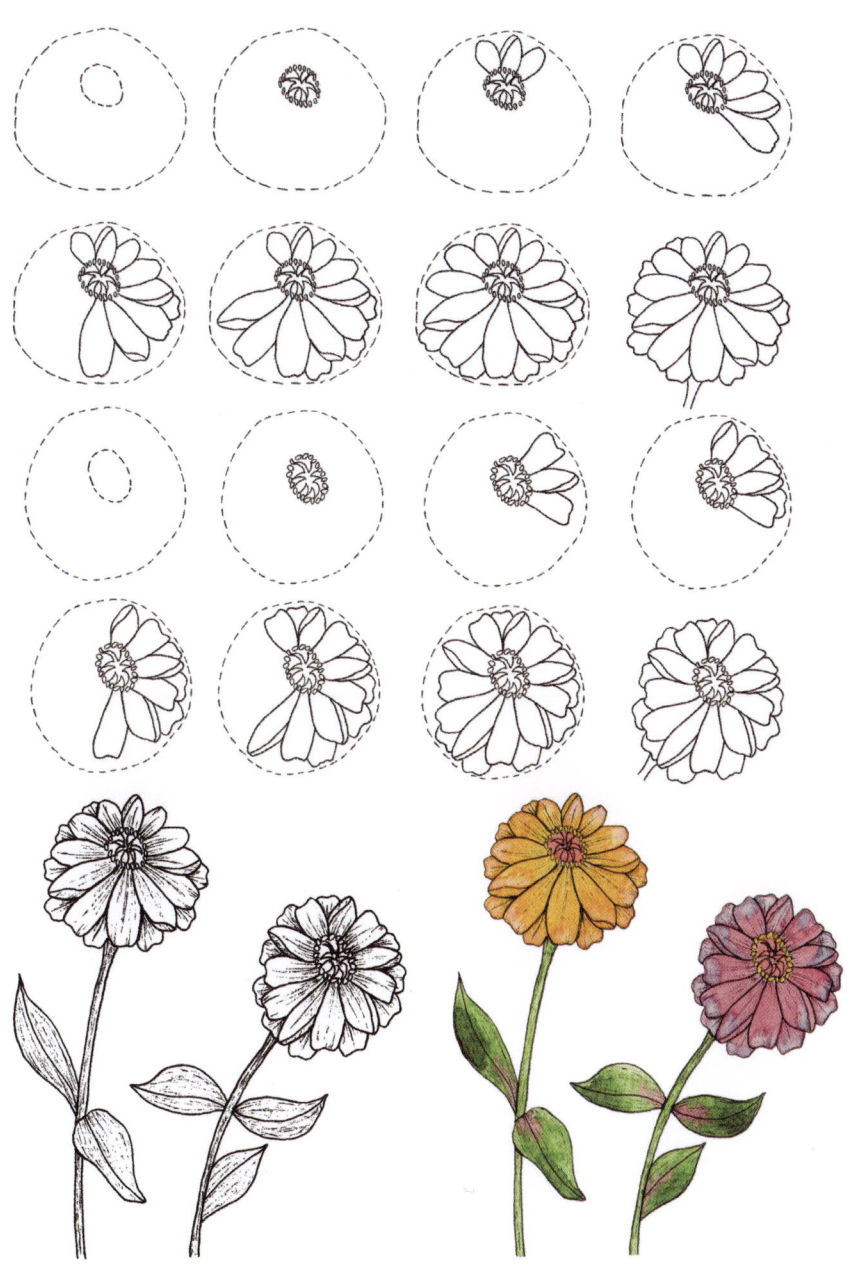

Dianthus

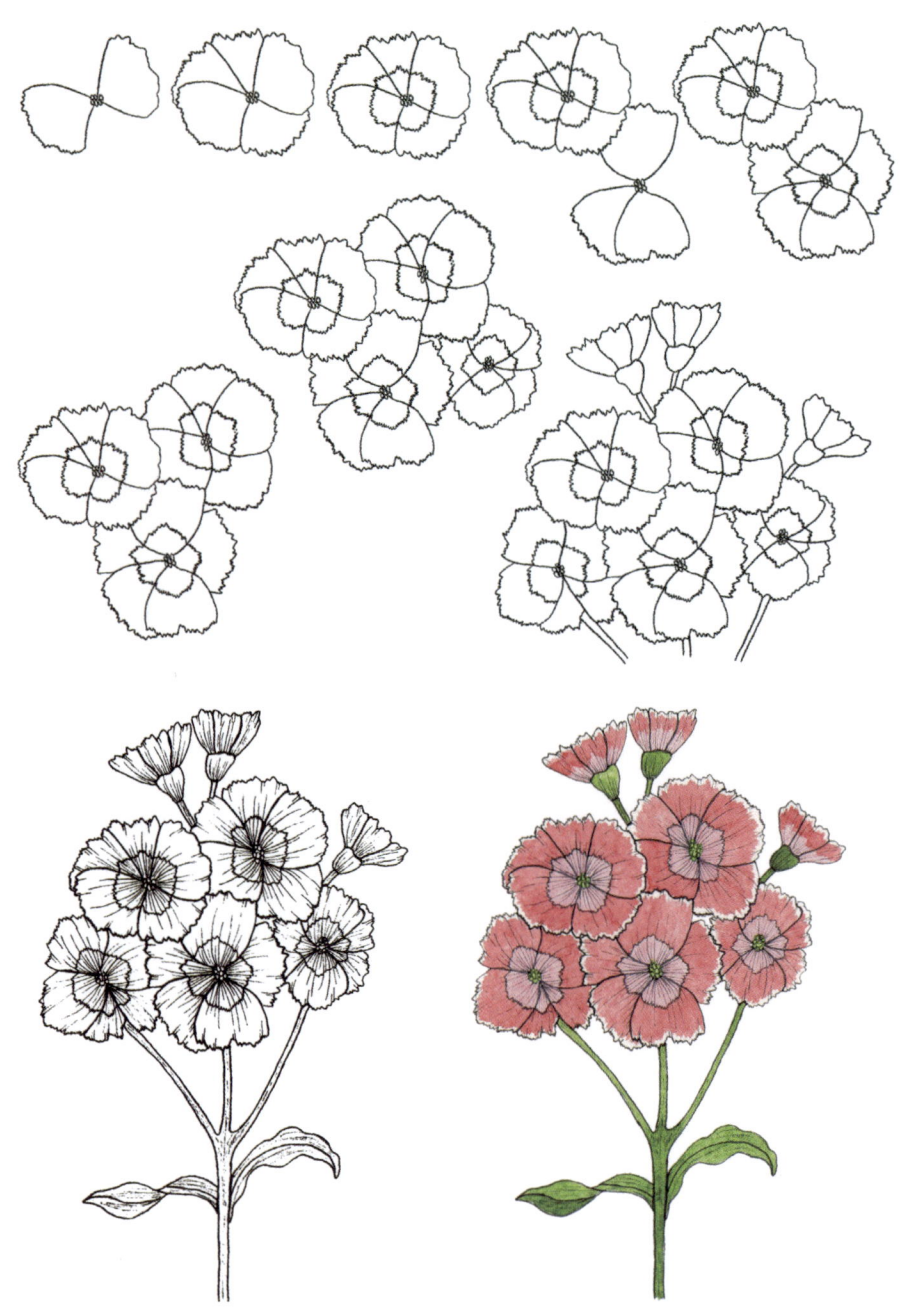

Forsythia

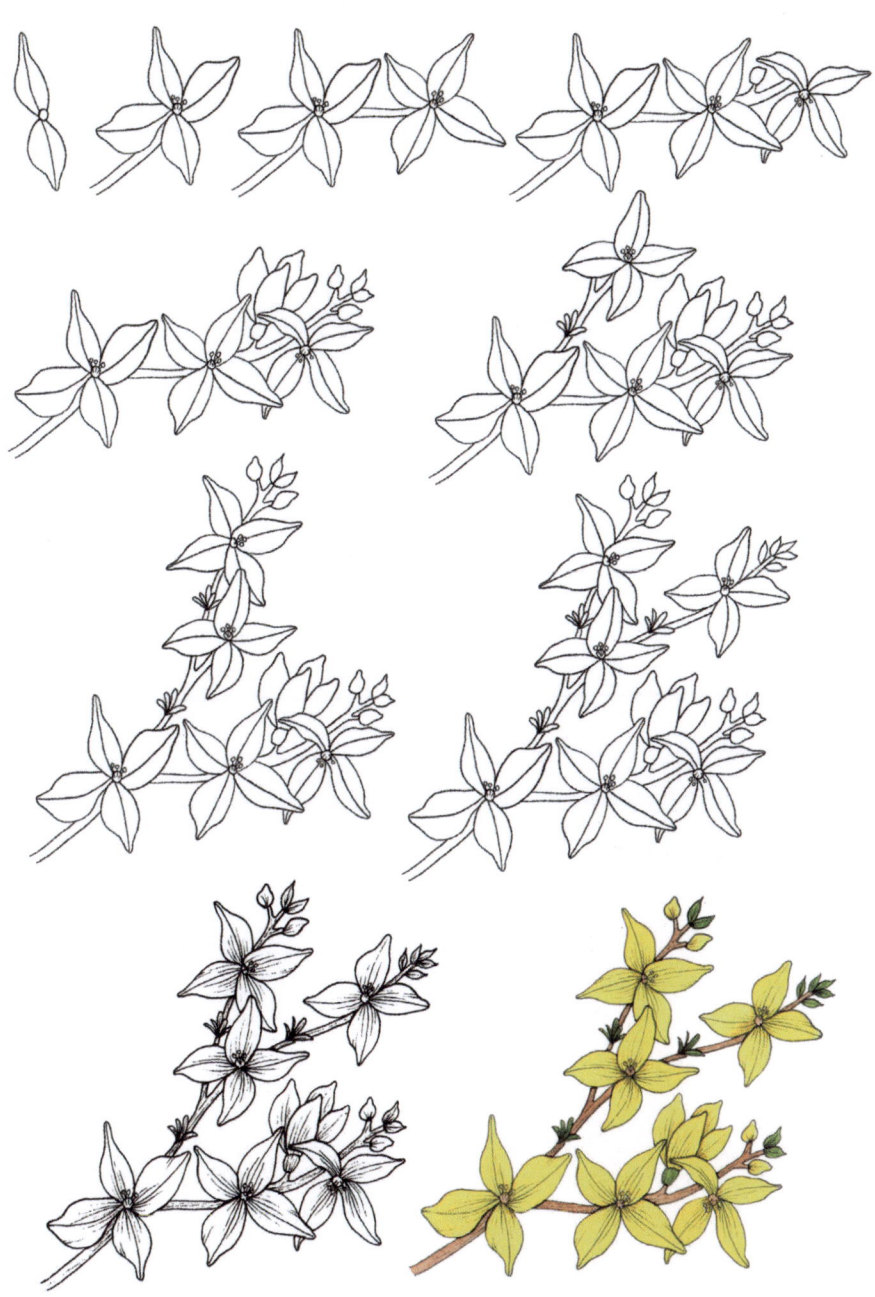

Agapanthus

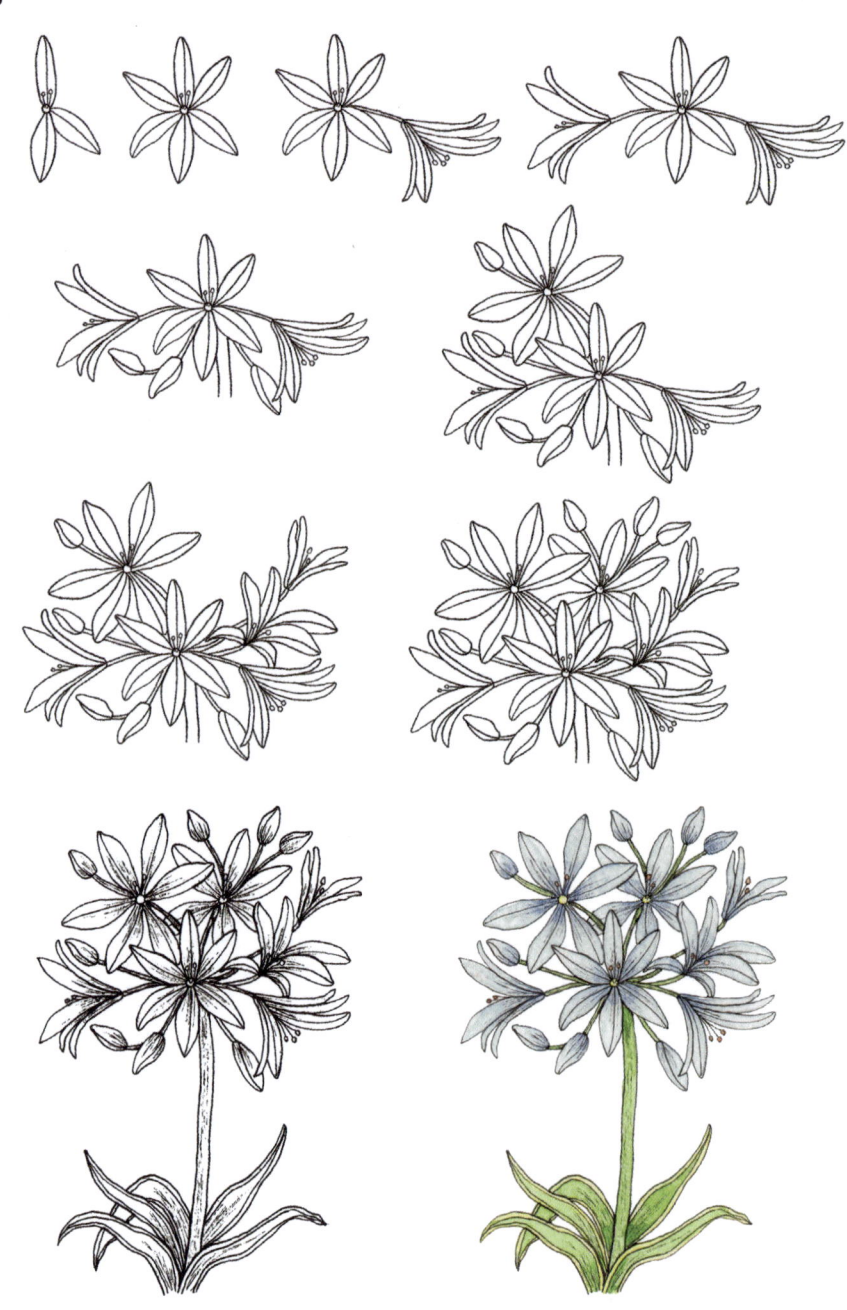

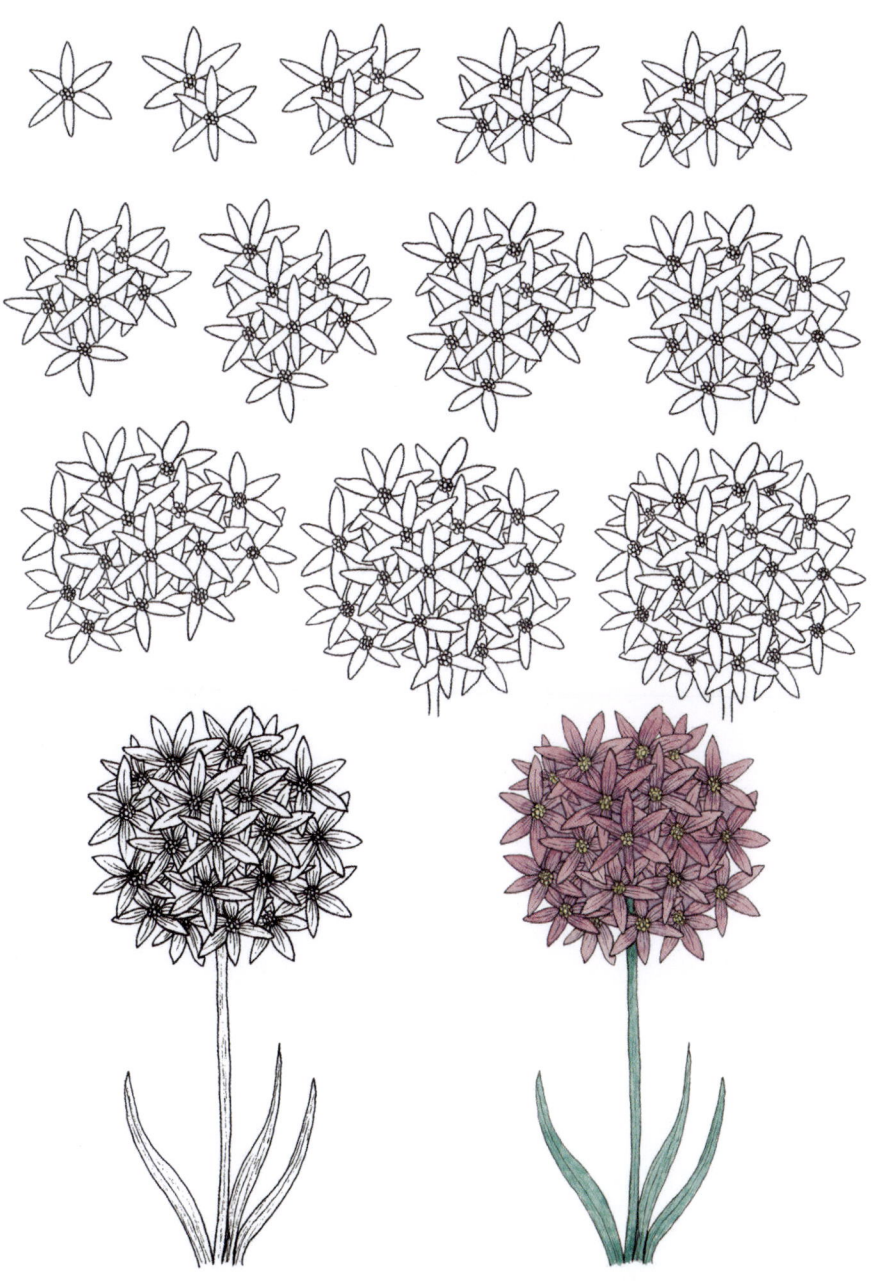

Amaranth

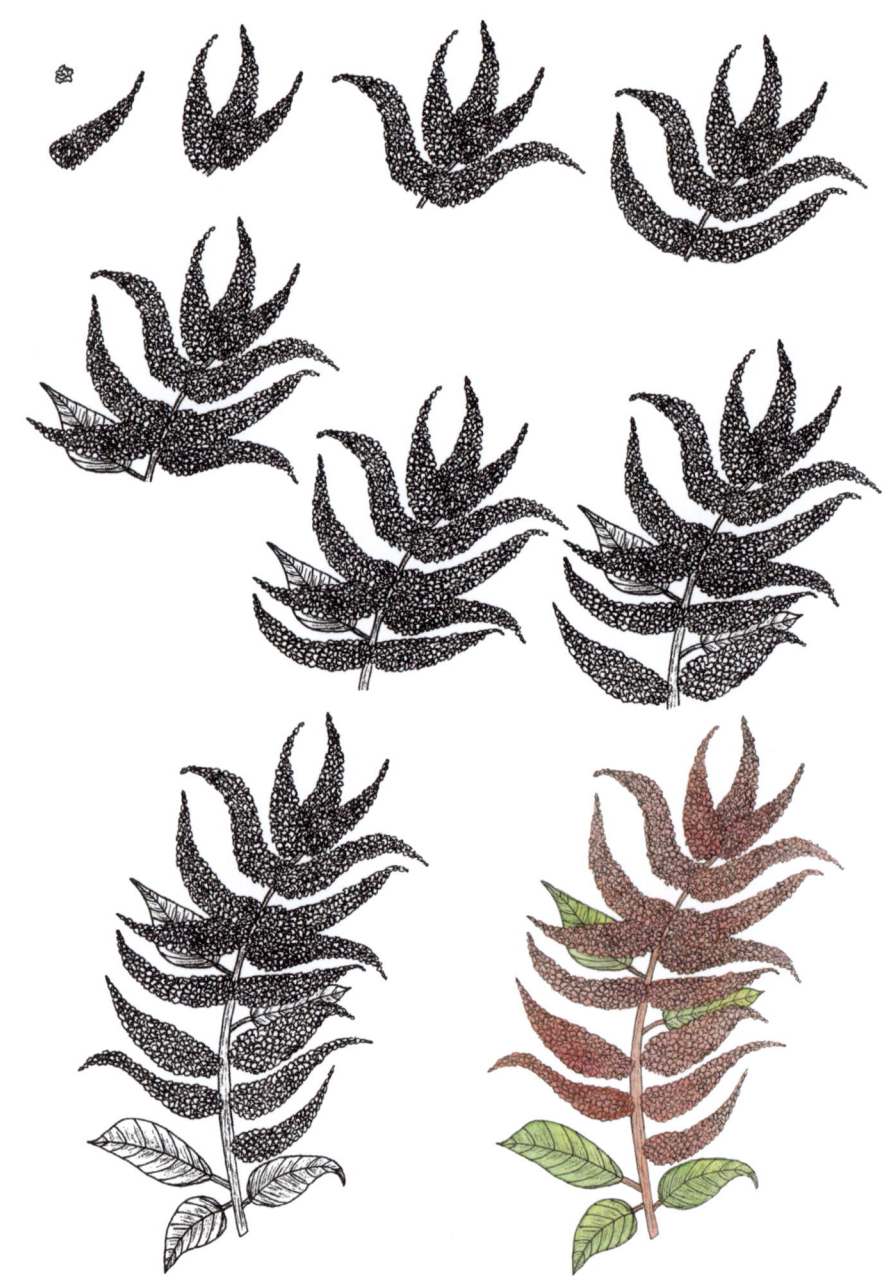

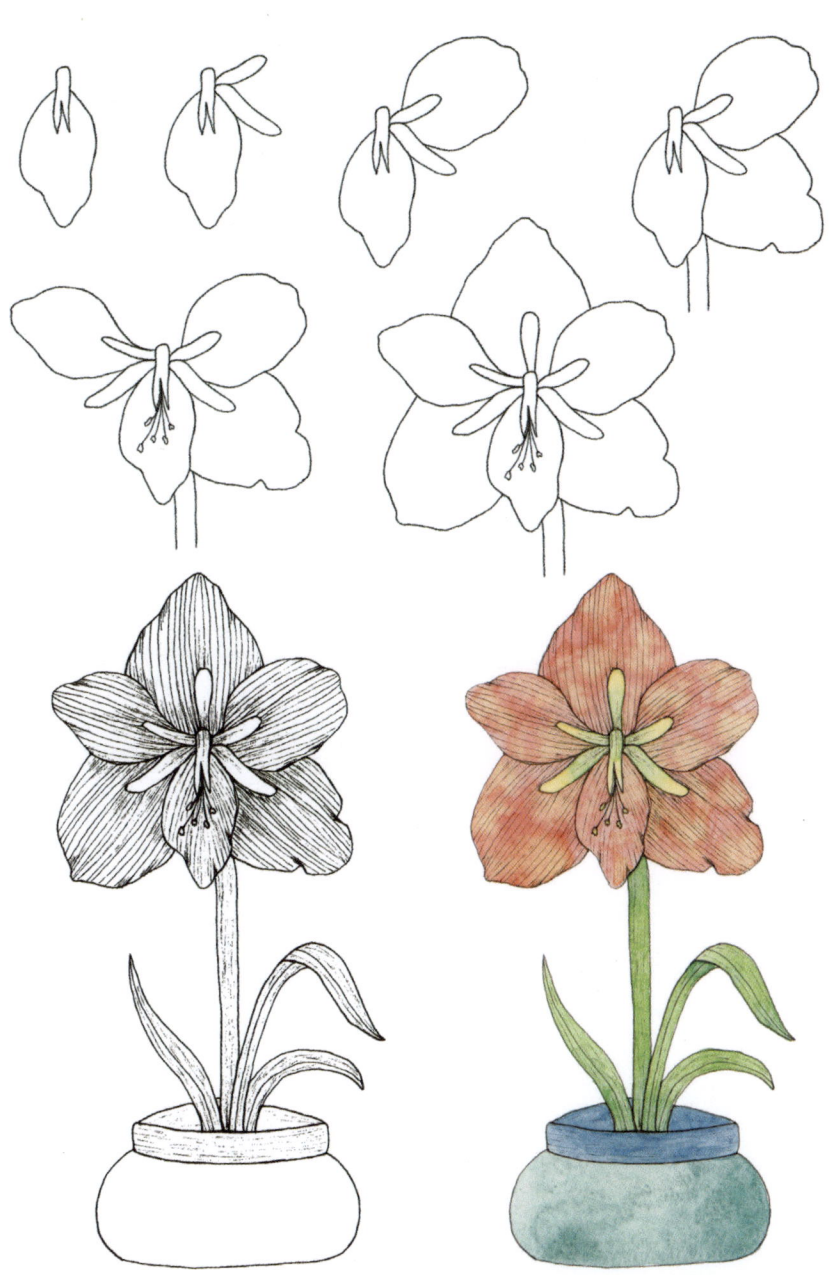

Sage

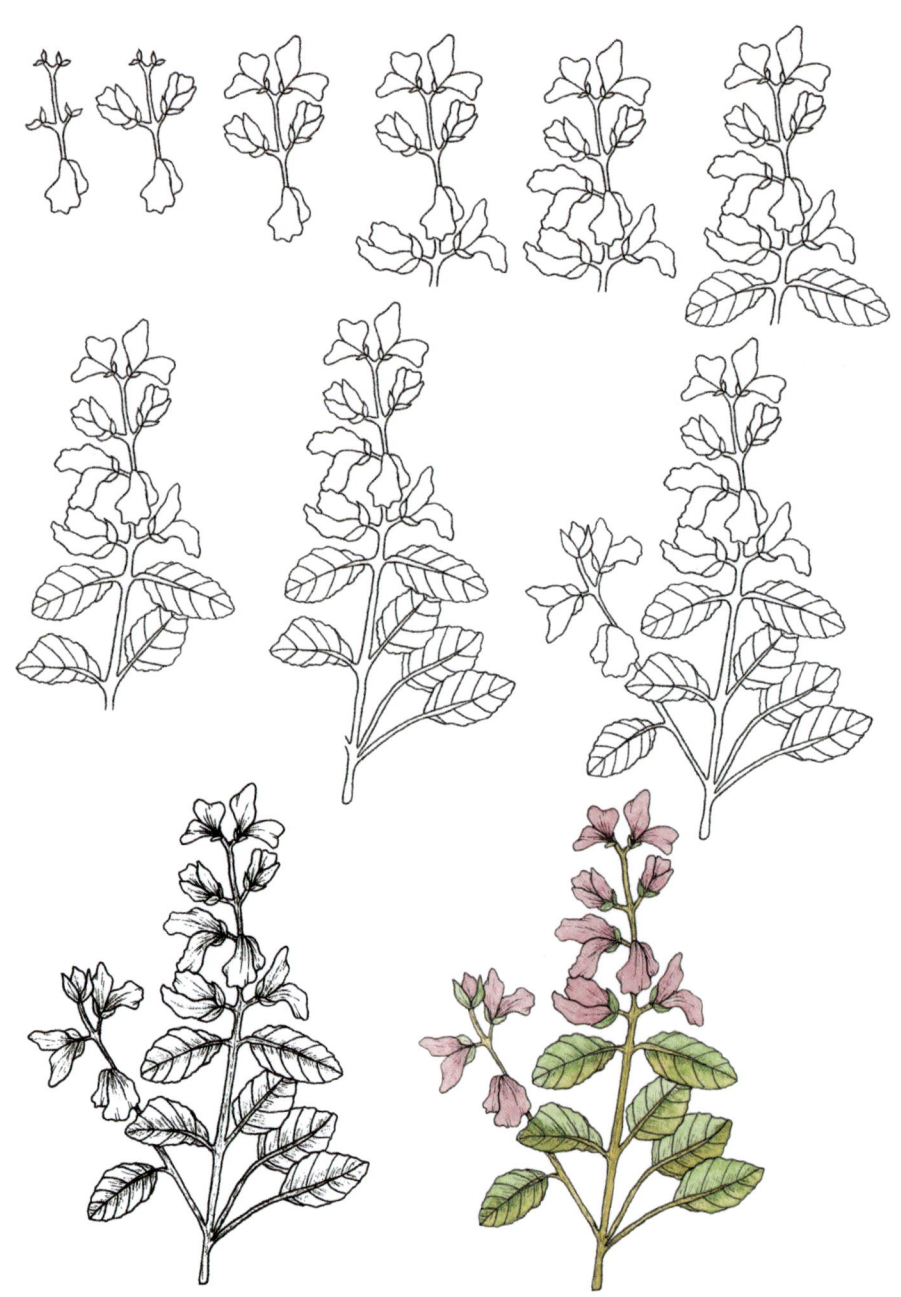

Celosia

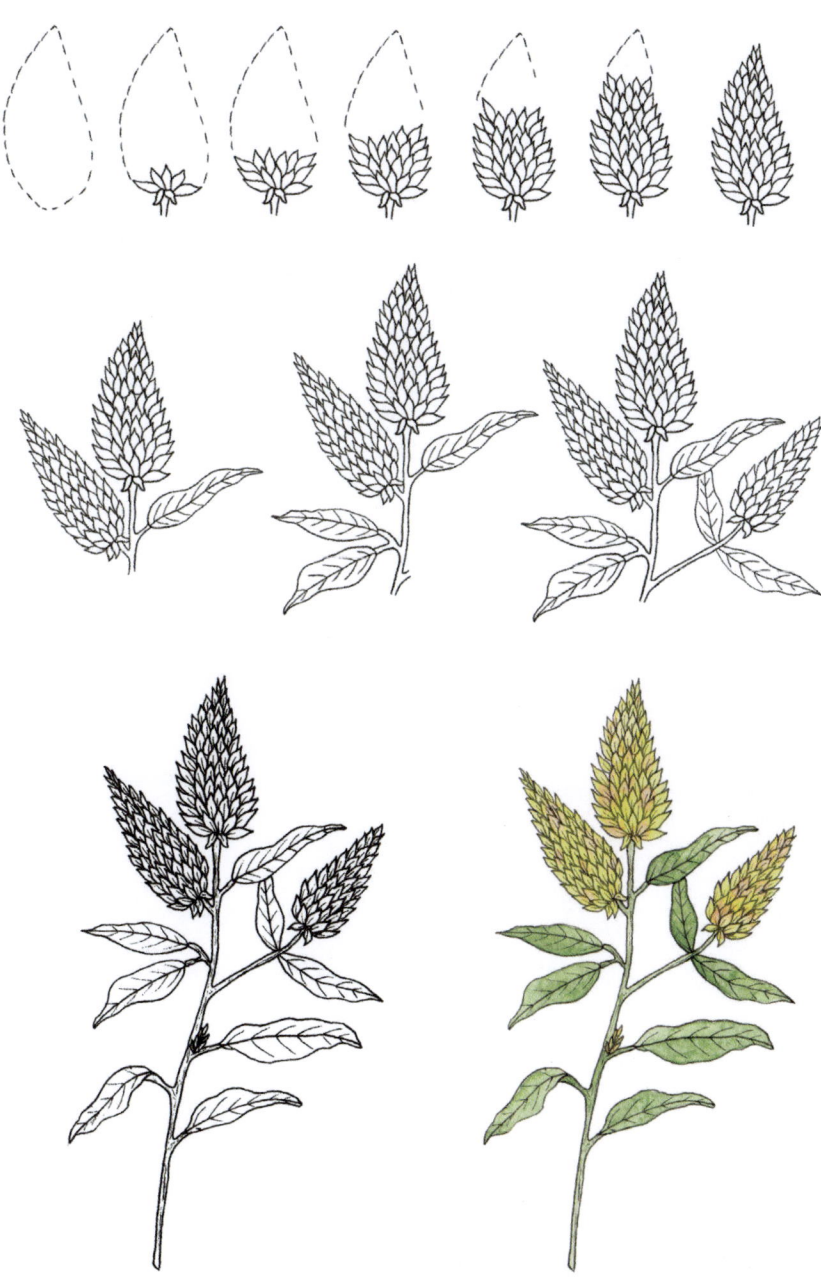

Common Comfrey

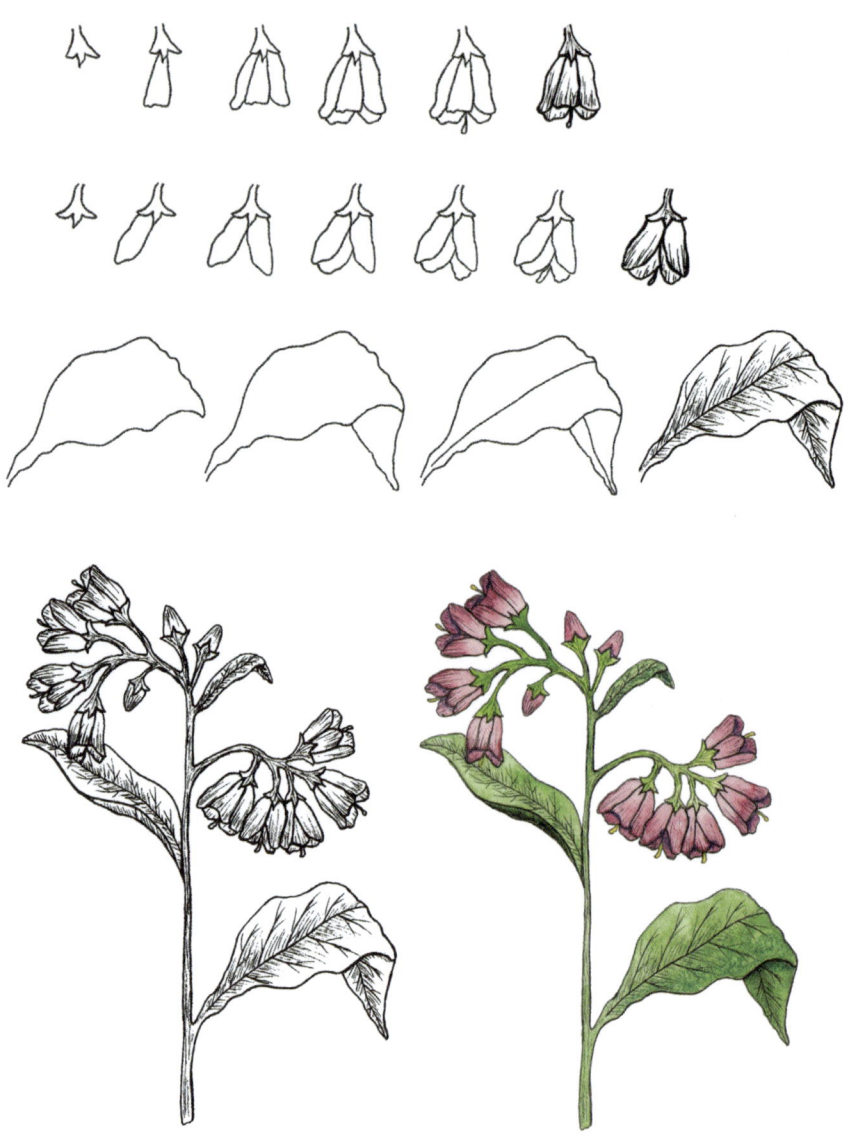

Larkspur

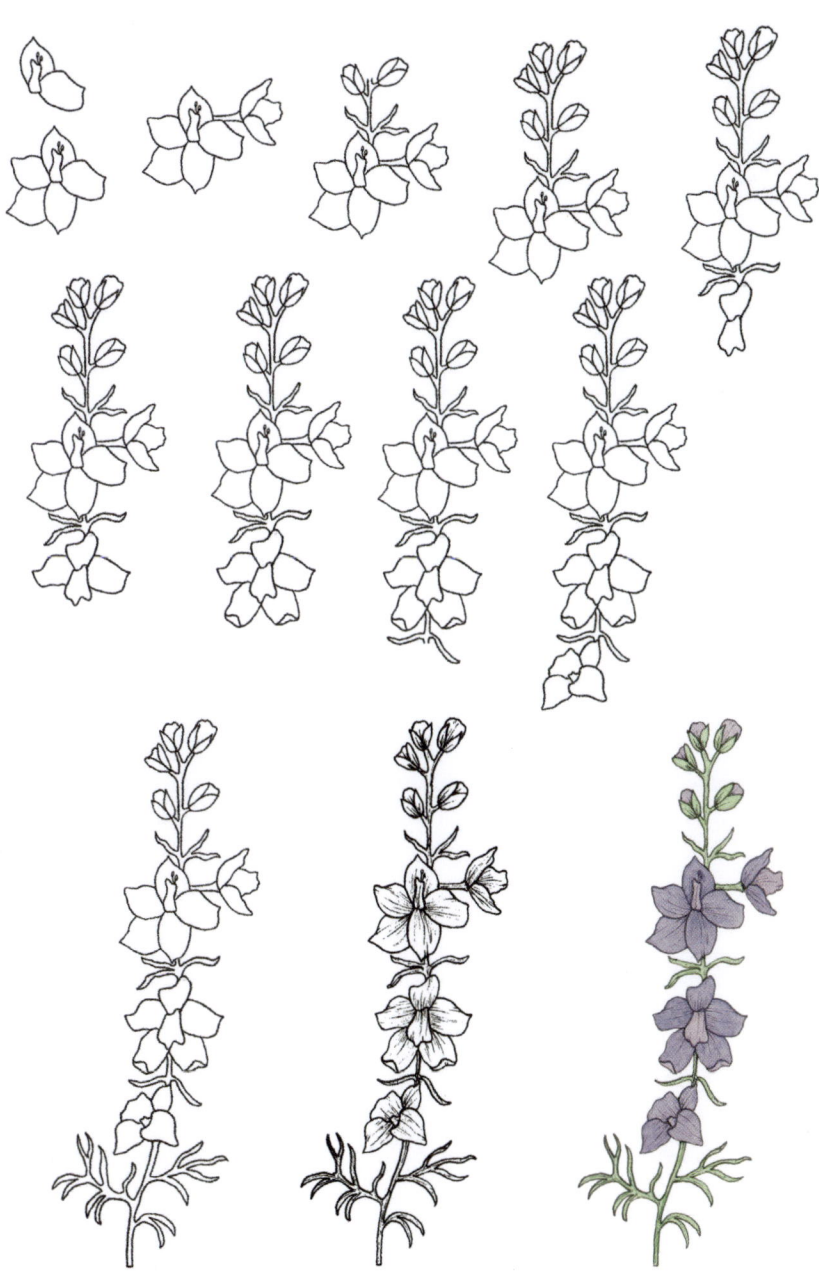

Cowslip

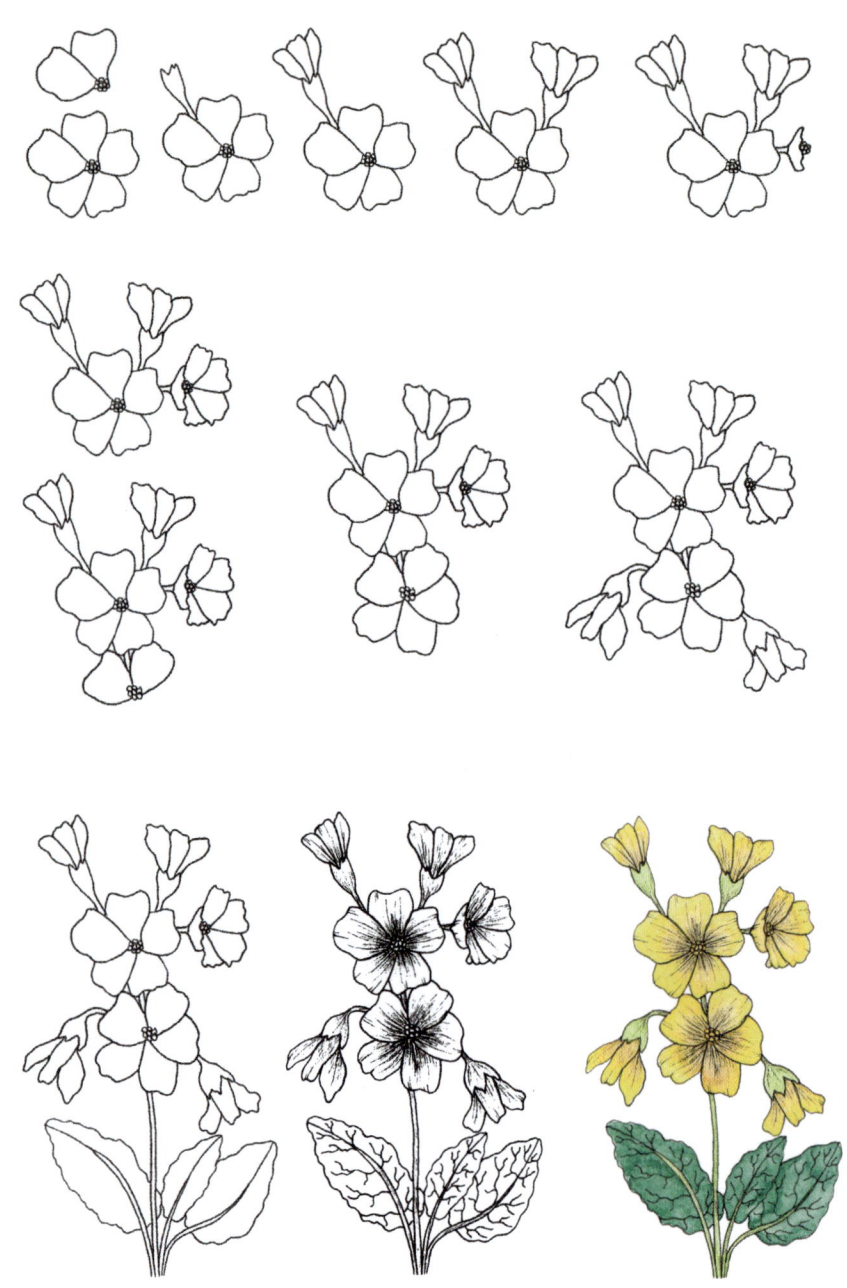

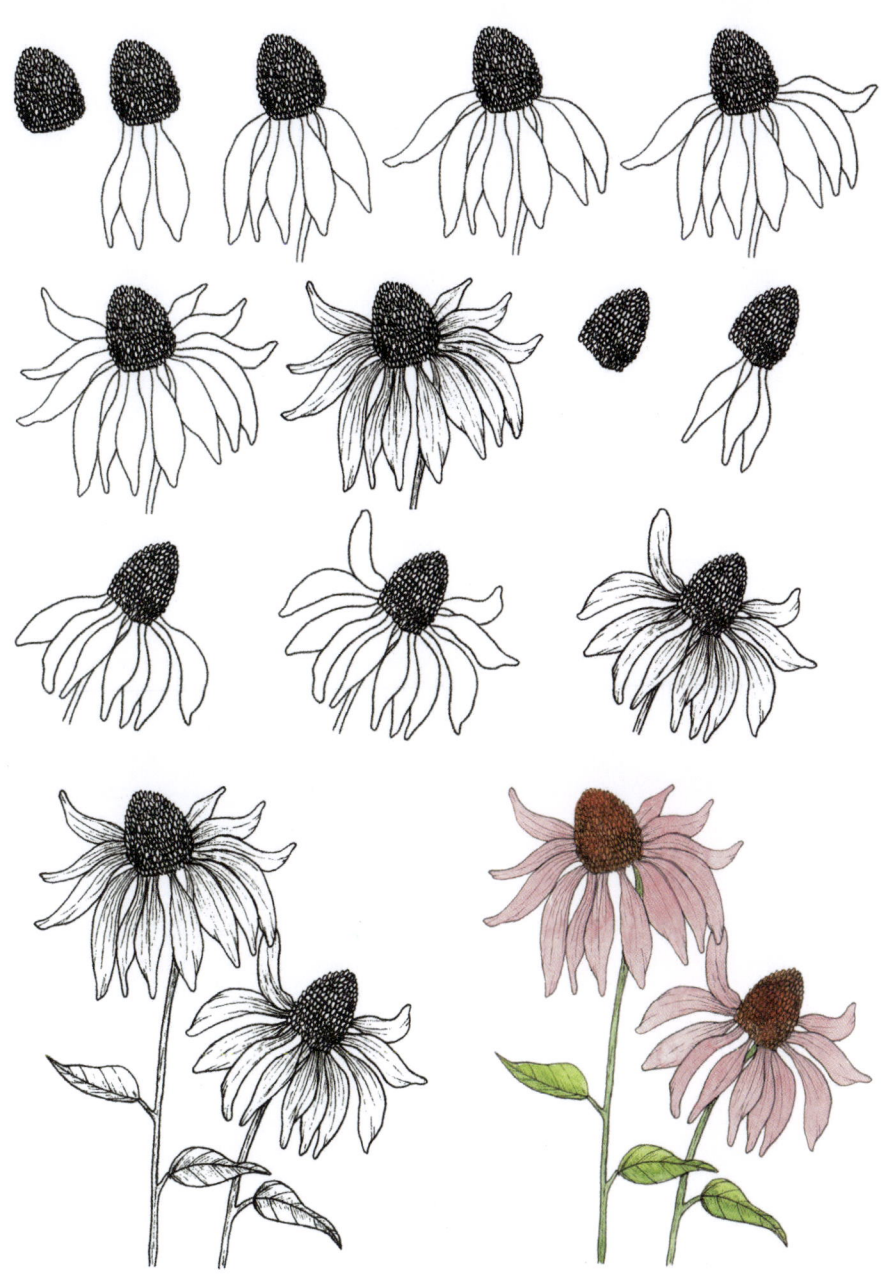

Geranium

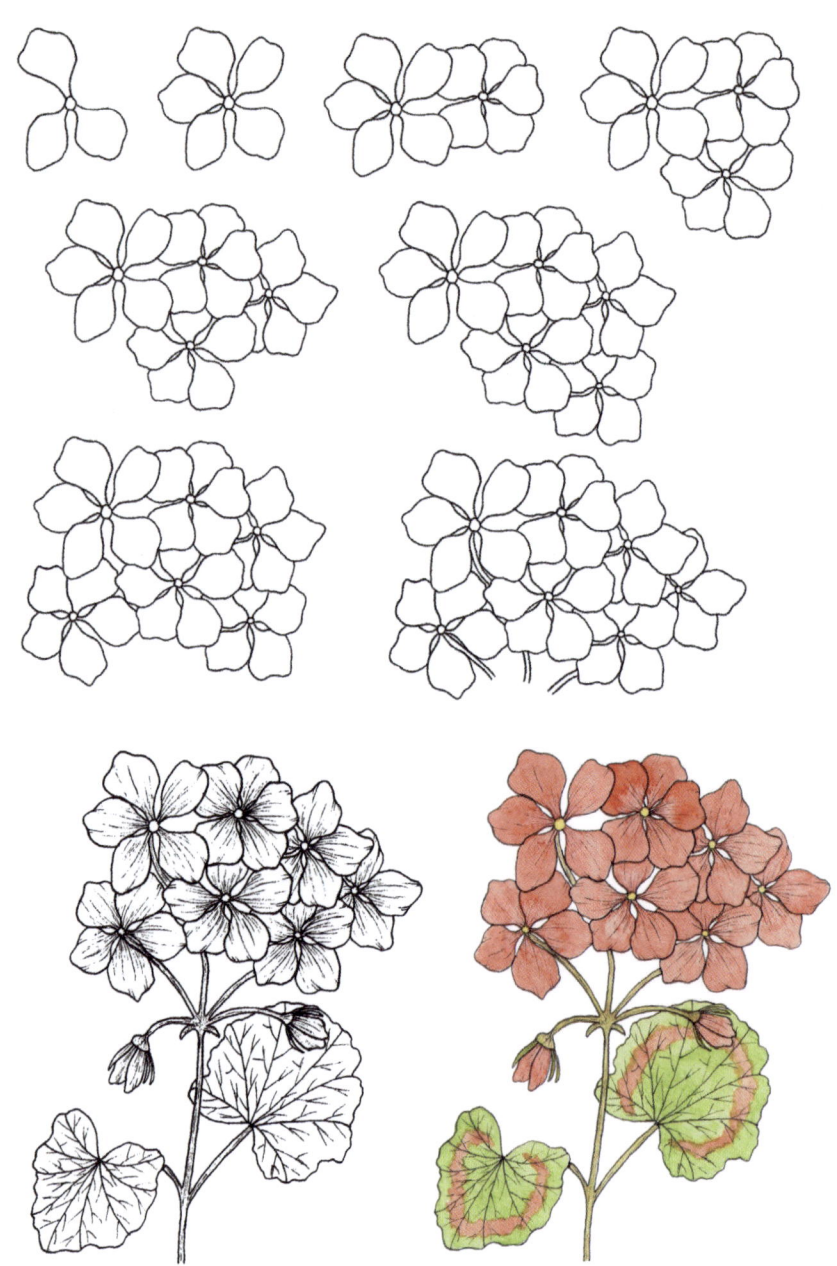

Gerbera Daisy

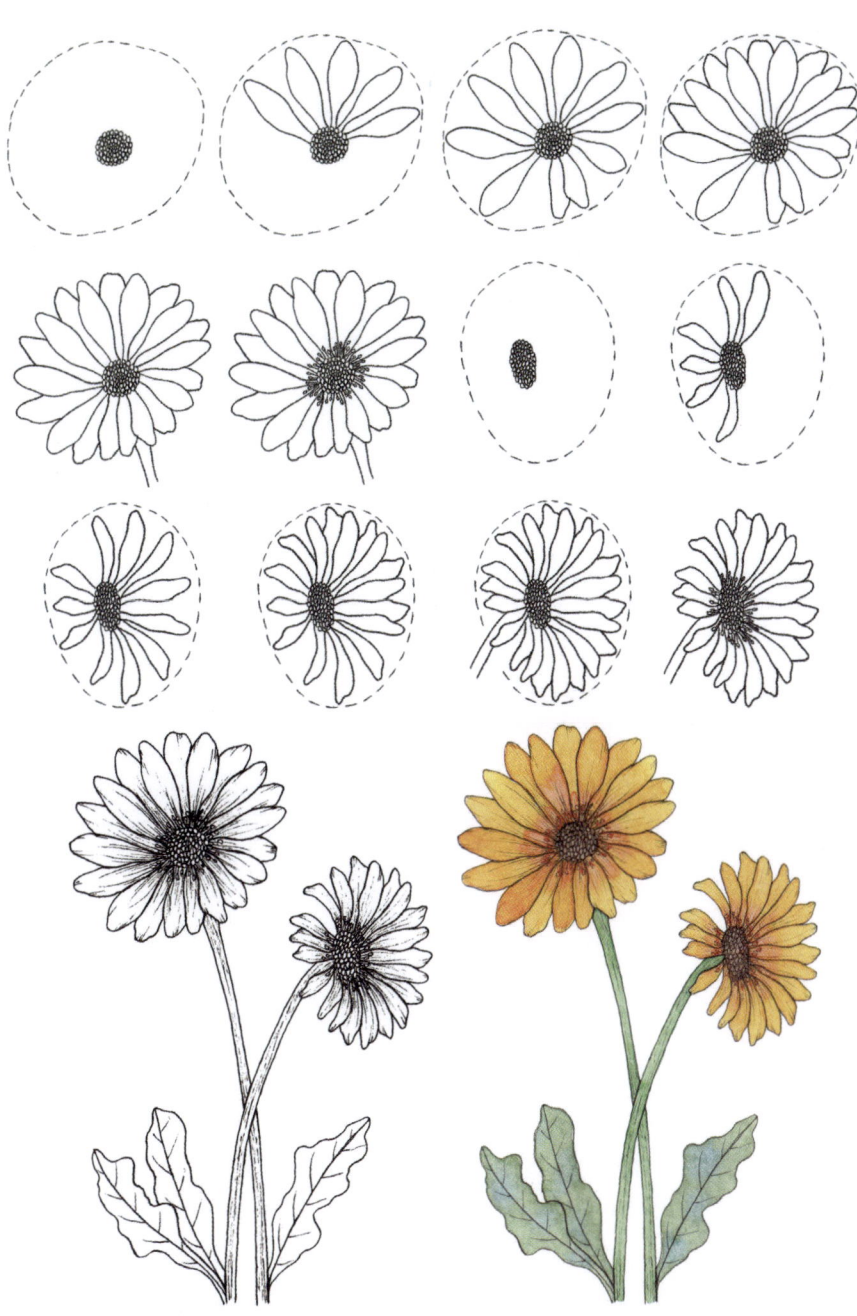

Lucile's Glory of the Snow

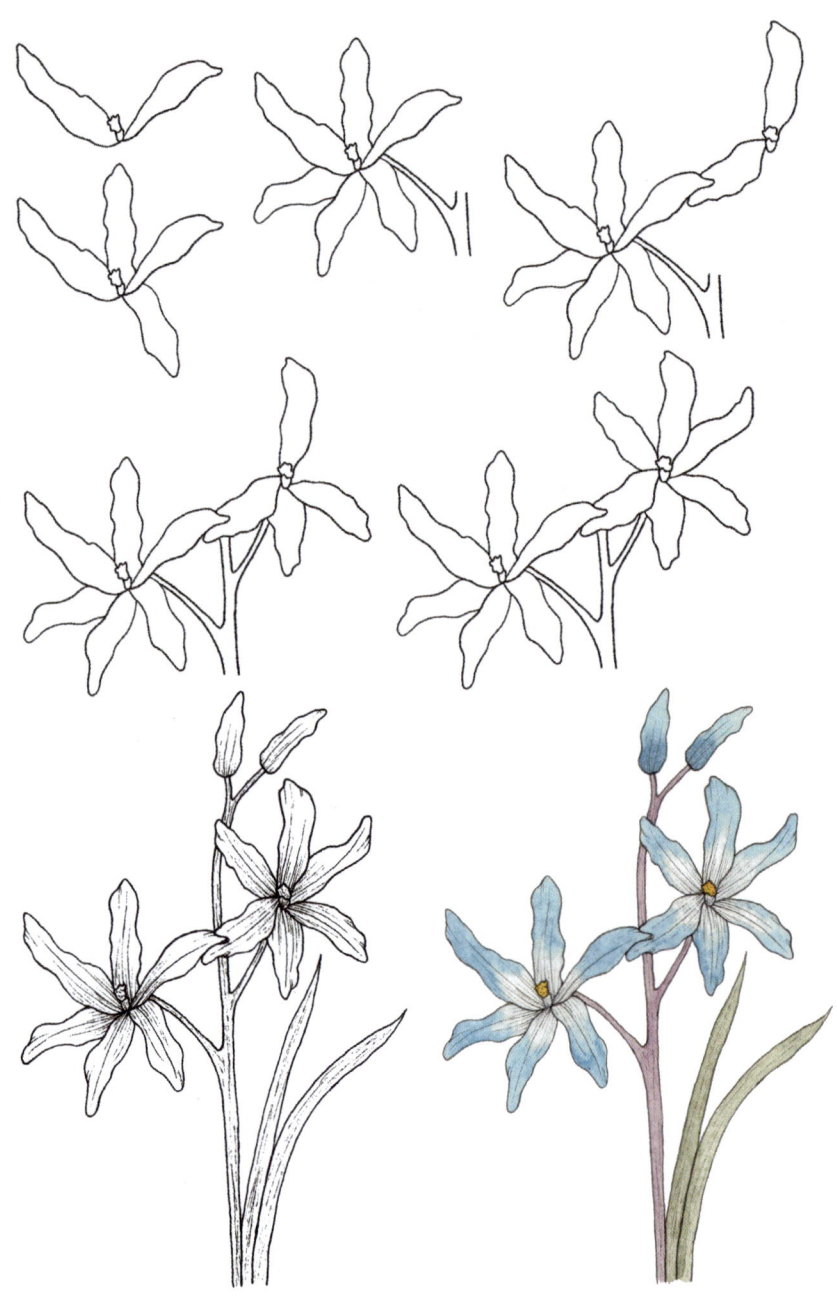

Hollyhock

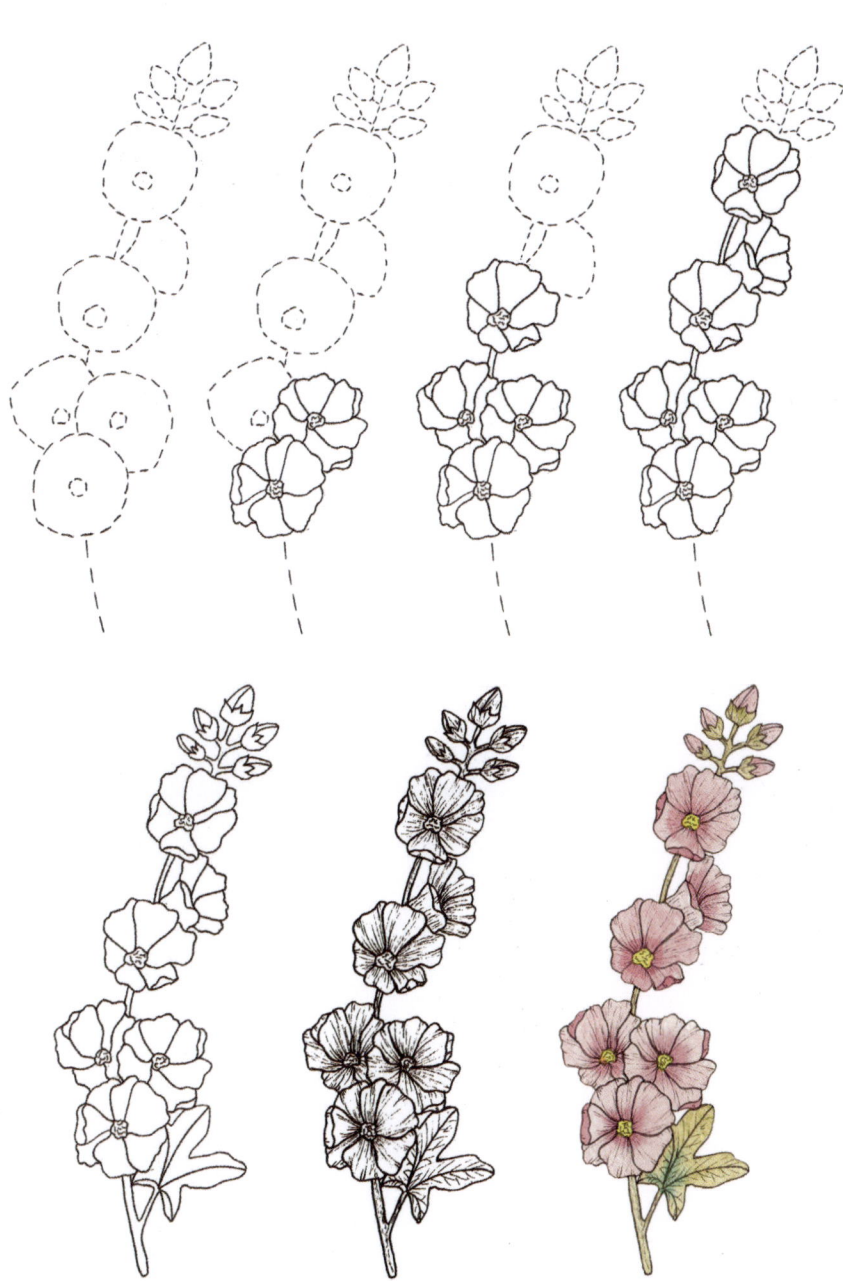

Hyacinth

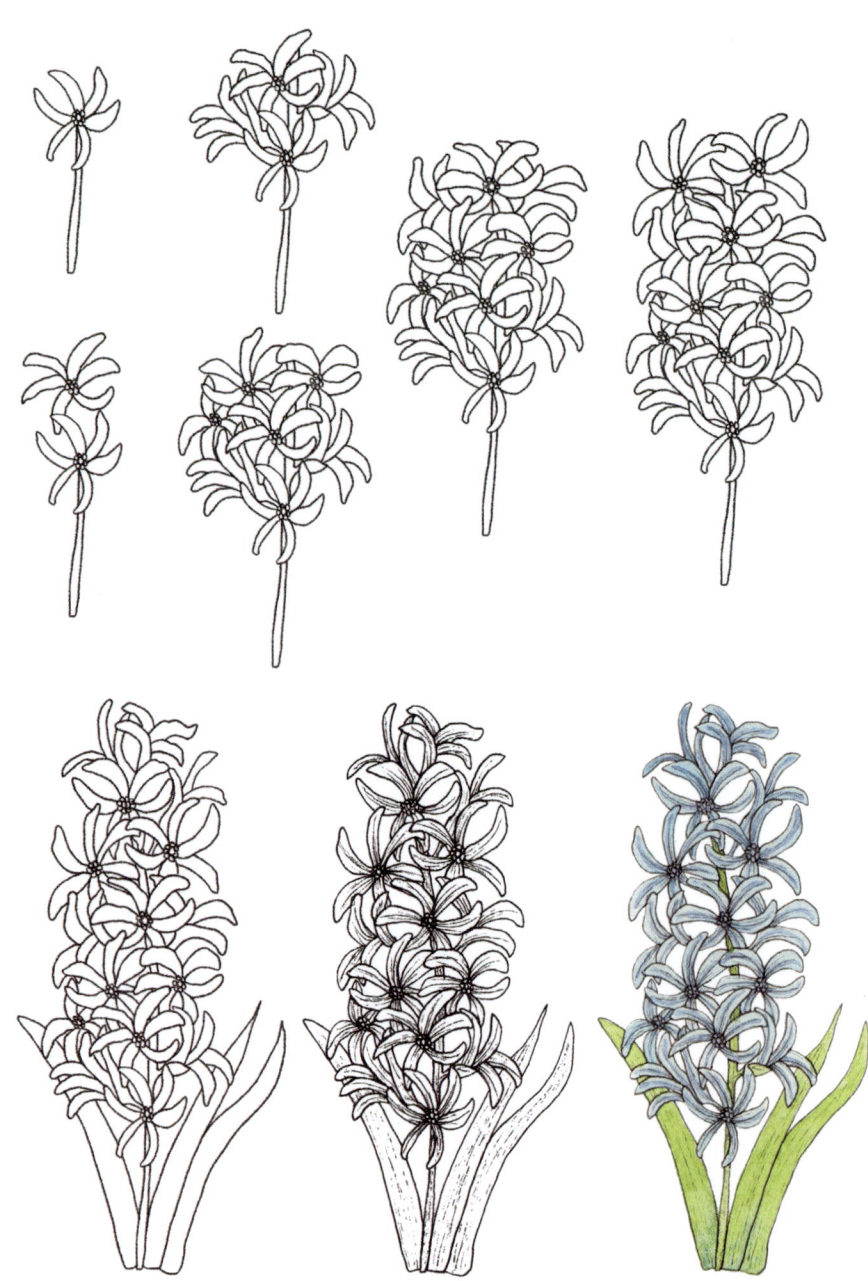

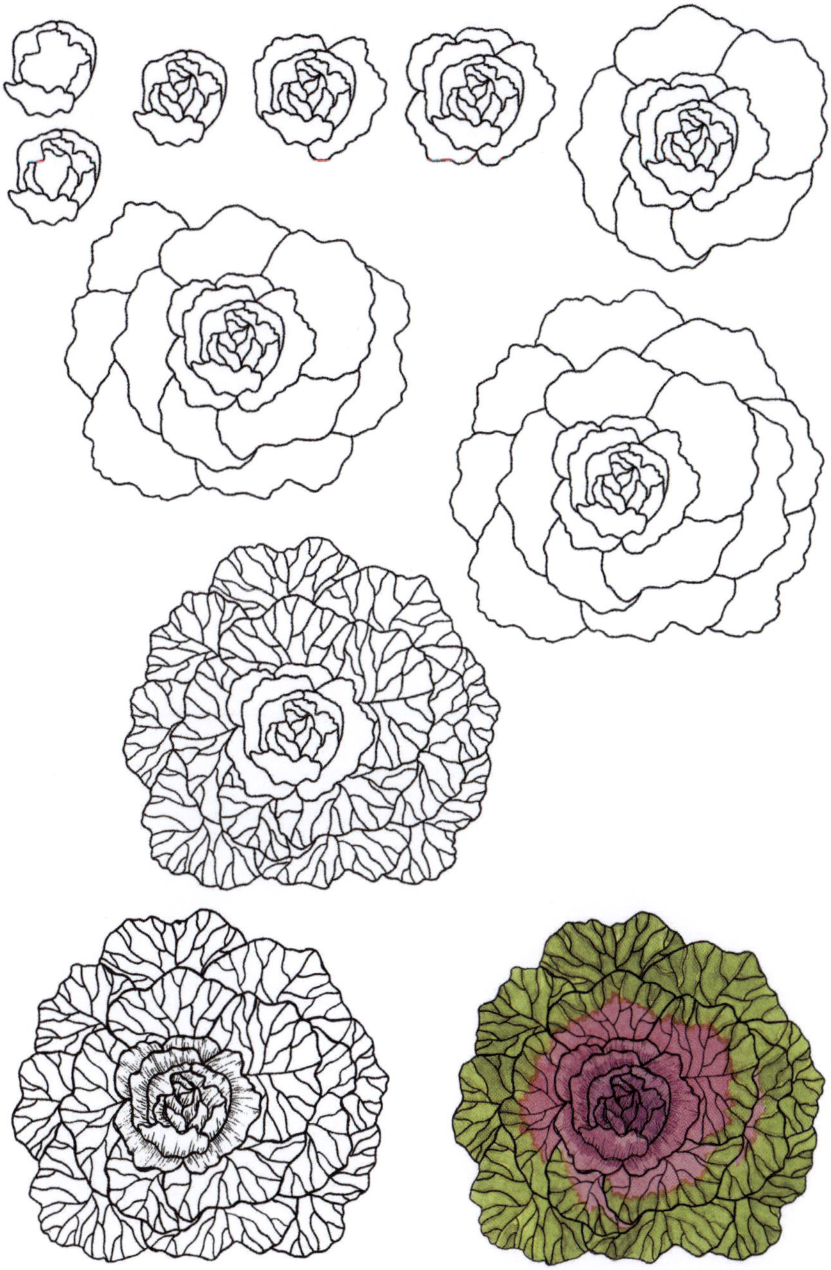

Periwinkle

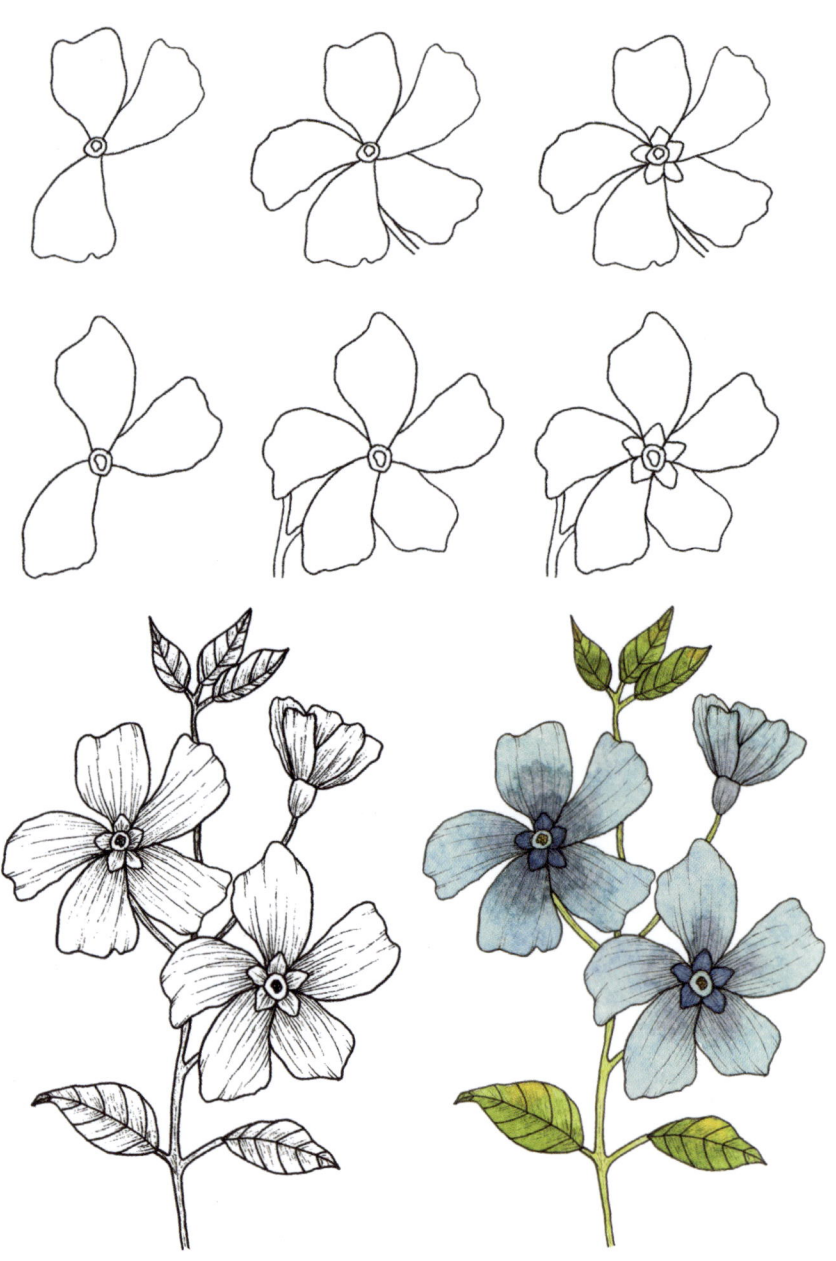

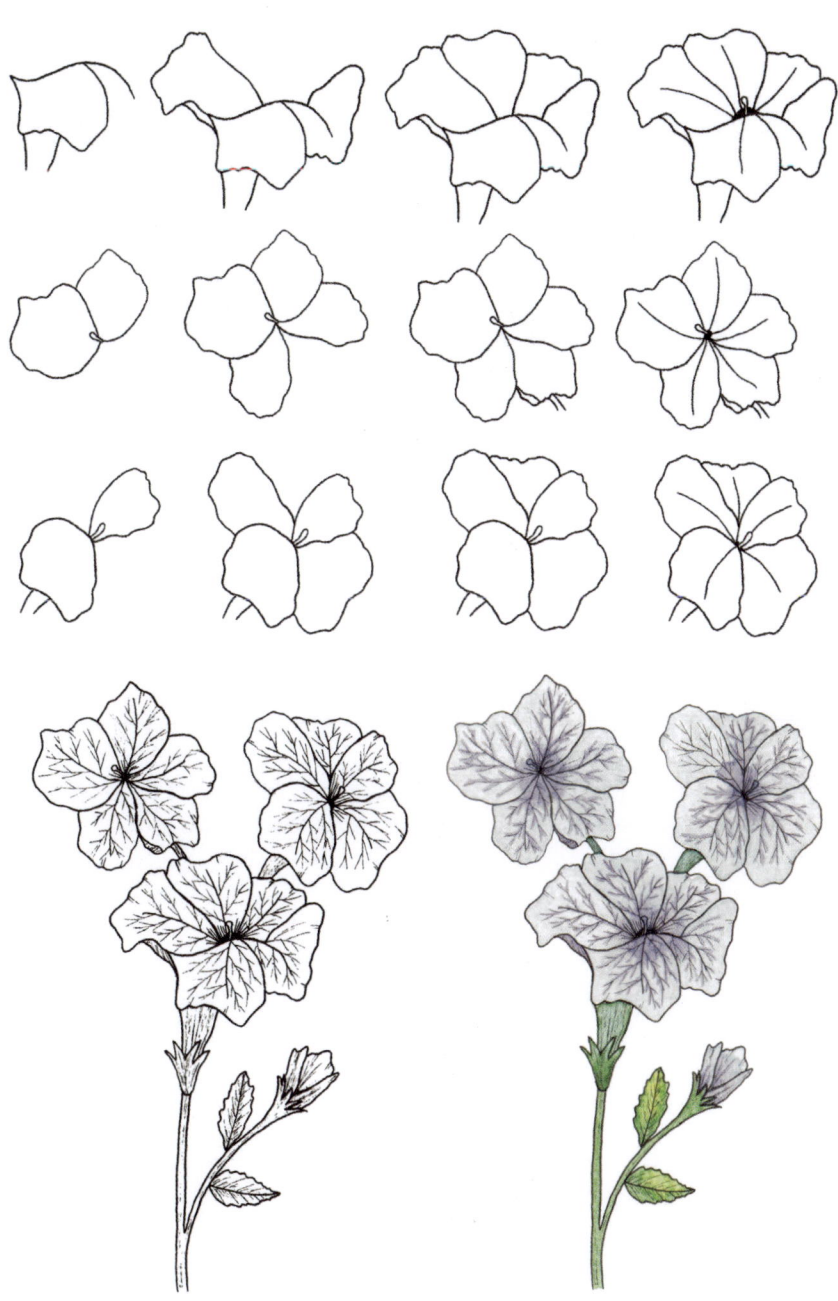

Tansy

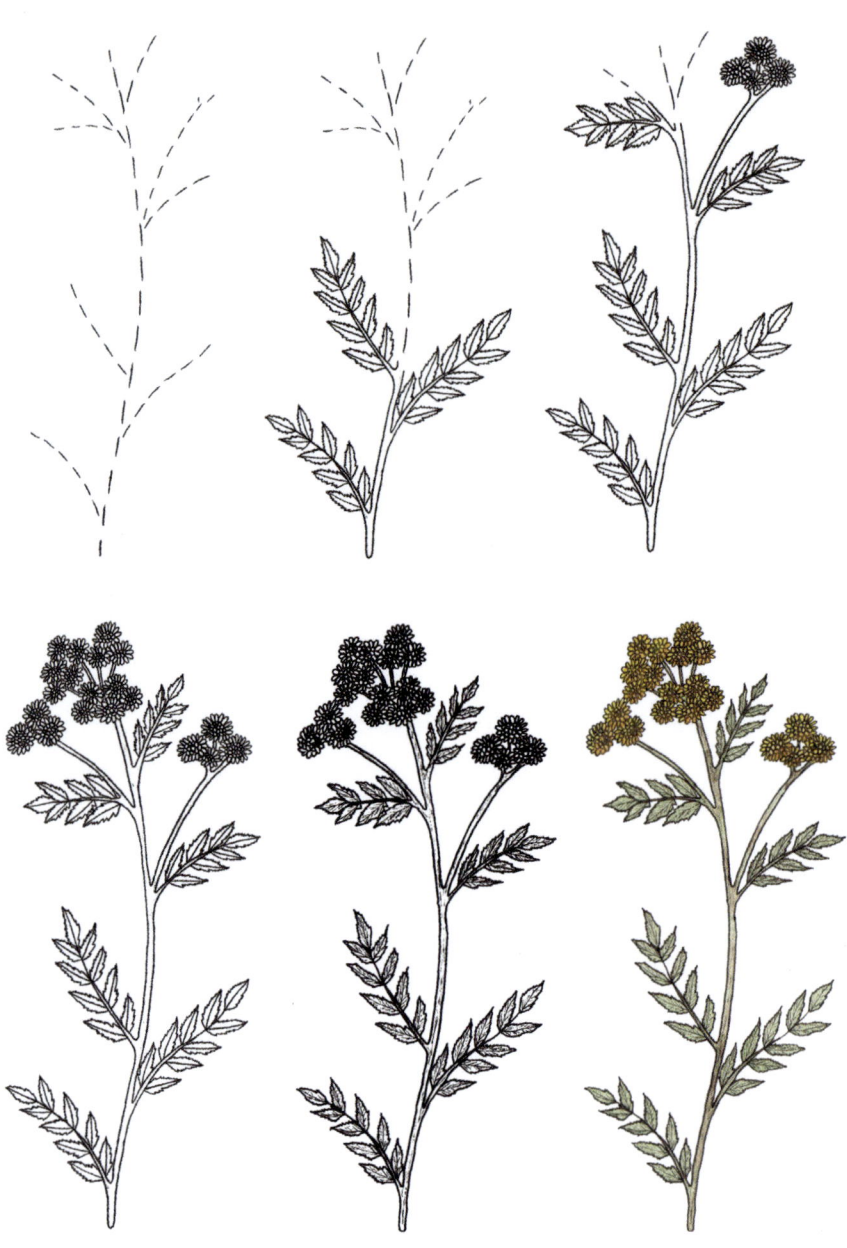

Heather

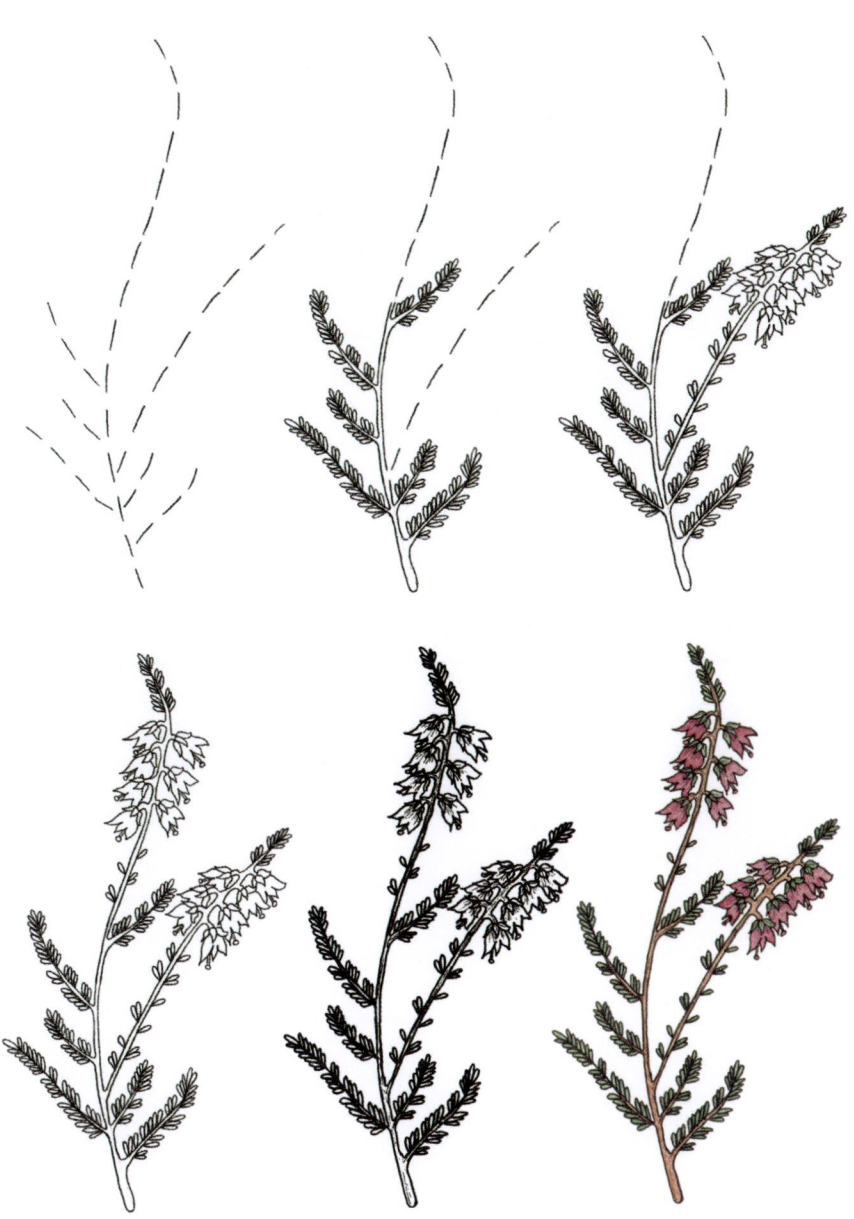

Yarrow

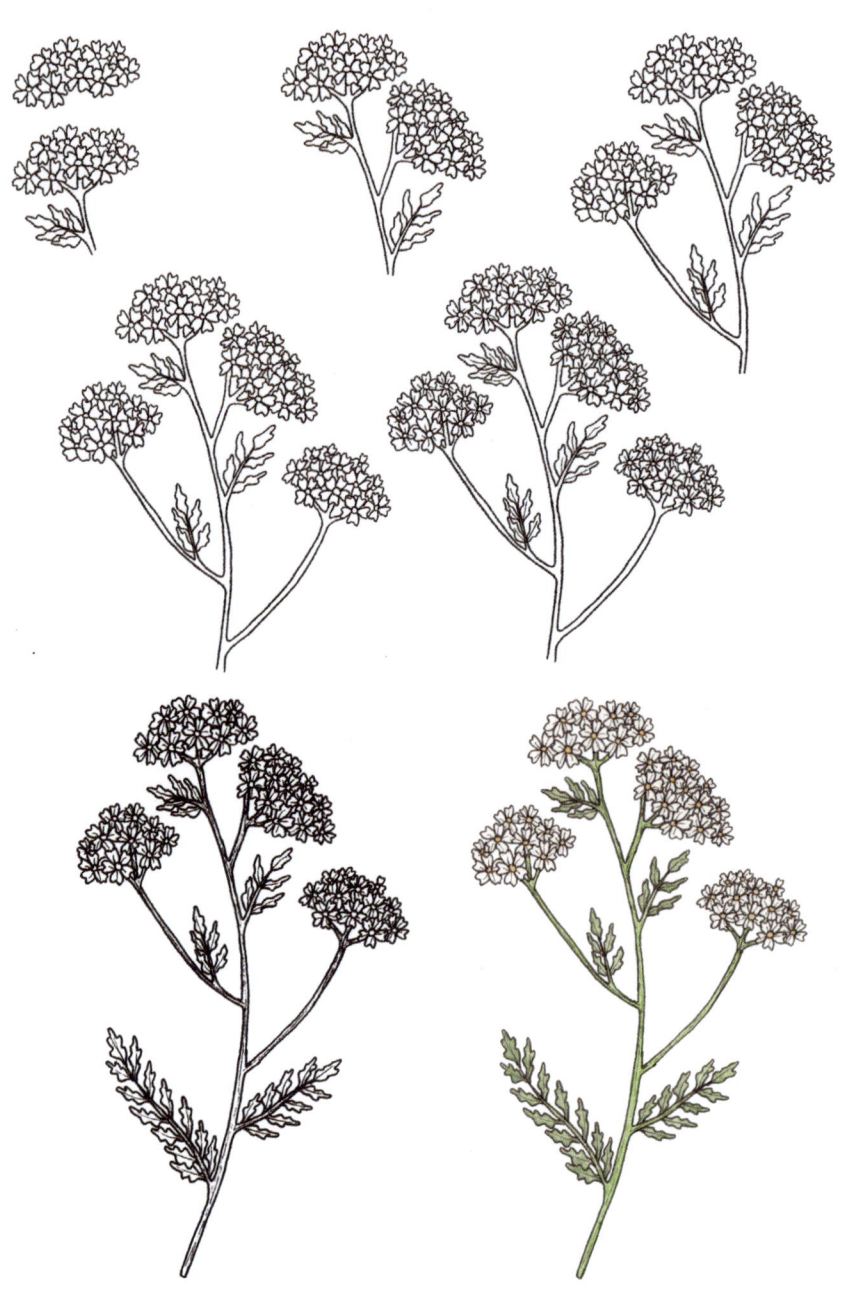

Cherry Blossom

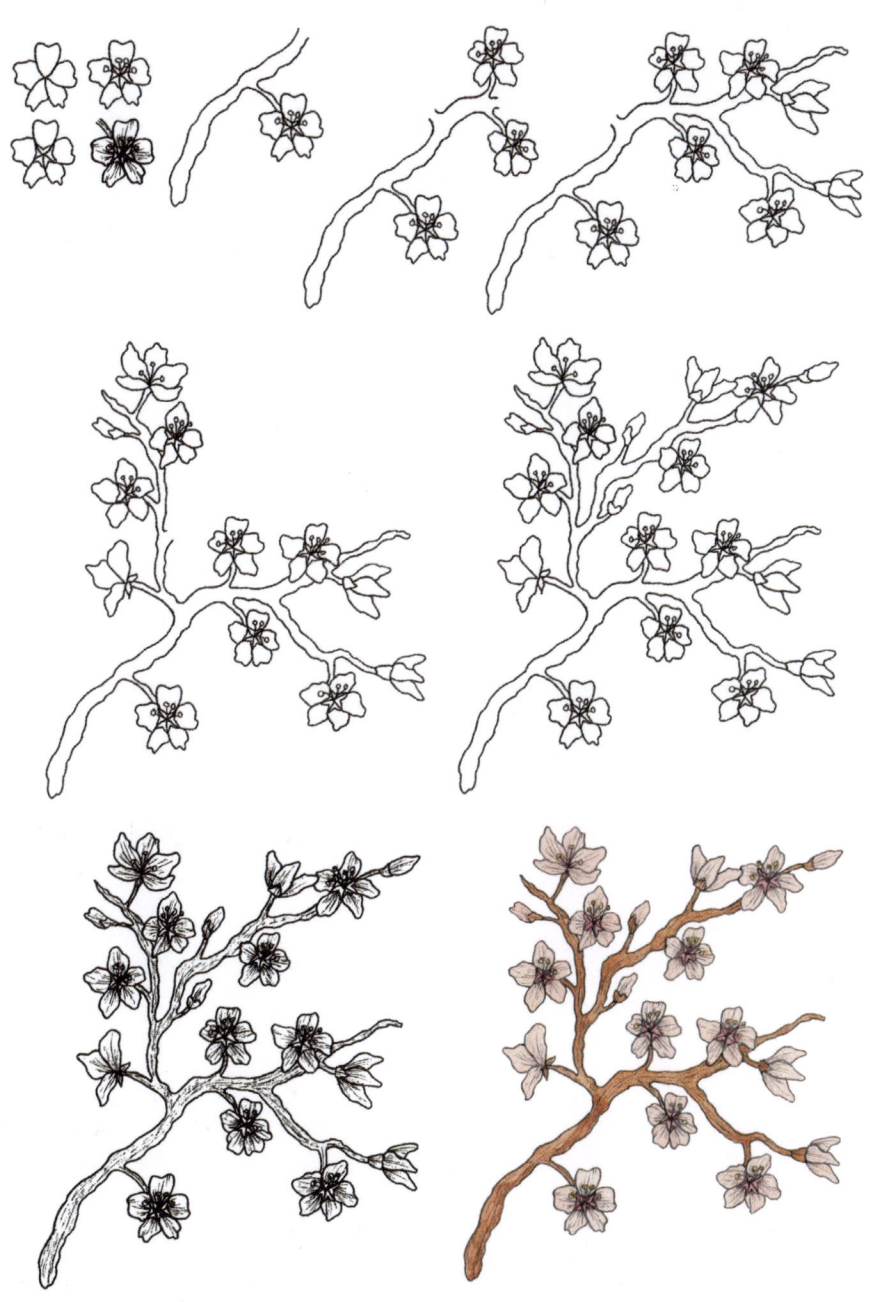

Leaves & Grasses

Whilst flowers are often considered the stars of the show, leaves and grasses provide wonderful structure and colour, often all throughout the year. If you decide to try out some floral composition drawings, I would highly recommend including some leaves and grasses too as they offer so much interest.

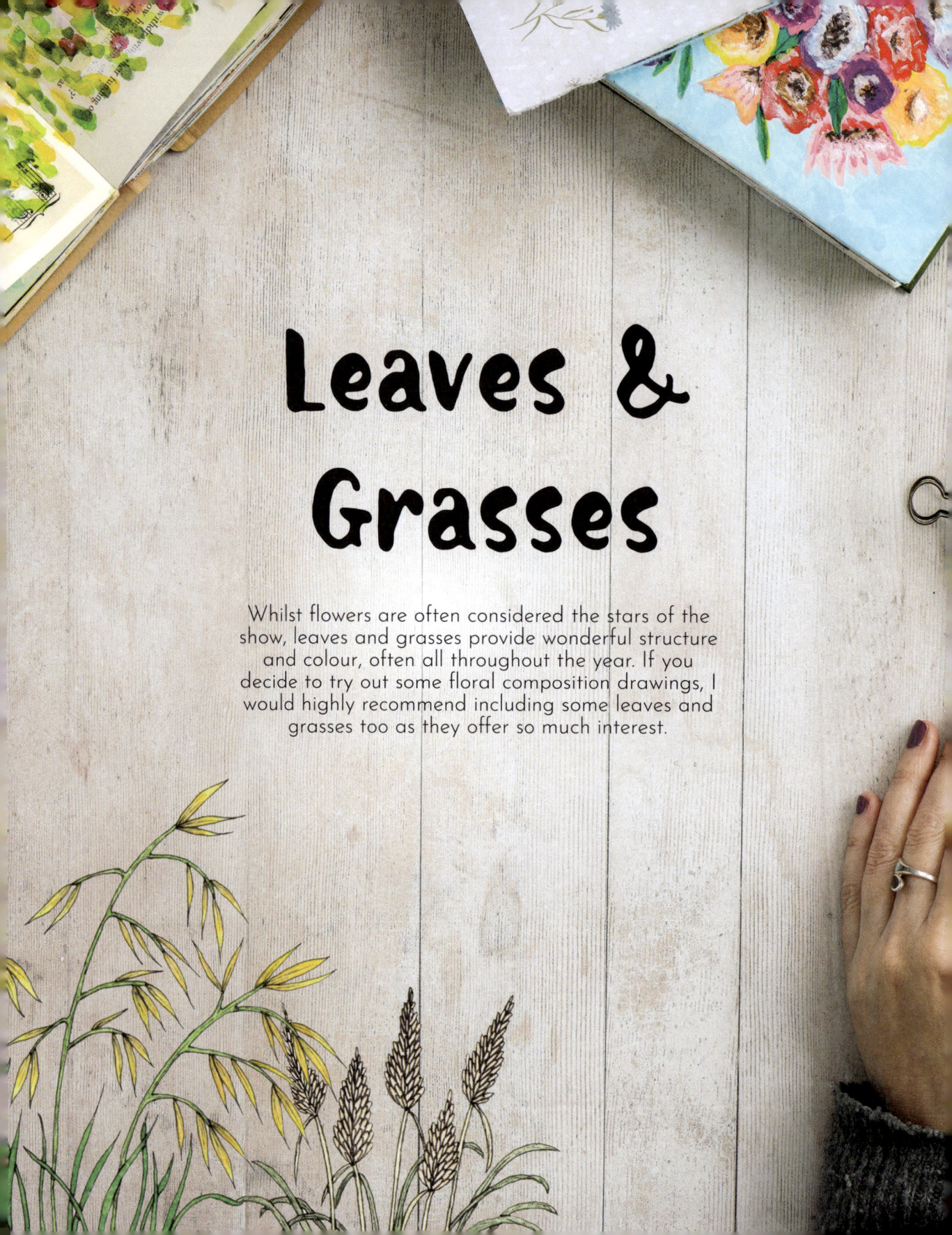

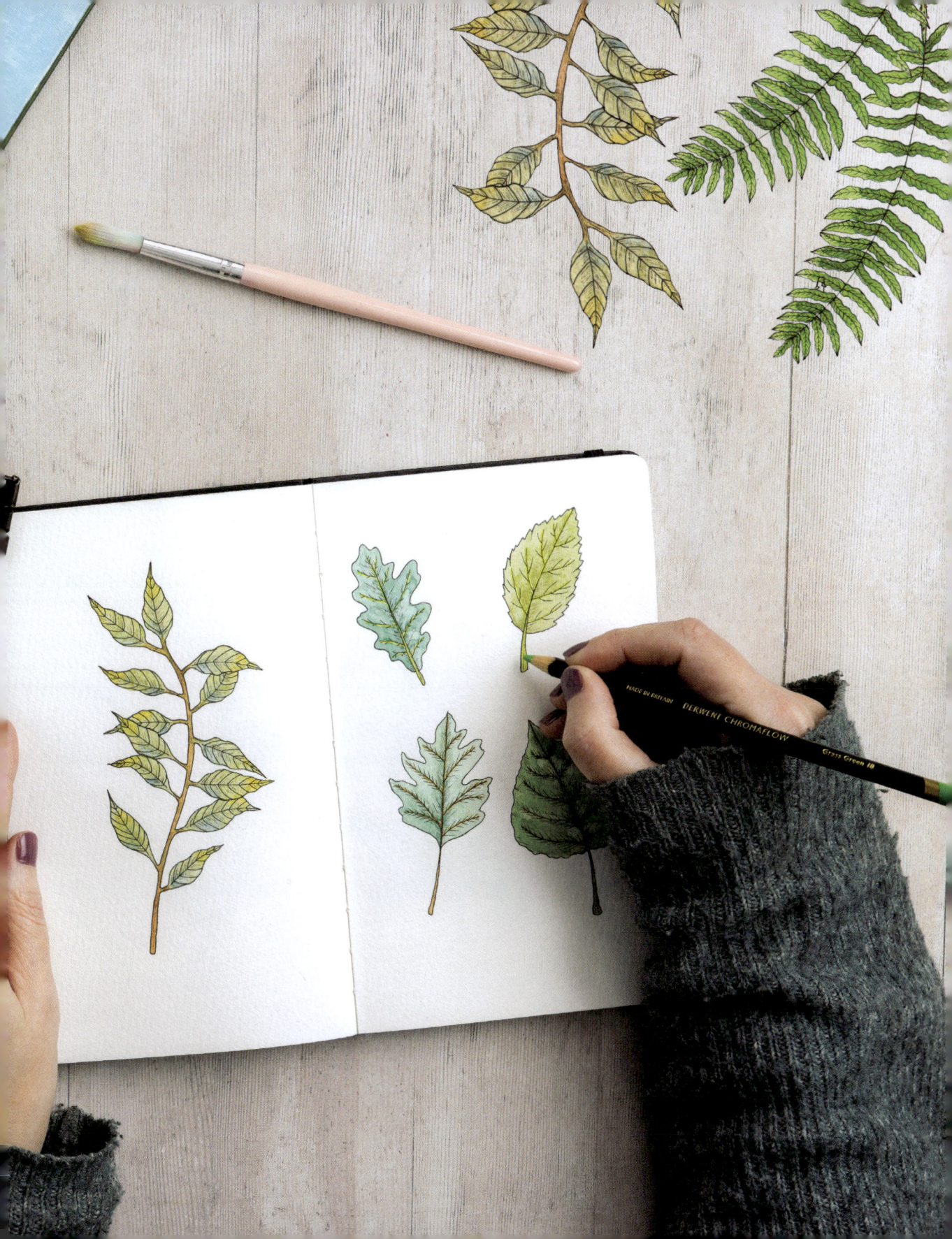

Pampas Grass

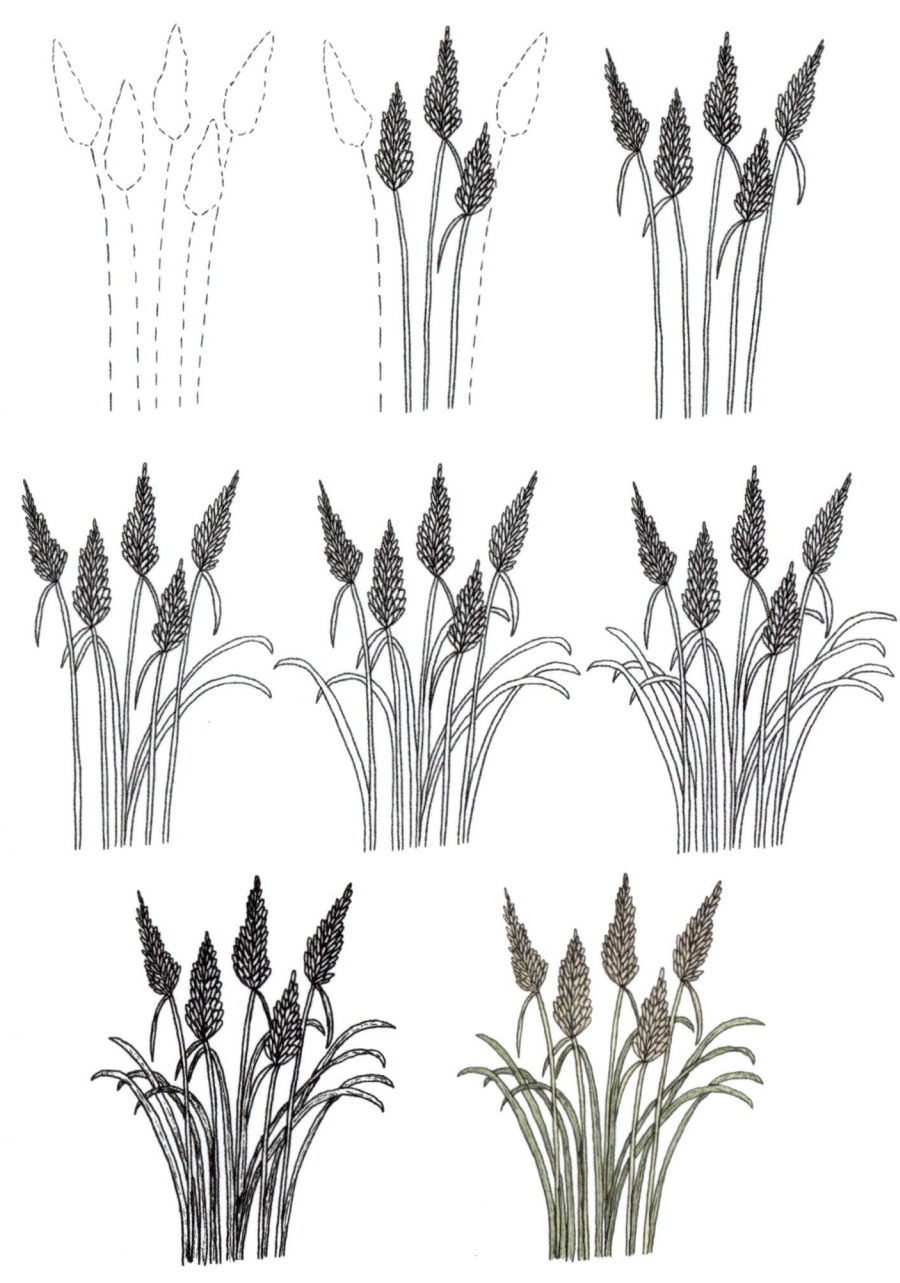

Purple Fountain Grass

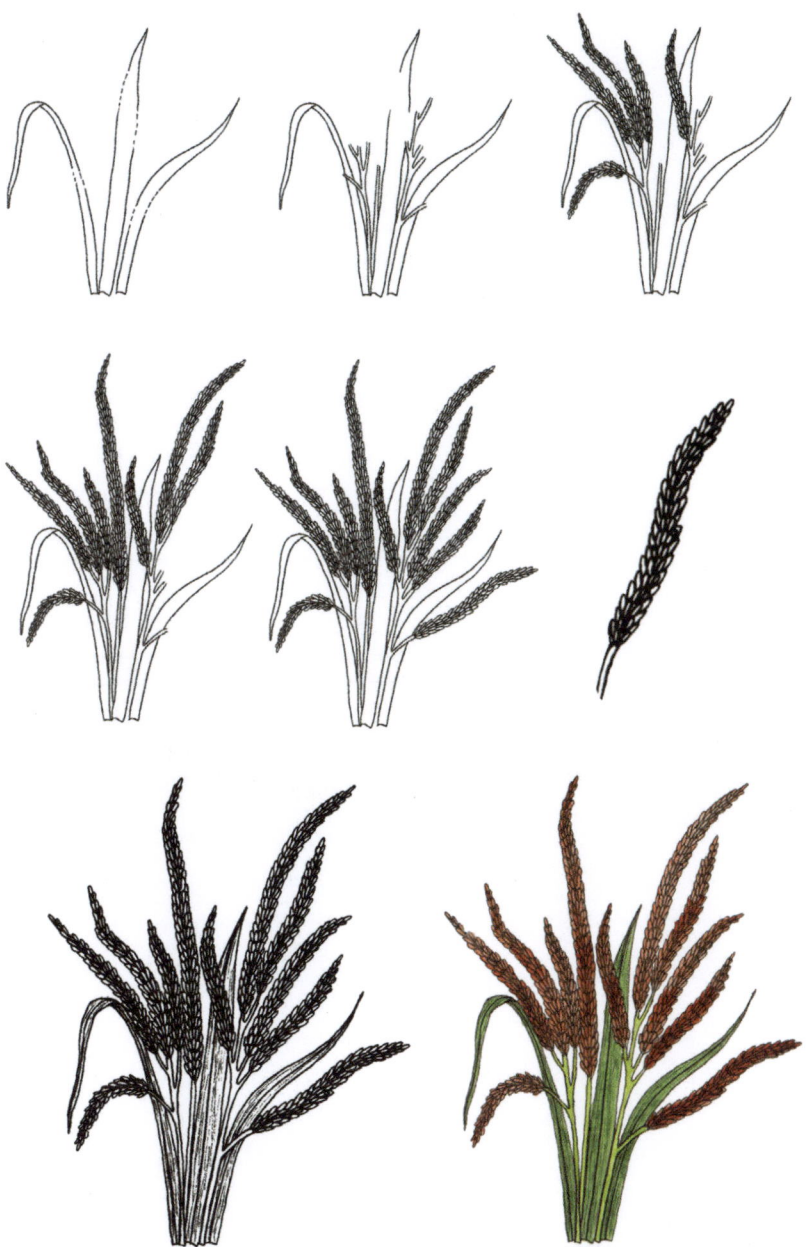

Golden Oats

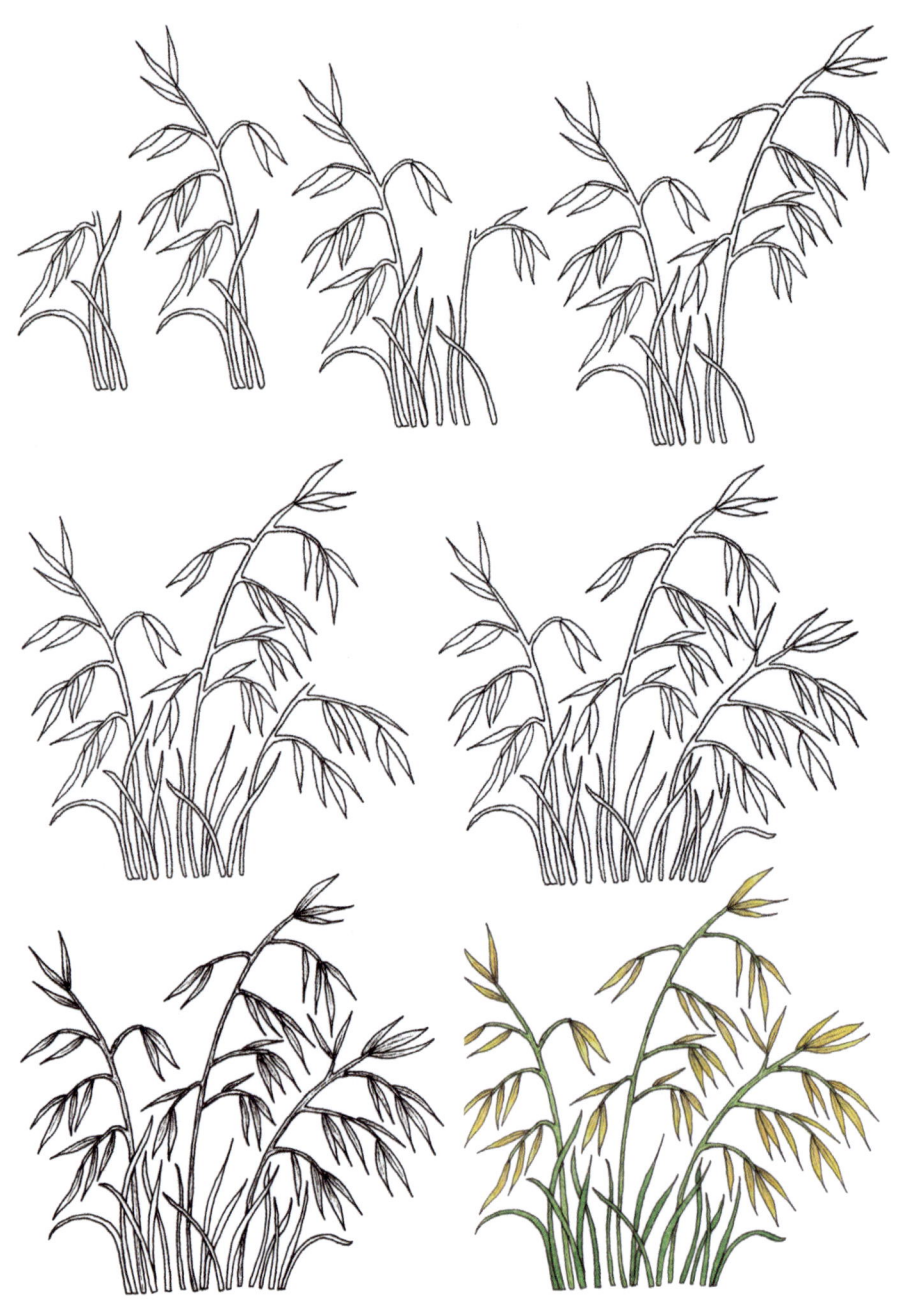

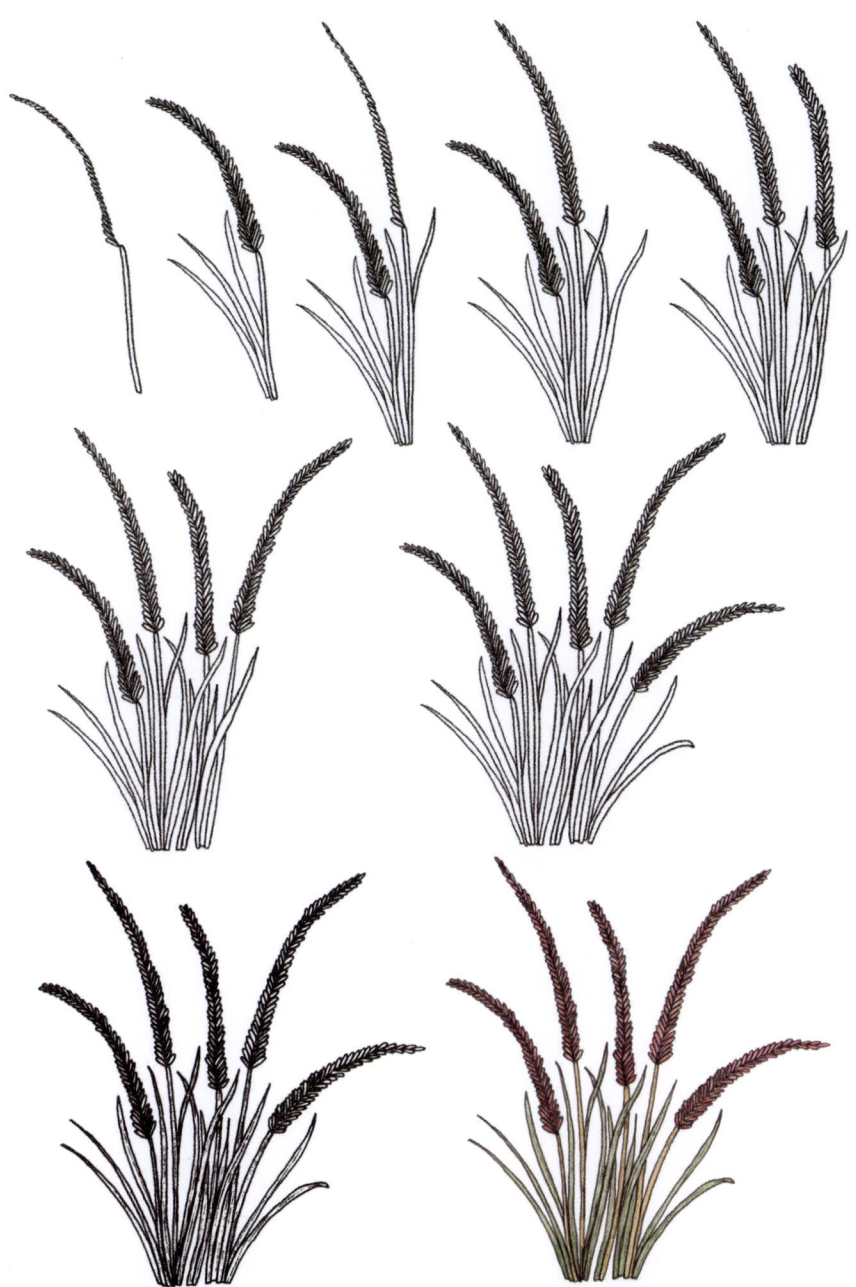

Fern Leaf

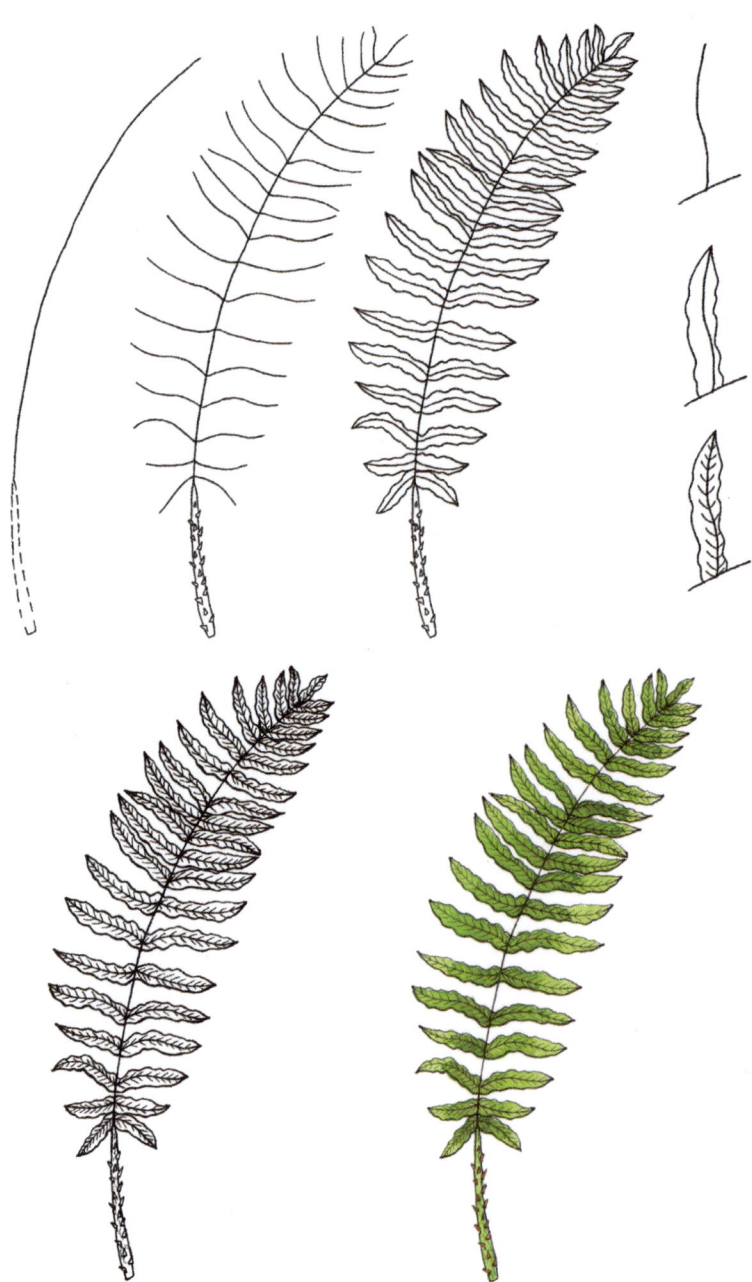

Leafy Branch

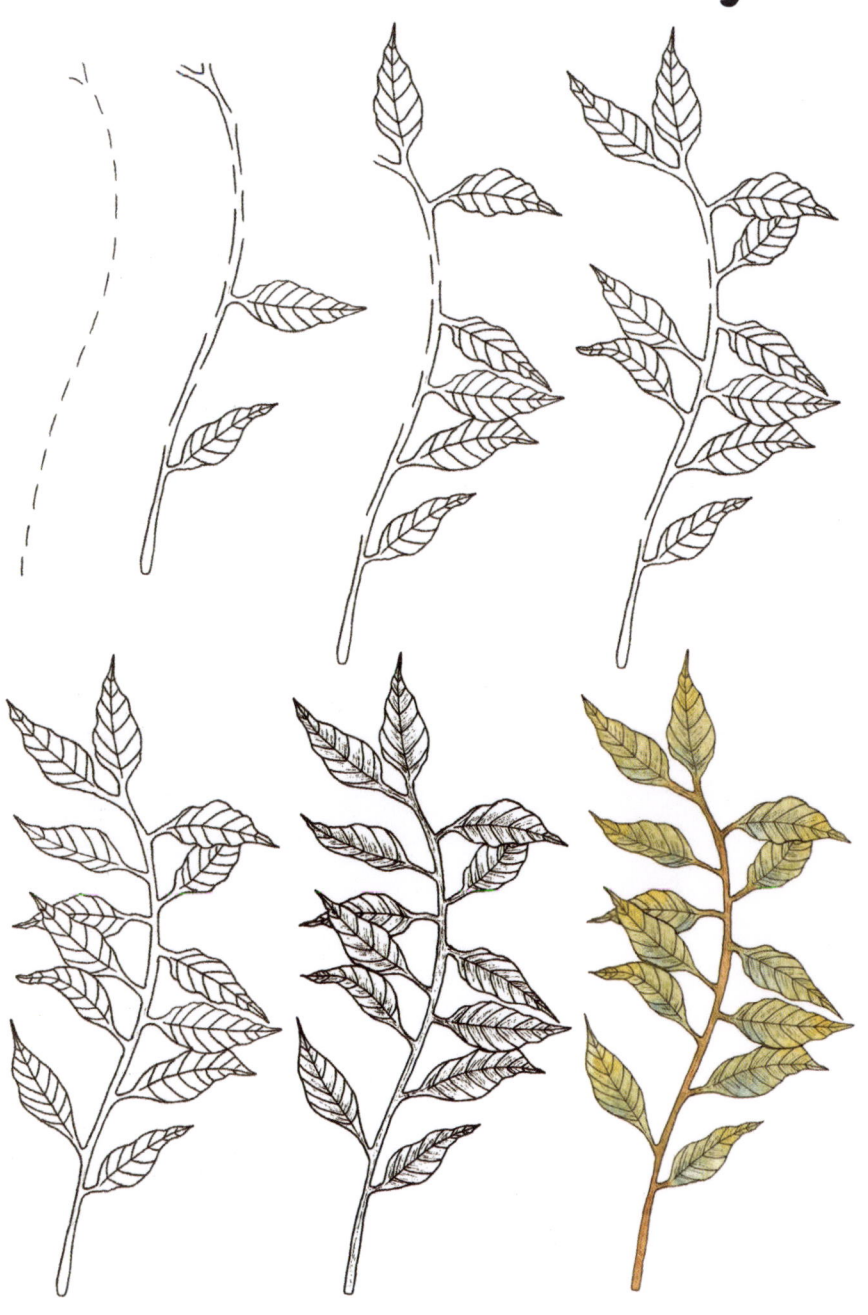

Leaf Selection

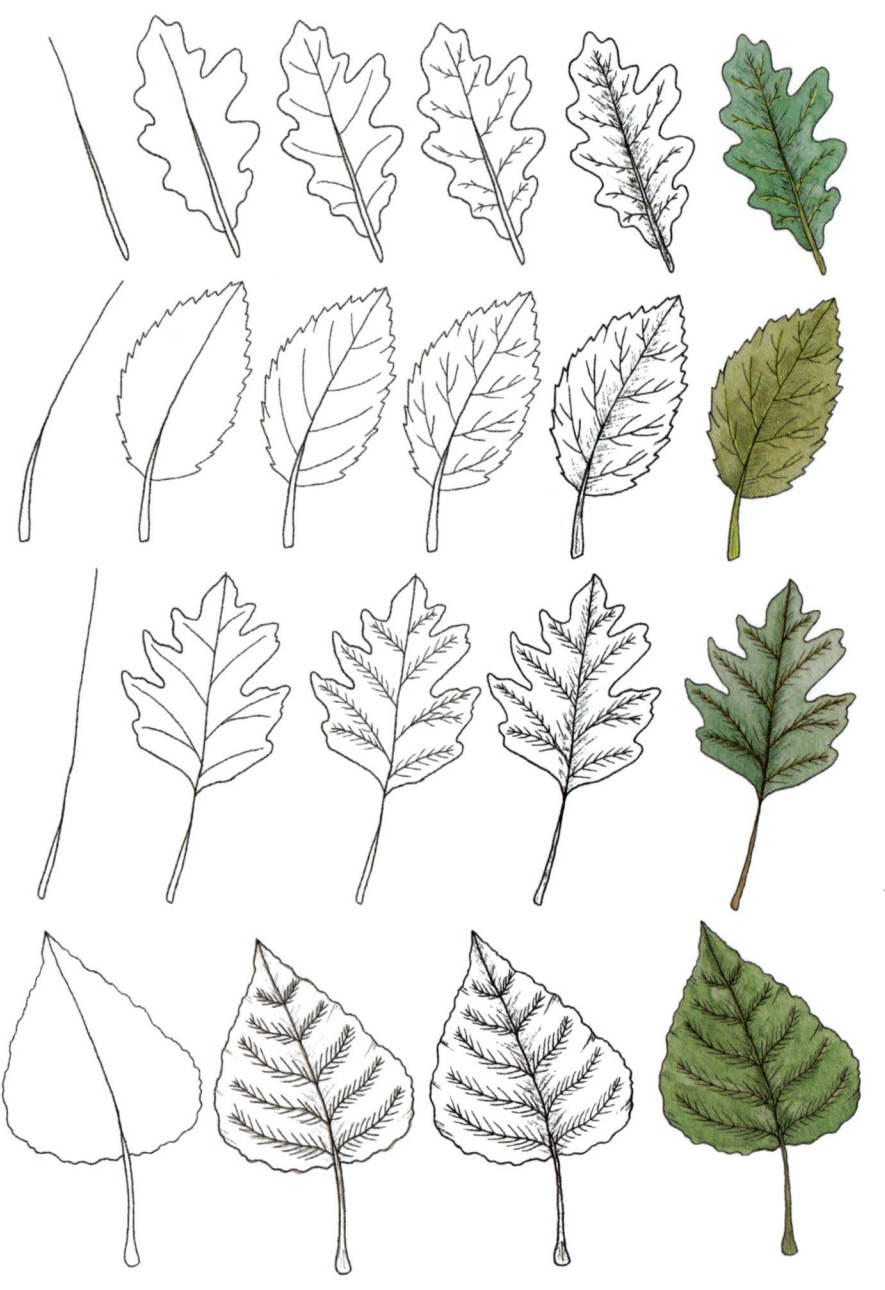

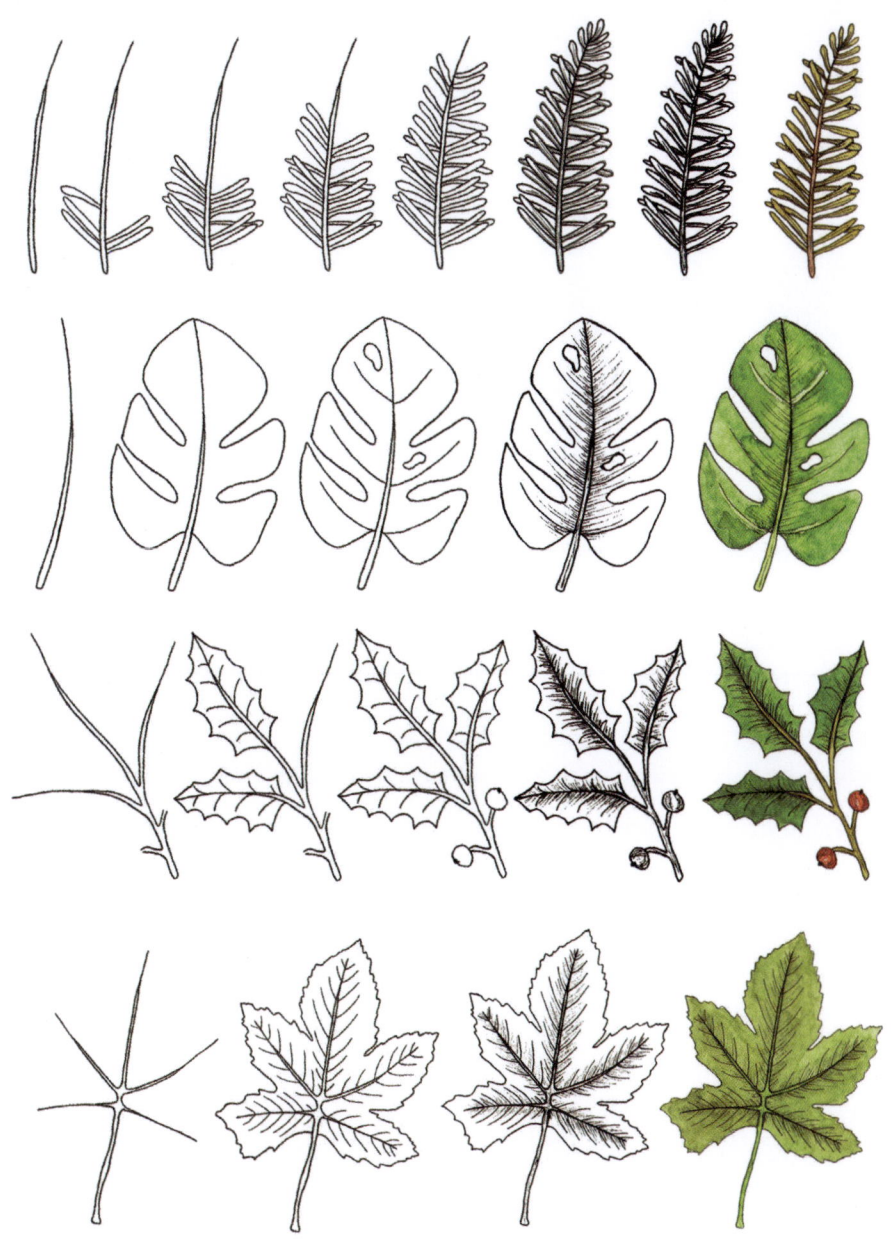

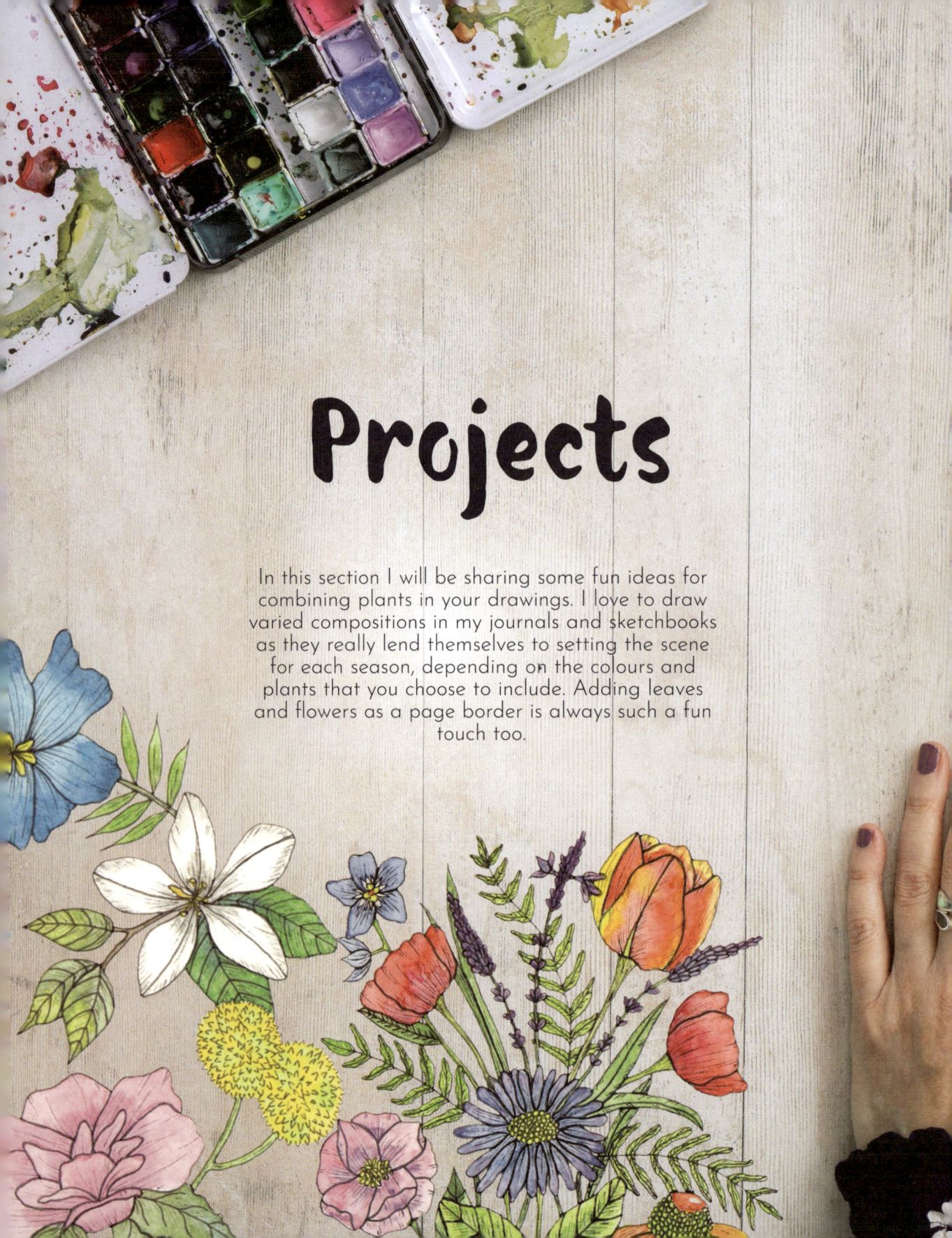

Projects

In this section I will be sharing some fun ideas for combining plants in your drawings. I love to draw varied compositions in my journals and sketchbooks as they really lend themselves to setting the scene for each season, depending on the colours and plants that you choose to include. Adding leaves and flowers as a page border is always such a fun touch too.

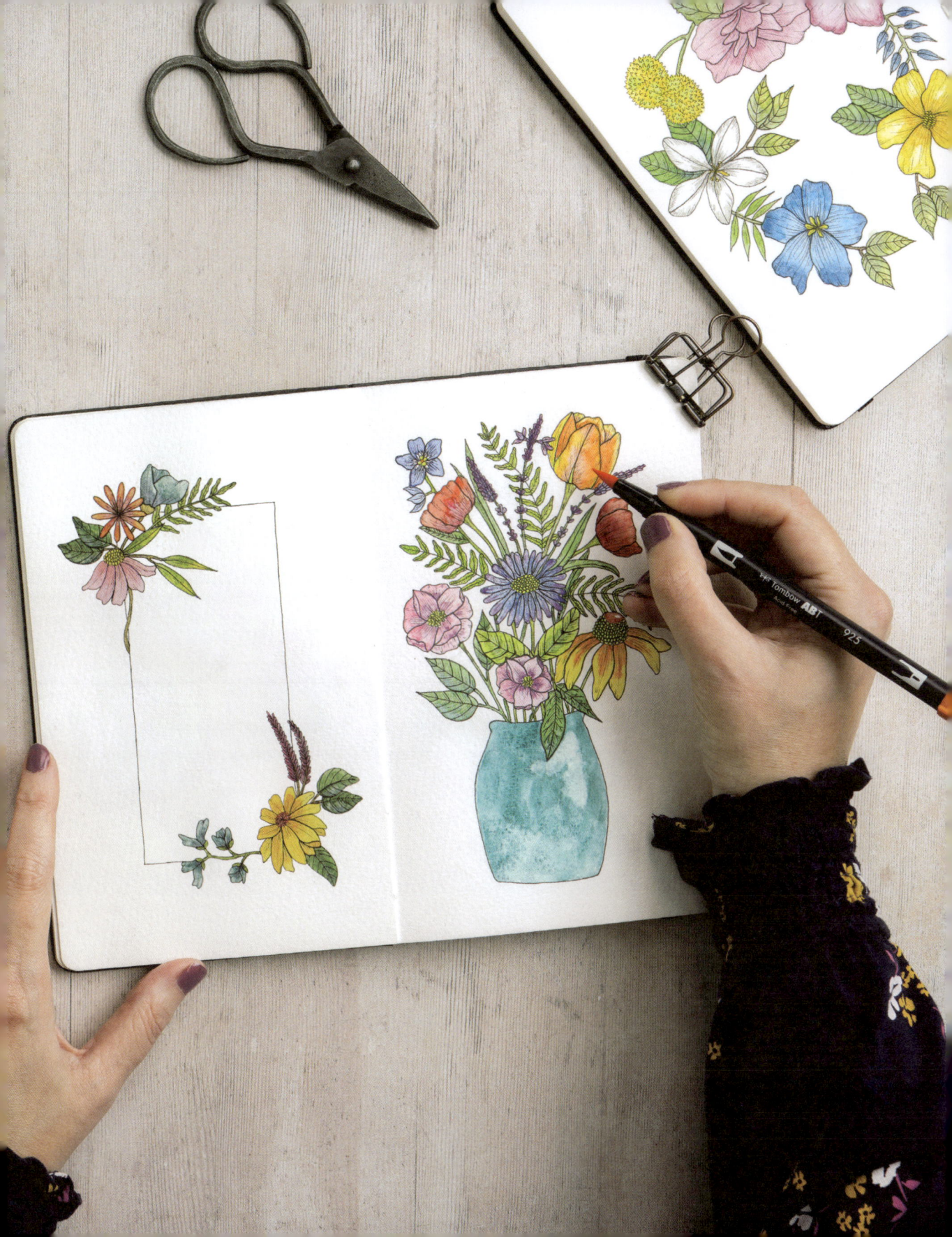

Vase Arrangement

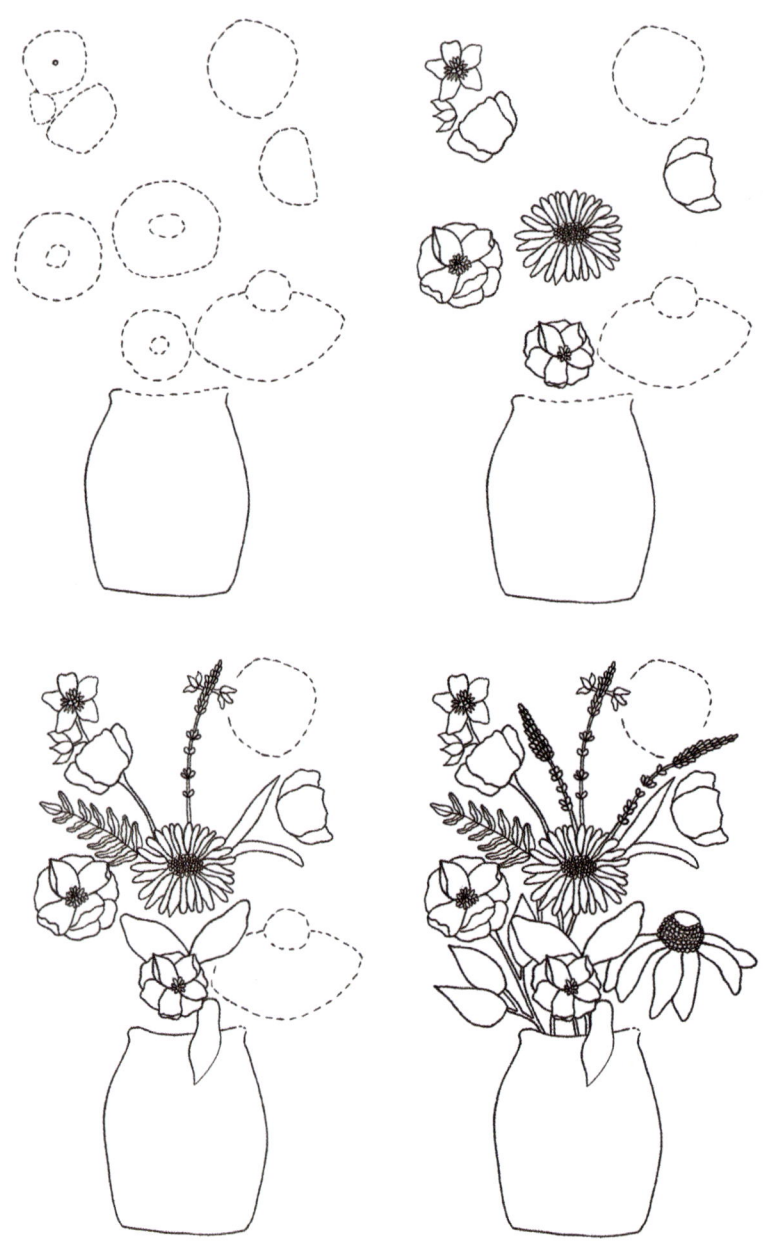

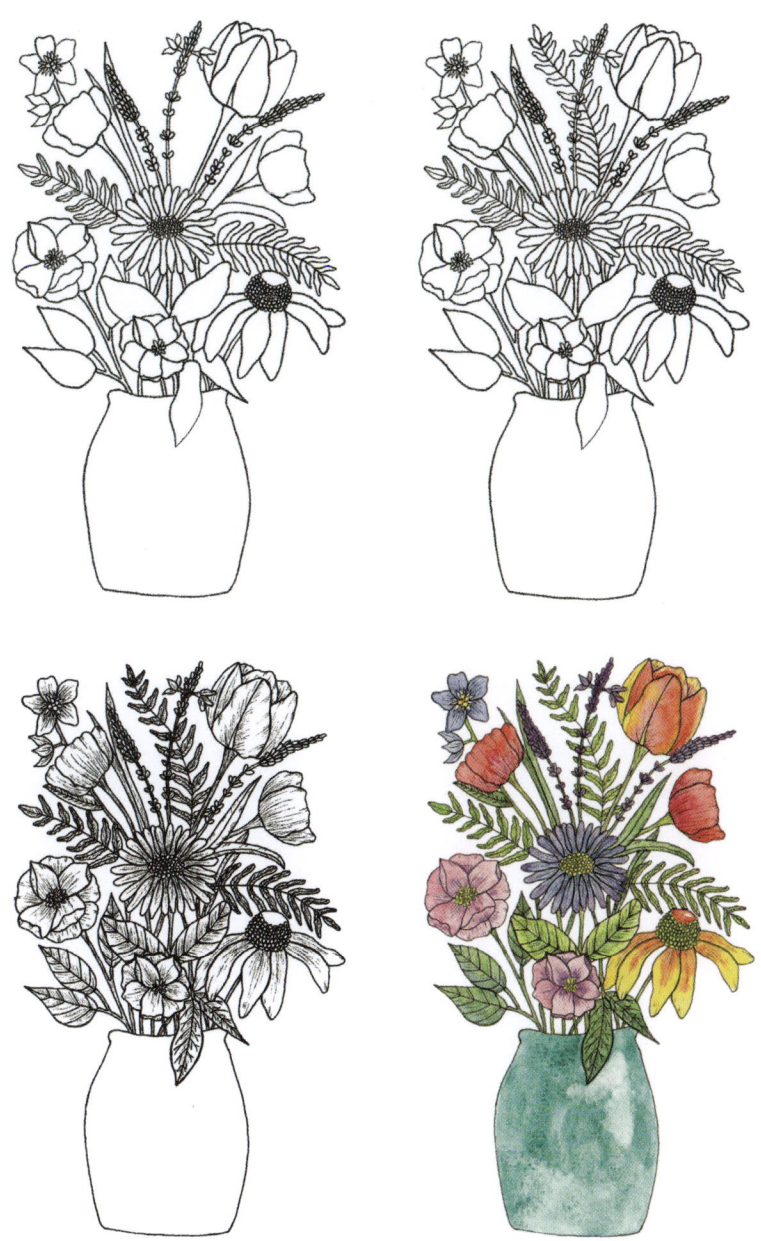

Wreath

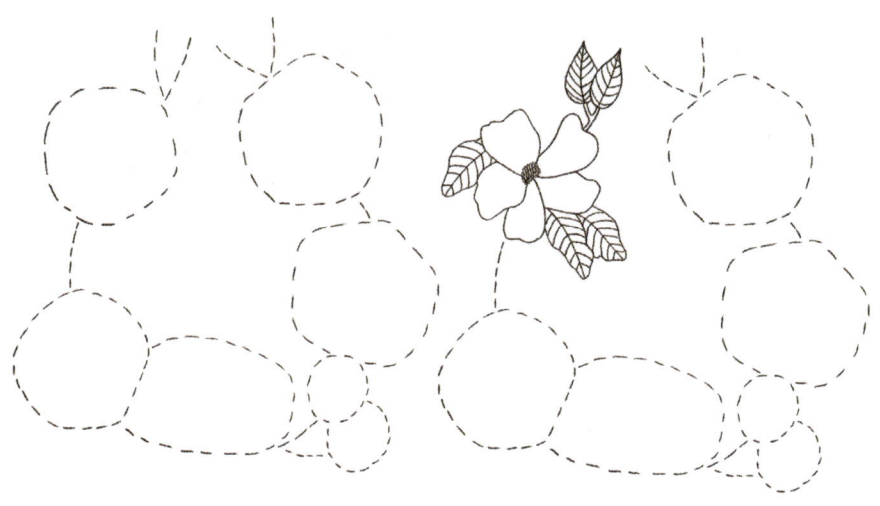

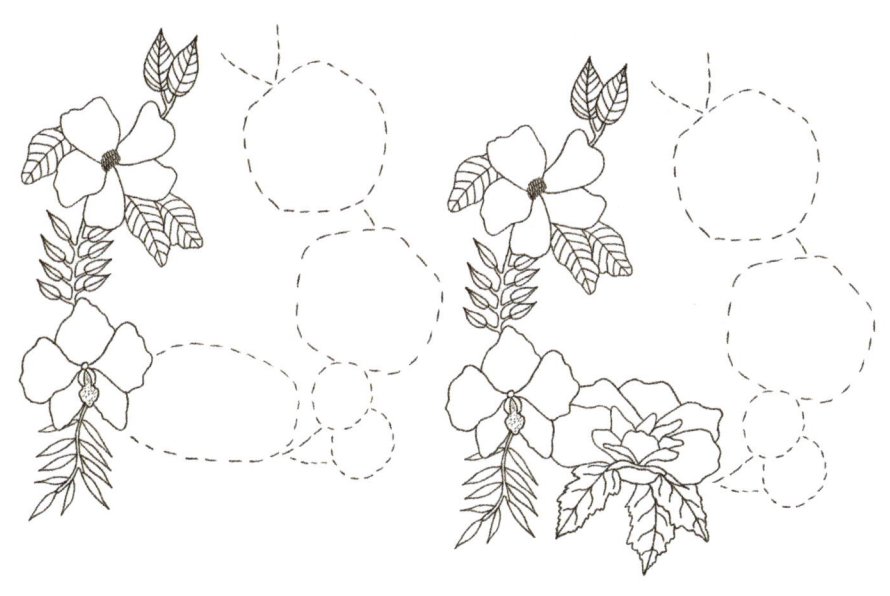

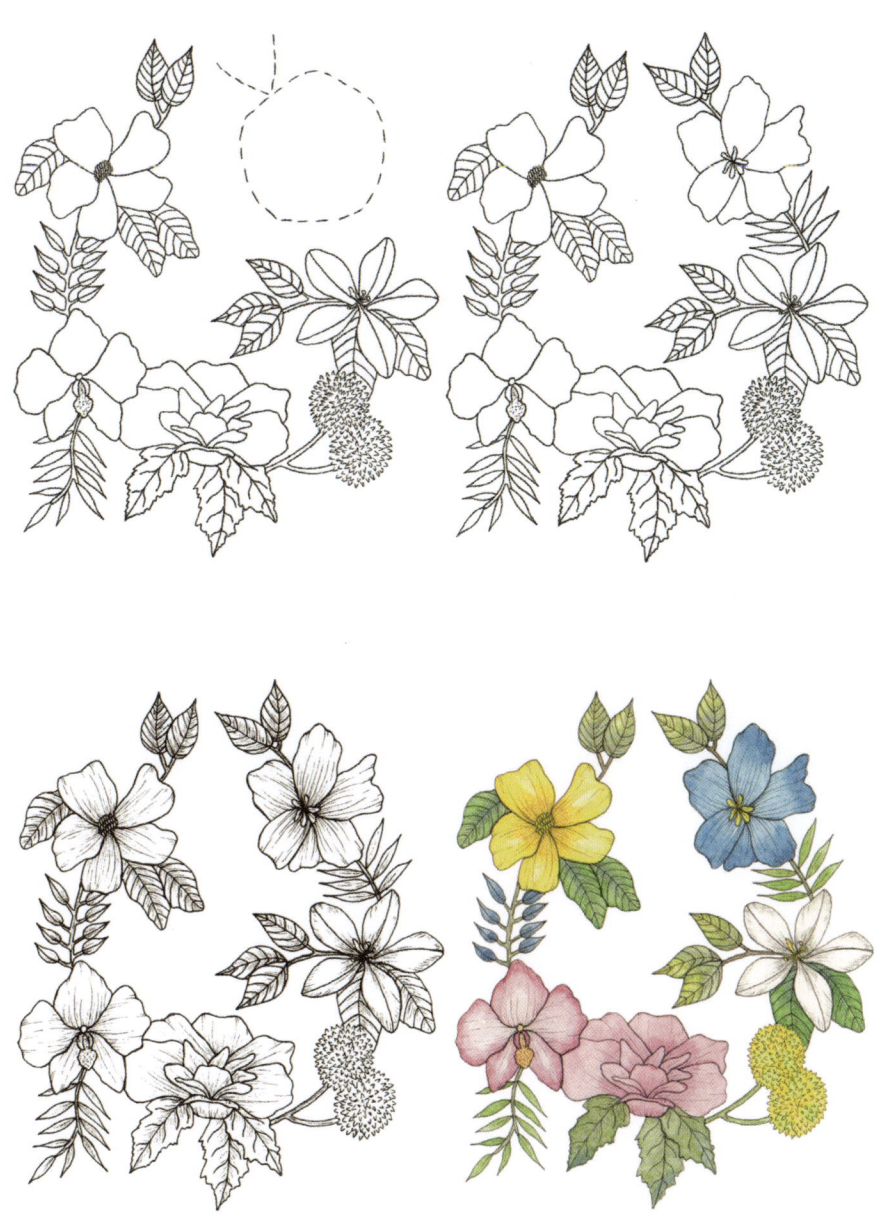

Decorative Border

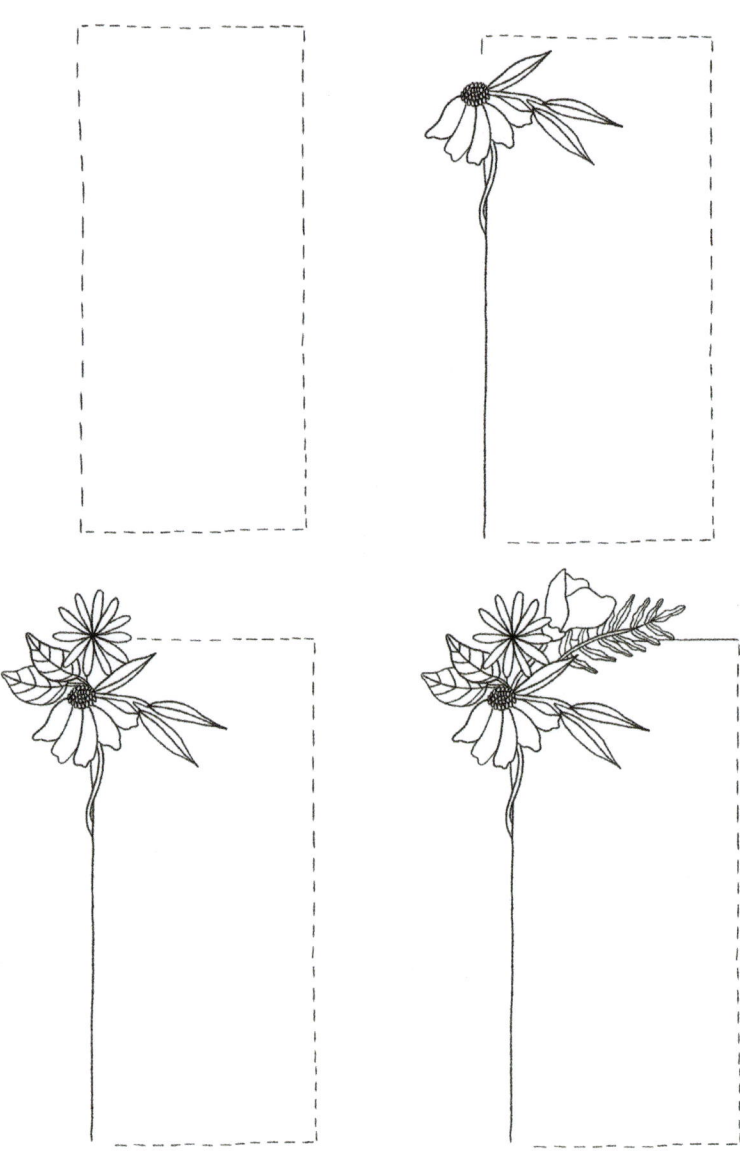

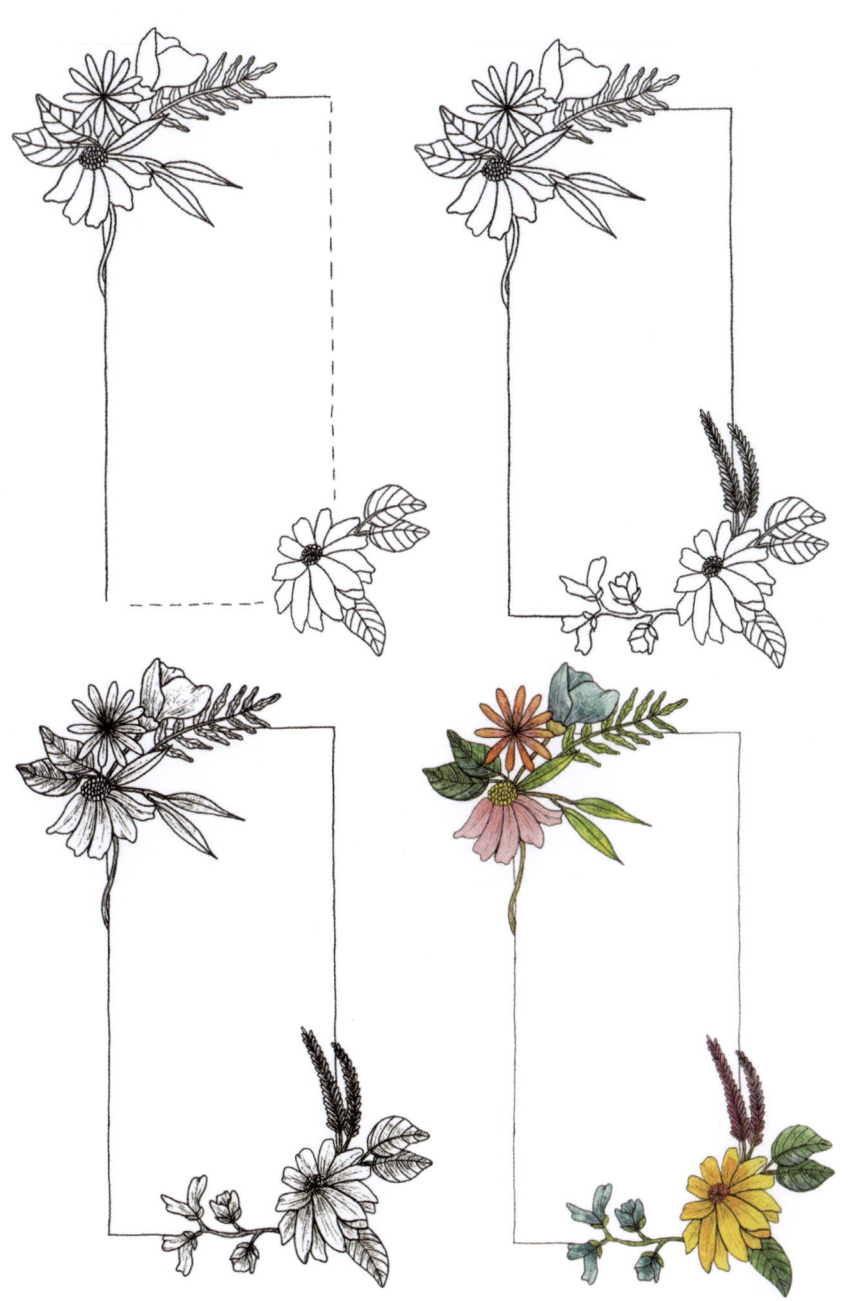

Project Inspiration

Now is the time to have lots of fun with everything you've learned throughout this book. I loved putting the designs on bookmarks, tote bags, decorative tags, envelopes, and greeting cards, as well as using them as embroidery guides. It's also really interesting to try drawings out on different backgrounds - like book pages or on top of a watercolour wash. I tried out some different inks too - like a white gel pen and a black paint pen which can bring such variety to your designs. I would absolutely love to see what you choose to create.

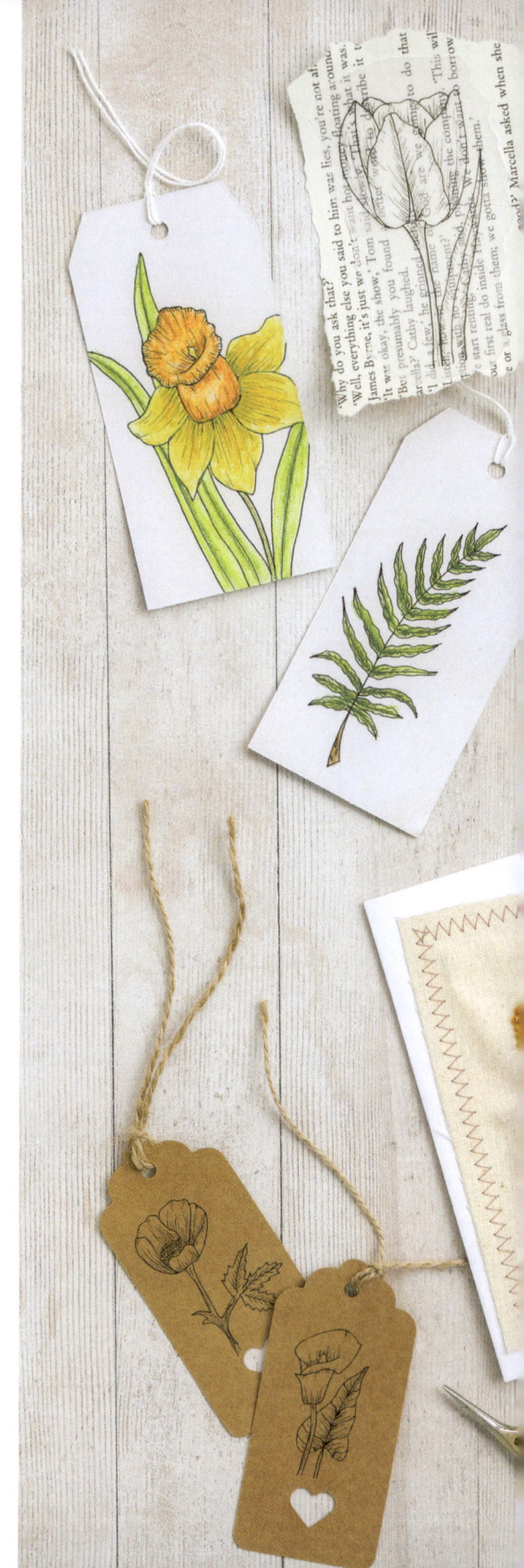

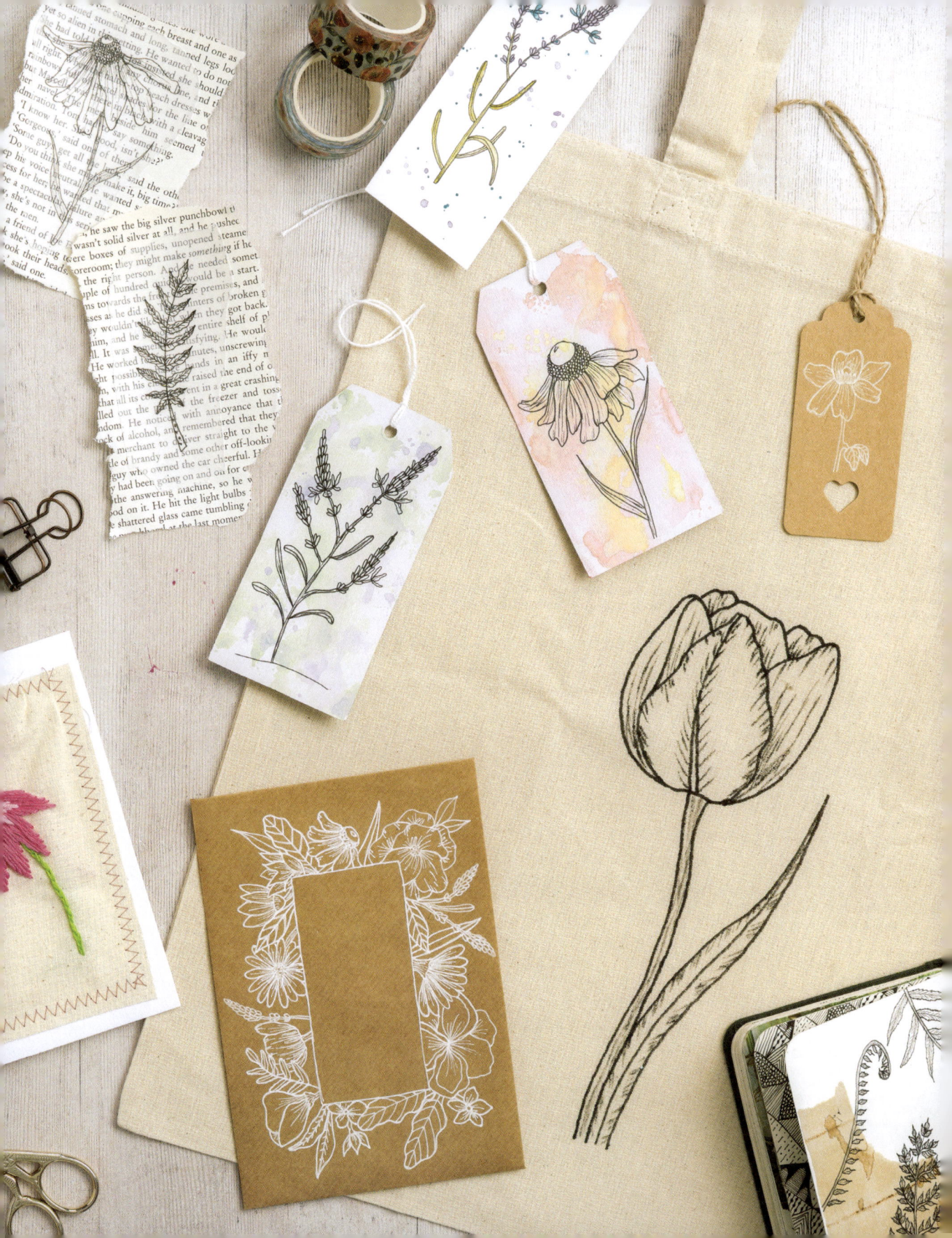

About the Author

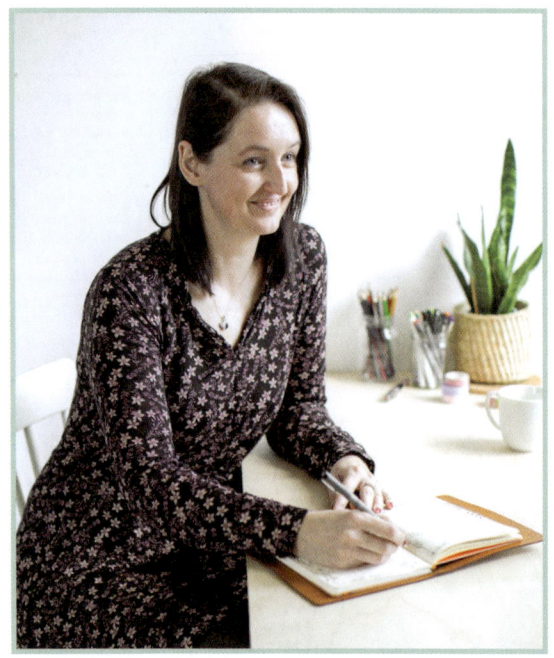

Helen Colebrook did not think of herself as creative until she found her "thing" – keeping a creative journal – and began her blog *Journal With Purpose* (www.journalwithpurpose.co.uk). Through getting creative in her journals, Helen grew in confidence and felt able to try out all sorts of new arty projects, including drawing the plants she saw on her daily walks. Being able to bring nature drawings into her journals has brought her so much joy and it's something she's really keen to share with others.

Helen's journal pages and sketchbooks have been featured in various books and blogs around the world. She's also been interviewed for and featured in various publications including Daily Mail, The Independent, and Grazia. She loves working with various stationery brands to showcase how their art supplies can be used in fun and interesting ways in both sketchbooks and journals too.

Alongside sharing her journals on Instagram, YouTube, Pinterest, and her blog, Helen also offers an online membership programme and workshops to support others in their creativity.

Helen would love to see what you create, so please do tag her in your posts on Instagram, using her handle @journalwithpurpose.

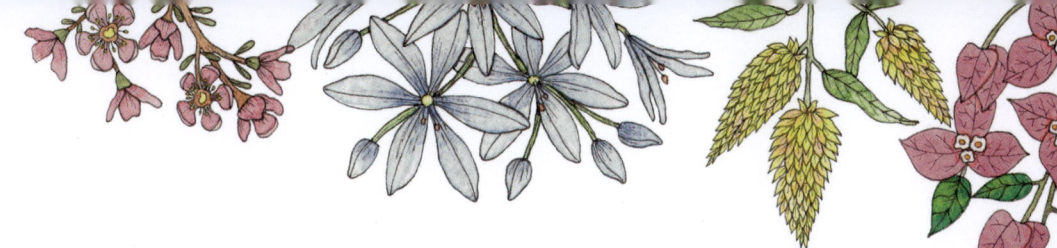

Index

A DAVID AND CHARLES BOOK
© David and Charles, Ltd 2026

David and Charles is an imprint of David and
Charles, Ltd, Suite A, Tourism House, Pynes Hill,
Exeter, EX2 5WS

EU GPSR Authorised Representative:
Logos Europe, 9 rue Nicolas Poussin, 17000,
La Rochelle, France
Email: Contact@logoseurope.eu

Text and Designs © Helen Colebrook 2026
Layout and Photography © David and
Charles, Ltd 2026

First published in the UK and USA in 2026

A catalogue record for this book is available from the
British Library.

ISBN-13: 9781446316771 paperback
ISBN-13: 9781446316788 EPUB

This book has been printed on paper from
approved suppliers and made from pulp from
sustainable sources.

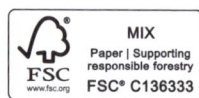

MIX
Paper | Supporting
responsible forestry
FSC® C136333

Printed in China by Asia Pacific Offset for:
David and Charles, Ltd
Suite A, Tourism House, Pynes Hill, Exeter, EX2 5WS

10 9 8 7 6 5 4 3 2 1

Publishing Director: Ame Verso
Senior Commissioning Editor: Nigel Browning
Publishing Manager: Jeni Chown
Editor: Jessica Cropper
Design: Sam Staddon
Pre-press Designer: Susan Reansbury
Illustrations: Helen Colebrook
Art Direction: Sam Staddon
Photography: Jason Jenkins
Production Manager: Beverley Richardson

David and Charles publishes high-quality books on
a wide range of subjects. For more information visit
www.davidandcharles.com.

Share your makes with us on social media using
#dandcbooks and follow us on Facebook and
Instagram by searching for @dandcbooks.

Layout of the digital edition of this book may vary
depending on reader hardware and display settings.

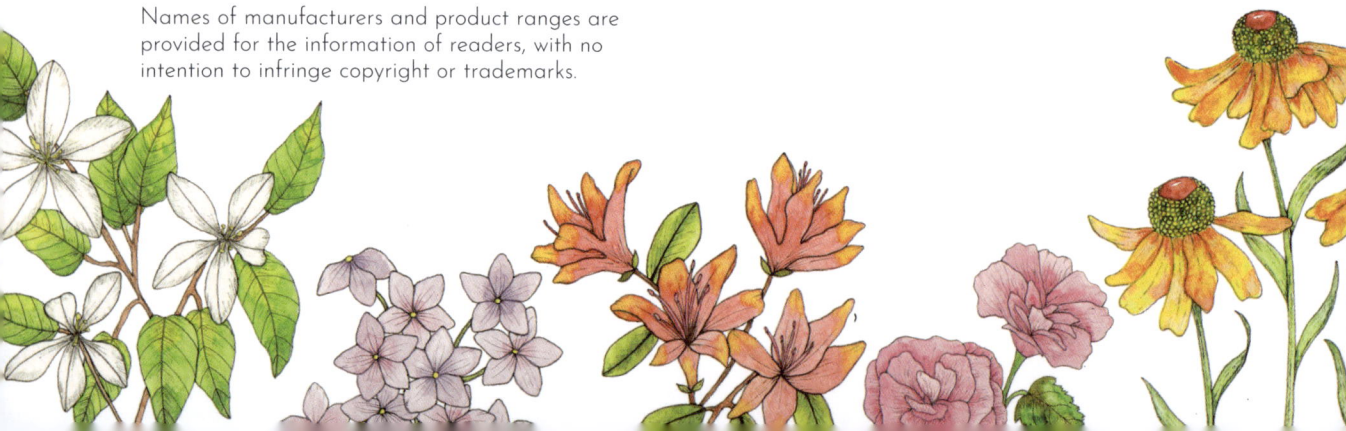